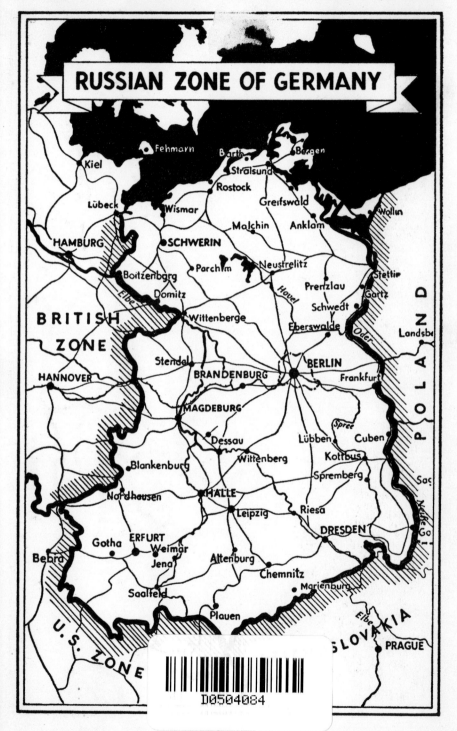

RUSSIAN ZONE OF GERMANY

Fehmarn
Kiel
Barth · Bergen
Stralsund
Rostock
Lübeck · Wismar · Greifswald
Wollin
HAMBURG · SCHWERIN · Malchin · Anklam
Boitzenbarg · Parchim · Neustrelitz · Stettin
Domitz · Havel · Prenzlau · Gartz
Wittenberge · Schwedt
BRITISH ZONE · Eberswalde
Landsb
Stendal · BERLIN
HANNOVER · BRANDENBURG · Frankfurt
MAGDEBURG
POLAND
Dessau · Spree · Lübben · Cuben
Blankenburg · Wittenberg · Kottbus
Nordhausen · Spremberg
HALLE · Sac
Leipzig · Riesa · Neisse
ERFURT · DRESDEN · Go
Bebra · Gotha · Weimar · Altenburg
Jena · Chemnitz
Saalfeld · Marienburg
Plauen · Elbe
U.S. ZONE · SLOVAKIA · PRAGUE

RUSSIAN ZONE

RUSSIAN ZONE

by

GORDON SCHAFFER

PUBLISHED FOR
THE CO-OPERATIVE PRESS LTD
BY
GEORGE ALLEN & UNWIN LTD
LONDON

FIRST PUBLISHED IN 1947

*Printed and Bound
in Great Britain by
Co-operative Wholesale Society Limited
at their
Printing Works, Longsight, Manchester*

CONTENTS

FOREWORD

THIS book is a record of the conditions I found in the Soviet-occupied Zone of Germany during a stay of ten weeks. In that time I had the best opportunity afforded to date to any foreign journalist to study the life of the people and to assess the changes that have taken place since the Russian occupation.

I interviewed scores of Germans in positions of responsibility—ministers of the various provincial governments, leaders of the political parties, of the trade unions, the co-operatives, the cultural bodies, and a host of other organisations. I met ministers of religion and shop stewards. I talked to the ordinary people in every walk of life, and I listened-in to them in the trams, in the queues, the railway stations, and the restaurants.

In some of the towns I visited I was the first foreign visitor, other than the Russians, since the outbreak of war. And I was welcomed almost like a visitor from another world. Some Germans I sought out, but once it was known I was in the town, they came to tell me about their work, bringing incredible quantities of newly printed literature dealing with their particular tasks, anxious above all things to re-establish their contacts with the west, and to break down the sense of isolation which all of them feel behind the zonal frontier.

Such a survey cannot attempt to paint the complete picture, for the Soviet Zone is not Germany and the present zonal frontiers, drawn at the Crimea conference for military reasons, have no political or economic foundations. The future of Germany—and with it many questions of vital importance to Europe and the world—depends on what happens in all the zones and on the ability of the Allies to co-ordinate their policies. It has not been my purpose to draw comparisons or contrasts between the policies in the various zones. Rather I have tried to set down a story which so far has not been told, and which the world ought to know if it is to judge the pressing problems of Germany aright.

G.S.

I

CONQUEROR AND CONQUERED

In this fascinating bit of Europe in which, almost unnoticed by the rest of the world, social and economic changes of the most far-reaching importance are taking place, you can gain a different impression every day.

Talk to an ardent anti-Fascist in charge of some measure of social or economic reform, and he will almost persuade you that a new Germany has already been born. Spend an hour listening to the cross-talk in a barber's shop and you will come out convinced that these people can never be redeemed. Examine the work put in by the Soviet administration, see how the Russians are sending the best products of their technical colleges and universities to help raise Germany to her feet, and you are lost in admiration at the creative drive and sense of purpose of a people who can register such achievements after a devastating war and the loss of millions of their best citizens. Check up on some acts of bureaucracy or petty tyranny by some unimaginative Russian official, and you wonder how such folly can be allowed to jeopardise the work to which their country is devoting so much effort.

Everywhere these contrasts exist. The foundations of a new society have already been laid in a way that very few people, even in the Zone, realise. The transfer of a considerable section of industry to the control of provincial governments has made possible a complete reorganisation of the economy. The division of the land has ended the rule of the Junkers, who have been the curse of Germany ever since she emerged as a state. Labour legislation and health services are much farther advanced than they were in the Weimar Republic. The trade unions have won rights for the shop stewards in regard to management and production which have changed the whole status of labour. The Co-operative movement, given back the property confiscated by the Nazis, is already re-emerging as an important factor in the life of the Zone. Cultural activities are being pressed forward with amazing energy.

Constitutions for the Lands and Provinces*—Saxony, Saxony-Anhalt, Thuringia, Brandenburg, and Mecklenburg-Pomerania—are already operating. They provide a more completely democratic form than has ever previously been achieved in German history.

All these things are there, but they have not been secured by the active pressure and the conscious effort of the masses. They have been achieved mainly by the activities of the anti-Fascists, who were thrown into positions of responsibility by the collapse and who have inevitably leaned very heavily on the Russian administration.

Significantly, however, in late 1946 and in the first months of 1947 when the situation in Germany was generally deteriorating, there were many signs that the people in the Soviet Zone were being drawn into the struggle for economic and social betterment. It began with the overwhelming plebiscite in Saxony in favour of taking over the property of war-criminals, and showed itself in succeeding months in an increase in activity by the democratic organisations, despite the all-prevailing hunger and cold.

To take one revealing incident: in January, 1947, the two Right Wing parties in the Parliament of Saxony managed to push through a measure to hand some of the state-owned factories back to their previous owners. Within a few hours of the decision's being made public, telegrams reached the provincial government in Dresden from factories all over the province threatening immediate strike action. The police are organised in the public employees' trade union and have their own elected shop stewards, and a number of police stations in the areas concerned wired saying they would back a strike. As one of the leaders of the Saxony branch of the Free German Trade Unions told me: " Within twenty-four hours we would have had a general strike in Saxony."

The Socialist Unity Party (the S.E.D.) was against any strike action because they feared it would destroy their working arrangement with the other two parties, the Christian Democratic Union (C.D.U.) and the Liberal Democratic Party (L.D.P.), but they could not stop the movement. Eventually three elected shop stewards, from one of the towns particularly affected, arrived in Dresden and announced they were not going to leave until the decision was reversed. The Prime Minister called a special meeting of Ministers to examine the

---

* Actually there are technically four "Lands" (or Lænder) and one "Province," but for the convenience of the reader, to whom the difference is purely academic, I have used the adjective "provincial" to describe them throughout.

position, in conjunction with the trade union leaders, and eventually agreement was reached to retain for the state all factories except one or two very small ones. The Russians did not come into the affair at all.

In various parts of the Zone strikes have taken place to force on reluctant employers the union agreement giving extensive powers to the shop stewards.

These incidents are significant. They did not come from exasperation at the difficult conditions of life; they were based on a clear belief in the importance of nationalised industry and trade union rights for the betterment of the conditions of the people. Such a development would have been impossible in the first months after the occupation when, with the exception of the proved anti-Fascists, the population seemed incapable of taking any decisions or showing any initiative. One Soviet General said to me: " For several months the Germans were pouring into my office asking for permission to do this and for permission to do that. Now at last they are making decisions for themselves. To me that is our biggest achievement so far in Germany: that we are beginning to develop initiative among the German people."

The propaganda of the various organisations in the Zone is directed constantly towards making the people believe in the reality of their new-found democracy, and it is not possible day in and day out to tell men and women that they have such a weapon in their hands without at some time reaching the point where they begin to use it. Moreover, the trade unions and the political parties, particularly the Socialist Unity Party, are conducting a campaign to educate their members to take up positions of responsibility.

The critics will reply that in the Soviet Zone the Russians are backing the Communists and placing them in key positions, and that the democratic structure is merely a façade. That general and widely circulated criticism can be answered only by the picture of the various aspects of life in the Zone which I have tried to give as objectively as possible in the succeeding chapters.

It may be of value, however, to deal at the outset with some of the more irresponsible criticisms and to fill in the human background against which developments since the occupation have taken place.

Many of the sedulously propagated stories about the Zone disappear into thin air once an observer comes into close contact with the people. No one, for example, challenges the fairness or the secrecy of the various elections for the provincial parliaments and the local authorities, and that view was shared by the Allied observers who were present in the Zone during the polling. It was expressed by one

of the American observers in a note which I saw in the visitors' book
at the Thuringian headquarters of the Soviet administration in
Weimar, in which he wrote: " This has been a most profitable and
enjoyable trip, the best answer to the innumerable lies I read daily in
our Press. I have been deeply impressed by the fairness of the
elections, the democratic way they have been conducted and the
outspokenness of the people in general."

These elections were fought with real controversy and in many
parts with bitterness. Some of the polemics would have come
within the law of libel in a British election. The Socialist Unity Party
(the S.E.D.) lost rather than gained votes because of its general
policy of friendship with the Russians. In Halle, the Liberals produced
a fake poster in which they falsely attributed to the S.E.D. a demand
to make the Zone a Soviet Republic and for this some of them landed
themselves in gaol.

Although the political life of the Zone is based on the " bloc of
the anti-Fascist parties," that is, the co-operation of the S.E.D., the
L.D.P., and the C.D.U., on a jointly formulated programme, the
political balance of any particular authority makes a big difference to
its approach to day-to-day problems.

In those villages where Liberals and Christian Democrats have a
decisive majority, there are endless tussles over the carrying out of
policies laid down by the higher authorities in which the Socialists
are stronger. And these authorities really do have responsibility for
administration. The Russians are there, but they are leaving the
Germans to do the job.

Religion, which was under constant attack by the Nazis, is
completely free under the Russians. This again is a fact which the
anti-Soviet elements—and there are plenty in the Zone—do not
attempt to challenge. Ministers of religion and leaders of the Christian
Democrats have both told me the same thing—that the Red Army
brought back the freedom of religion which Hitler destroyed.

There are no signs of Russian pressure on the German administration or on the people. Soviet troops are surprisingly few. Officers
and men join in the rush for the crowded tramcars, they drink thin
German beer in the crowded beer-halls, they wait their turn in the
barbers' shops, without demanding any privileges. The people are
not afraid to express open criticism of the administration. You can
hear it everywhere—voiced in a way that would have landed those
responsible in gaol during the Nazi regime.

This is a people conditioned for years to a life of fear, to the
knowledge that a Gestapo informer might be listening. Now they are

speaking freely, even though they know that their country is under Russian occupation. The conclusion seems to me inescapable—their freedom is a reality.

In my opinion, one of the best developments from the Russian point of view will be the breaking down of the foolish barriers prohibiting the exchange of newspapers and publications between the Zones. When the Germans in the East read some of the stories about their Zone appearing in the British and American Press and the Press of Western Germany, the obvious absurdity of the stories will do a good deal to discredit the rumour-mongers.

What is the truth about the most widely circulated allegations of all—the stories of crimes committed by Soviet army men against the German population? It is impossible to check up on all the reports, but two facts emerge. First, the Soviet authorities took and are taking the most ruthless measures against any of their own people convicted of criminal acts, and they are not afraid to discuss the problem with the Germans.

At a public meeting in Weimar, one of a series which the Russians organised in the Zone to explain their policy to the German population, the Russian major who had spoken on " The tasks and aims of the Soviet Army," was asked about incidents caused by the occupation troops. He assured the meeting, in the name of the officers and men of the Soviet Army, that any such incidents would be stopped. " Any Soviet soldier," he said, " who besmirches the honour of the Soviet Army will receive the most drastic punishment." At the same time he pointed out how many crimes were wrongly attributed to Red* Army men.

That is the second fact: criminal elements both among the Germans and the large number of foreign nationals constantly posed as Russians. Towards the end of the war the Nazis used the Vlassov army of renegade Russians for the deliberate purpose of terrorising the population and some of these elements still exist, although large numbers have been rounded up.

Walter Jurich, Police President of Leipzig, told me: " It is only necessary for a bandit to put on a fur hat and speak broken German for the word to go round that there has been a crime committed by the Russians. Girls who want to explain an awkward pregnancy always find it easy to blame a Russian." I was shown statistics by the German police in a number of towns setting out the cases in which

---

* Officially the Red Army has now become the Soviet Army, but the old term is still widely used.

Germans and foreigners posing as Russians were caught, and these showed a negligible percentage proved against the Russians. The incidents I came across personally showed that the Russian authorities were only too anxious to take action to put matters right. In one small town a Russian took a motor-cycle. The owner went to the local commander to report the theft. The next day he was called to the Russian barracks and found every motor-cycle in the hands of the Russians set out for his inspection. He picked out his own. It was handed to him with apologies and an assurance that the offender would be punished.

Another sidelight on the problem was expressed to me by a Russian. He said: " Some of our men come from villages completely wiped out by the Germans. Now if they are caught taking anything from the Germans, they get ten years. That's pretty hard."

With the rounding up of bandits the incidence of crime in the Zone has been reduced to a surprisingly low level, and cases of indiscipline by the occupation forces have been extremely rare since November and December, 1946, when a big proportion of the men who had been through the war were demobilised. During the whole period of my stay in the Zone, I heard shots fired only once. It was in the early hours of the morning and I discovered later that they were fired by German police rounding up a German gang. Since the very early days of the occupation, there have been only a few minor cases of proved pro-Nazi activity. There were, however, some cases of arson in state-owned factories in the autumn of 1946, the origin of which appears to be uncertain.

There is plenty of talk still going the rounds about occurrences during the first days of occupation. Some bad incidents took place. The Red Army had fought its way from Stalingrad to Berlin through thousands of miles of Russian countryside devastated with sadistic thoroughness by the Germans. The men had seen the tortures inflicted on their own people. They came to Germany to find homes stuffed with loot. Millions of the best of Russia's manhood, trained in the principles of a Socialist army, had perished. The units which eventually reached Berlin contained many elements, even criminals who had been given the chance to redeem themselves by fighting for their country. Some of them got out of control. But when you hear the stories from the people on the spot you find that there is general agreement that order was very quickly restored.

Some of the incidents were amusing rather than tragic, as for example the woman in Dresden who told me how one Red Army man came in to demand her watch, but was followed by a second who promptly threw his companion out and gave her a large sausage as a

peace-offering, or the "very nice young Russian" who politely
collected sewing machines from a whole street because the Germans
had taken every one from his native village and he was determined to
make restitution. I heard just as many stories about the Americans
in the areas which they captured before the Red Army took over,
but these incidents were not used by the world Press to discredit the
American Army.

In the last days the Nazis ran amok, and large sections of the
population indulged in organised looting, so that much of the losses of
property were the result of German and not Russian depredations.
The only stabilising element in this chaotic situation came from
the various anti-Fascist groups, some built up in the last months of
the war, others formed spontaneously, often with the help of released
victims from the concentration camps. In many districts they took
control while the Nazis, the landlords, police officers, and other
pro-Fascists were trying to escape to the West.

In many towns and villages I learned the story of events preceding
and during the entry of the Red Army. The pattern was usually the same.

The story of Leipzig is typical. It was told me by Hans Schlosser,
who was imprisoned for the first five years of the Nazi regime and
eventually released because, so the Nazis told him, "a man who
spends his time in prison studying Hegel can't be dangerous."
Schlosser succeeded in getting an illegal anti-Fascist group going in
Leipzig during the last months of the collapse. "But," he told me,
"the Nazis' rule was effective to the last. Even the progressive
elements among the workers were thinking in terms of 1933."

In the last days before the Americans reached the city a Committee
for Free Germany was formed and tried to maintain some sort of
order. On one occasion a crowd of several thousand was bent on
plundering the food stores. Six members of the committee faced
them, in danger at any moment of being trampled underfoot. There
were moments of tension and then someone from the crowd shouted
"these are the right people." The mood of the crowd changed and
they eventually dispersed.

Action by the anti-Fascists stopped the mass plundering all over
the Zone. In Riesa a Social Democrat, Richard Wunderlich, stopped
the looting of the Co-operative stores by explaining to the crowd
that, with the destruction of the Nazi regime, they would be able
to demand the return of co-operative property.

I was given copies of the posters which the Leipzig Free German
Committee somehow succeeded in printing in the first days of
liberation and with which they plastered the town. These called on
the people to stop looting and explained that by denuding the stores

the looters would threaten the town with starvation, and called on all sections of the people to begin the reconstruction of their country.

The Americans were the first to enter Leipzig and the anti-Fascist committee at once came out with posters and proclamations asking the people to help the American authorities in the restoration of order and the arrest of the Nazis. Very soon, however, there was a clash. The Americans installed a certain Dr. Vierling as burgo-master and the Free German Committee issued posters exposing his record as a banker and German nationalist.

During this period, the Communist and Social Democrat members of the Free German Committee formed a close working alliance, a link which remained until the two parties merged into the Socialist Unity Party. Then the Russians came in, bringing manifestos printed in German repeating Stalin's words: "Hitlers come and go but the German people and the German State remain," and declaring that their task was to destroy Hitlerism and Fascism. The anti-Fascist Committee became the basis for the government of the town and Dr. Vierling and others like him were quickly out of office.

In varying forms, that story could be repeated for most of the towns taken over by the Russians, except that things happened more quickly where they were the first occupying troops. During those first weeks some of the Nazis and Nazi sympathisers met with rough justice, particularly at the hands of the foreign workers. In some districts the Red Army took the job of liberation too literally and opened up not only the prisons and the concentration camps but the lunatic asylums as well! Many criminals were loose in the general chaos. But the Russians had one clear principle—if a man or a woman were a proved anti-Fascist, that was sufficient guarantee. A high Russian officer put it to me quite simply when he said: "When we found a man who fought Fascism in Spain or who suffered years of imprisonment because he refused to assist Nazi tyranny, then we accepted him as one who would work with us in destroying the rem-nants of the Nazi regime." Not every Red Army man understood these principles and there was much heartburning among anti-Fascists who came into contact with occupation forces conscious only of what Germany had done to their country.

Nevertheless, this principle of accepting the help of the anti-Fascists enabled the Russian occupation to get over many of the initial difficulties, and despite the hardships which followed they have kept alive this sense of liberation among the best elements of the German people and, I am convinced, are drawing behind them a widening section of progressive opinion. That, I believe, is why in the Soviet Zone one finds among the democratic elements an atmosphere of hope and not of frustration, despite disappointments and setbacks, and why in the Soviet Zone the occupation forces—albeit slowly—are gaining rather than losing prestige.

Inevitably, the alliance of the Russians with the anti-Fascists has created the possibility of a cleft between the anti-Fascists on the one hand and the mass of the population on the other. And on this question it is always necessary to remember that denazification has removed tens of thousands of Nazis from well-paid jobs and positions in which they not only exerted authority but also enjoyed graft at the expense of the people. Many of these Nazis have been forced to take up manual work, and though they dare not come into the open as Nazis, they seize on every opportunity to discredit both the German and Russian administration.

Their activity takes various forms. In times of acute shortage it is always easy to start the cry that officials, party leaders, and so on are receiving preference at the expense of the rest of the population, and the pro-Nazis are making maximum use of it. To some extent the allegation is true, for certified victims of Fascism who are very largely in key positions have had special privileges conferred on them by legislation. They receive a higher food category, a special rebate in taxation, and deliveries of coal and other commodities through the Victims of Fascism organisation. Recognised " Fighters against Fascism "—that is the men and women who suffered in the concentration camps or in some other way proved their active resistance to the Nazis—secure an additional preference.

I visited many former concentration camp inmates in the luxurious flats from which Gestapo leaders and other Nazi criminals had been ejected. In this respect, too, they have privileges, for with the flood of refugees, or " resettlers " as they are called, from the new Polish areas and the Sudetenland, the housing position is terrifyingly acute and the ordinary householder is liable at any time to have a family billeted upon him.

There is a danger here. Naturally concessions to the anti-Fascists give support to the cry about " Communist dictatorship," but as far as the Russians are concerned they view the situation quite objectively. They say that it is a very good thing that the mass of the people should be made to understand that there is a difference in the attitude of the administration towards the great bulk of the German people who actively or passively backed Hitler and the minority who fought against him. The victims of Fascism are selected not by the Russians but by a joint committee of the three parties, and they include people of all political views and many without party such as Jews who have lost their relatives.

B

Hostile elements use every means to try to discredit the Russians. I was told of one meeting at Dresden where a German who was speaking on Russian culture was persistently interrupted by cat-calls. A musical programme followed at which the work of German composers was listened to in silence while items of Russian music became the signal for whistling and talking. In the queues there will usually be someone to explain that " Germany is short because the Russians are taking all the food " and that " things are far better in the West."

An incident in a Leipzig tram occurred while I was there. A German deliberately pushed two Russian women. One of the women turned and reprimanded him in Russian. The man turned to the other occupants of the tram and declared his views about " Russian vermin." A German girl, white with rage, retorted: " You can think yourself lucky that the Russians don't treat people like you as you deserve. After what the Fascist vermin did to the Russian people it's a wonder they don't tread people like you into the ground." There was an uneasy silence and the man got out at the next stop. I met a number of Germans, many of them not actively political, who expressed the view that the authorities give too much freedom to these elements who are busy trying to undermine the new democratic foundations which are so painfully being built.

Talk of a coming war between West and East is widespread. Again and again I was asked the question whether such a war was coming. One woman came to me weeping and asked: " Is it true that the Americans are going to drop atom bombs on us ? Haven't we had enough of war ? " I told her that though differences might arise between the Allies, the people in all the countries would see that there was no new war and that Germans who tried to split the Allies were the worst enemies of their country. She ran out with tears in her eyes, shouting to the rest of the people in the house, " Gott sei dank, the Englishman says that there will not be a new war."

Unfortunately those Germans who do wish to split the Allies receive constant encouragement from the anti-Soviet campaign in Britain and America and in the Western Zones of Germany—and also from the anti-British and anti-American atmosphere often reflected in the Press of the Eastern Zone. It is a campaign which is dangerous, not so much for Russia as for Europe, for it feeds on masses of Germans still completely oblivious to the part that they played in Hitler's crimes. The story of a woman employed in a Government department of Saxony is typical. She complained bitterly that a Russian took her bicycle during the Red Army advance through her town. The very next day the discussion turned on wireless sets and she said brightly: " Oh, I've got a lovely radio set. My husband sent it to me while he was serving in France."

The new German frontiers with Poland offer a much more tangible means of fostering discontent. Germany has not only lost resources of coal and steel and foodstuffs, but the refugees from the area have created a shortage of housing, furniture, clothing, and so on, which brings new burdens to the whole community. Already the frontier problem has become the " King Charles's head " of a big section. I had Germans almost weeping on my shoulder, telling me that the new frontiers and reparations were beyond endurance, in much the same way as they used to weep and tell you that the Jews and the Treaty of Versailles were responsible for all Germany's sufferings.

When you see the picture at close quarters, you realise how tenuous is the democracy which is being developed in Germany. The basic conditions are still there for any demagogue to recreate a movement of revenge and nationalism.

The Germans in the Soviet Zone, as in all the other Zones, are much more ready to pity themselves than to recognise their guilt and to join in an effort to make amends to the nations they wronged and to purge their life of the Fascism that brought all their suffering. When you see the whole picture you are torn between the two sides. You are inspired by the self-sacrificing efforts with which the best elements in the German people are facing the terrific problems before them. You are overwhelmed with sympathy when you see the suffering everywhere. Then you talk to the victims of the Nazi terror.

Take Leo Loewenkopf, for example, leader of the Jews in Dresden, who was imprisoned in Maidanek in Poland, and who escaped death by posing as a Pole, when the order came from Berlin to exterminate all Jews. Loewenkopf watched while 18,000 Jewish men, women, and children were stripped naked, machine-gunned, and buried in layers in a mass grave. He came back to Dresden. There he found that where there used to be 5,800 Jews, all but 133 had been murdered.

These stories of horror have become a commonplace, but they assume a new and awful reality when you hear them re-told in a German home. You leave, seeing vast numbers of the people around you who still have only one quarrel with Hitler—that he lost the war. You see the ruins of Dresden and you almost have a savage feeling of satisfaction that here, at least, is a lesson the Germans will not be able to forget, a grim reminder of the destruction Nazism brought upon the world.

This psychological aspect of the German problem cannot be overlooked in any assessment of the developments in the Russian Zone. Had there been a German revolution at any time before the collapse, the Red Army would have marched in as liberators. As it was they came as conquerors, with a bitter hatred for the Germans responsible for the devastation of their land and something of a contempt even for the anti-Fascist forces because they had proved so weak and so incapable of saving even a few Red Army lives.

Apart from the type of incident already referred to, their attitude from the beginning was correct. There was no ban on fraternisation, but in most areas Red Army men preferred to keep to themselves. Organisation of administrative machinery in the early weeks was largely a matter of improvisation, and varied according to the temperament and ability of the commander who happened to be in charge of any given district. The remarkable thing, however, was the speed with which the Soviet administration got down to creating machinery of government. And here one finds the key to much that has happened since 1945. The Russians, after fighting for four terrible years, had no cut-and-dried plan for taking over their area of Germany. They had not been able to train special staffs for the various jobs. But they knew what they wanted and had worked out a set of guiding principles.

They had taken to heart Stalin's statement that the German State would go on and therefore, despite their bitterness, they took immediate steps to give the Germans an opportunity of rebuilding the trade unions, the anti-Fascist parties, and other mass organisations.

In their propaganda during the early months the Russians made many mistakes, but the constant use of those words of Stalin, spoken, not after victory, but at the time when Germany was aiming at the destruction of Russia, had a tremendous effect on the German population. From the beginning the Russians encouraged these democratic organisations, and they pushed as much authority as possible on to them and on to the anti-Fascists who had been placed in administrative positions all over the Zone. Thus there were improvised German ministries for the principal sections of government operating for the whole Zone within a few weeks of the occupation. In conjunction with the Soviet administration, these bodies began to tackle the most urgent problems—the campaign against epidemic disease, the starting of industry, and so on.

From the beginning food was used as a lever to make people work. Banking accounts were stopped so that people could not live on the profits of Hitler's war. The ration cards were granted so that those doing the heaviest work received the most food.

Above all, the Russians came with a positive rather than a negative approach to denazification. They were determined to get the Nazis out, but they preferred to give the Germans an opportunity to do it themselves and they gave every encouragement to plans to train new teachers, new judges, new administrators to take their place. One of the lesser-known differences between Eastern and Western democracy is that the Russians see nothing out of the way in turning a plumber into a judge.

Moreover, the positive approach to denazification meant that the Russians backed the anti-Fascist parties in attacking, not only the Nazis, but the economic causes of Fascism. That is why from the beginning their main broadsides were reserved for the monopolists and the great landowners, whom they regarded as the creators and principal supporters of the Nazi regime.

Slowly these developments created a new situation. A genuine co-operation began to grow up between the Russians and Germans engaged in common tasks—not as between conqueror and conquered, but as between colleagues. The Red Army began to sort out their own specialists for the various tasks; other specialists came from the Soviet Union. The German in charge of a particular section of administration, either at the centre or in the provinces and towns, found that his Russian opposite number was an expert at his job. That in its turn had important repercussions. The Russians in key jobs in Germany began to fight for concessions from Moscow, not out of sympathy for the Germans but because they were determined to make their work in Germany a success. That was one of the factors present during the period of dismantlement of German factories which ended when, at the beginning of 1947, Marshal Sokolowsky ordered that no more machinery was to be scheduled for dismantlement and a specified division was to be made between reparations and goods for the German market.

The destruction of German war factories and the taking of a portion of her industrial plant as reparations were methods agreed upon by the Allies to ensure against a revival of German aggression and to provide some compensation for the countries which Germany devastated. To suggest that the property taken by the Russians has destroyed or crippled the industrial capacity of Eastern Germany is plain nonsense. The fact is that under Hitler—even before the war—so much industry was switched over to armaments that to-day Eastern Germany has a bigger potential for peace production than at any time since the Nazi armaments drive began. What Eastern Germany lacks are the raw materials which formerly came from the West.

Nevertheless, dismantlement caused grave difficulties and quite a lot of tension even between the genuine anti-Fascist section of the Germans and the Russians. It was not easy, even for trade union leaders and shop stewards who understood the necessity for and the justice of reparations, to explain to workers that the factories they had painfully restarted were to be packed up and sent to Russia. Sometimes a factory would be scheduled for dismantlement which broke a whole chain of production and threw the plan for a whole area out of gear. Dismantlement was directed, not by the Soviet administration in Germany, but by a special department in Moscow, and sometimes the dismantlement squads carried out their work in such a way as to cause maximum hostility among the German population.

There were many cases, however, where the local Soviet administration fought hard to retain certain factories in Germany. I heard of one instance where a factory, which was the only one of its kind in the Zone was scheduled for dismantlement. In this case the officer in charge of the dismantlement realised the consequences to German economy and co-operated with the shop stewards in getting it stopped. He delayed the work for some weeks, while the workers organised a deputation to the Soviet headquarters in Berlin and eventually secured a reversal of the decision.

The last assignments of machinery to go to Russia were from a number of mines which had been ear-marked before the order declaring dismantlement at an end. There was a long fight to secure a reprieve, but Moscow was adamant. The Russian mining areas had suffered such complete devastation that they would not forgo their claim. To the men in Moscow struggling to rebuild thousands of square miles of what was once Russia's greatest industrial area, the claims of the country responsible for the crime were not so likely to find a sympathetic hearing as they would to the Russian whose main concern was the immediate problem of German recovery.

There were cases where machinery was badly handled during dismantling or was allowed to deteriorate before being transported to Russia, and naturally these were the subject of widespread propaganda. I visited a number of factories, however, where dismantlement had taken place, and German technicians, many of whom were quite ready to criticise bitterly the actions of the Russians, all agreed that the Russian engineers responsible for the work were experts at their job. Moreover, in very many factories a specified percentage of machines remained and great care was taken to leave enough of each type to enable the plant to be restarted.

In this matter one cannot do more than cite a few cases, personally investigated, but it seems obvious that the Russians who desperately needed the German machines and who at the same time were clearly trying to help the recovery of German peace industry, would not, generally speaking, be so foolish as to do the job of dismantling inefficiently. Those people who still believe the story that Russia does not possess skilled engineers will no doubt go on believing it.

Similar problems arose over the question of reparations from current production. There were Russian commanders in some localities who set out to get maximum reparations in rather the same spirit with which they would push up production in their own country, and naturally bad feelings were evoked among the German population.

I think there can be no doubt that from the point of view of the German problem dismantlement was too drastic and the original proportion of reparation goods was too high, although from the viewpoint of devastated Russia, any burdens imposed on Germany could be justified up to the hilt. The Russians, however, clearly recognised the situation when they called a halt to dismantlement, returned a large number of factories earmarked as reparations to the German people, specified the proportion of production which must remain for German consumption, and declared that goods made from German raw materials should remain in the country.

Other factors enter into the question of reparations from current production. From the viewpoint of the German worker the effect of reparations is psychological rather than practical. He is actually in no different position from the British worker who makes goods for export which he knows are needed on the home market. In any case German workers have never in history been consulted about the destination of the goods they made.

It is also clear that, apart from necessities like clothing and furniture, which are now being diverted in fairly substantial quantities to the Germans, it would be futile to place other goods on the home market before the food and cigarette situation improves. If German cameras, typewriters, and similar goods were put on sale at controlled prices, within the shortest possible time they would be swelling the black market and many of them would reach the Western Zones to be exchanged for English and American cigarettes at the black market price of 3s. 6d. each.*

---

* Actually the price of a cigarette in terms of 1944 costs at which present prices and wages are controlled is nearer 10s. In transforming German marks into English money I have taken the rough figure of fifteen to the £ when dealing with salaries, budget figures and so on. This represents a fair comparison in terms of controlled prices.

It is against the background of these problems that an assessment
of the Soviet Zone must be made. The Russians certainly have no
illusions about the difficulties of their task. They know how far
Germany must progress before the danger of a revival of Fascism is
over and the German people are ripe for a complete democratic
development. At the same time, they are convinced that only by
destroying the basis of Fascism and encouraging the democratic
forces can the difficulties be overcome. Under military occupation
there can never be complete democracy, and the Soviet administration
will always keep a tight hold on the situation. In the last resort, the
Russians are the rulers of their zone of Germany and they will not
allow the forms of democracy to be used to provide a cover for the
revival of reaction. That is why they have not permitted a succession
of splinter parties, nor have they allowed so-called independent
candidates at elections. There are, however, many organisations in
the Zone embracing the main political viewpoints, the trade unions,
the co-operatives, women, youth, and various cultural activities.
The test for a political party, as the Russians see it, is not whether it is
Left or Right in its policy but whether it is anti-Fascist.

No doubt most Russian administrators find it easier to get on
with the S.E.D. representatives than with some of the others, but
officially there is equal treatment for all parties.

As far as the divisions between the Left are concerned, the Russians
regard the decision of the Communists and Social Democrats to join
together in the Socialist Unity Party as a matter entirely for the
Germans, and they say that they have not yet received any application
by the Social Democrats of the West to organise in the Zone. At the
same time, the Russians, in my view, will not allow a party to operate on
a platform of hostility to the Allies and particularly to themselves,
whatever title it may adopt. That is to say if Schumacher, the leader
of the Western Social Democrats, comes to the Soviet Zone to tell the
people that " the Communists are the Nazis of to-day," as he did in
Berlin, I imagine he will be stopped. To the Russians a complete
parallel would be if in the British Zone a German political party
adopted as its policy the slogan that Mr. Attlee is no different from
Hitler.

To the purist that is no doubt a negation of democracy, but the
Russians, remembering why they are in Germany, prefer a more
practical approach. As for the argument developed in the West that
the various mass organisations are not democratic because the
Communists play a leading part in them, that is the viewpoint among
some members of the Labour Party in Britain regarding every
movement based on broad progressive forces if the Communists are

taking a share in it. It may be a tenable policy in Britain, but it certainly is not practical politics in the Soviet Zone of Germany.

A much more pressing consideration is the over-shadowing influence of the food situation on the political and cultural developments in the Zone. One of the big advances in the Zone was that the various democratic organisations were sufficiently well founded by the winter of 1946–7 to keep going despite all the difficulties. But future progress depends in a very large degree on the ability of the Allies to solve the economic situation sufficiently to provide some improvements in the general standards.

Rations in the Zone vary from 1,500 calories for the lowest card to something over 2,000 for the heavy workers, but calories do not make up for the shortage of fats and vitamins, and there is no doubt that the population is hungry, although by no means starving. The hard winter of 1946–7 imposed further hardships and it was a great feat of organisation to ensure that although supplies were sometimes irregular, all through those bitter months ration cards were invariably honoured and it was an even greater feat that early in 1947 several millions in the then lowest category had an increase. The biggest blow of that winter was the destruction of large quantities of potatoes by the heavy frosts which penetrated to the storage clamps. That meant losses of vital food which had been carefully hoarded to bridge the gap before the new harvest. Purchases of various substitute foodstuffs from Czechoslovakia partially made good the deficiency.

The hunger and the shortages conceal from most people in the Zone the very real progress that has been made, but when these are overcome the extent to which the foundations for a new life have been laid will become apparent. How far these foundations have been laid, the difficulties still remaining and the possibilities of the future, I have sought to set out in succeeding chapters.

2

CONTRASTS

THE contrast between the passive hostility adopted by a fairly large section of the German population and the enthusiasm shown by those who are pressing forward with the tasks of rebuilding, overshadows everything. To get the picture in perspective and to assess the difficulties facing both the Germans and the Russians, the reactions and the potentialities of both these sections must be constantly kept in mind. Let me try to crystallise this contrast in three pictures of life in the Zone to-day.

First, a typical " little man " in post-war Germany—not a Nazi, but one of the millions who helped to put Hitler in power and who " heiled " him until the final defeat. I found this particular person in a rather curious way, but there are hundreds of thousands like him to be met everywhere. He had been commander of a prisoner-of-war camp in Saxony, with a mixed population of British and Russian prisoners. His rule in the camp was fair, so much so that a friend of mine in England, who was one of his prisoners, gave me his address and asked me to look him up. Although not a member of the Nazi Party he never disguised from the English prisoners either his support for Hitler or his fear of the consequences of the Russians' getting to Germany. I found him back in his hairdresser's shop in a small town in the Zone.

In the last months of the war he was removed from his post as camp commander because a Gestapo informer reported that he had disobeyed regulations by allowing a coffin for the burial of a Russian prisoner. As a punishment he was sent to the front. He was taken prisoner in Czechoslovakia and put to dismantling the barricades in Prague. He attempted to escape and was thrown into gaol with a number of Gestapo and S.S. men who were due to be tried. He was there a fortnight before he was taken to other quarters.

He told me of his sufferings and then launched into a long tirade on the ill-treatment which he and other Germans had received in this Czech prison. I asked whether he included the S.S. prisoners among those he was defending. " I say," he said, " that they are all human beings."

Did he think that of the Germans who operated the gas chambers ?

Compared with the sufferings he had endured, the gas chamber was easier, he answered.

Did he realise that the gassings were not isolated examples of brutality, but were the result of a definite policy which resulted in the deliberate murder of millions of men, women, and children ?

He hesitated: Was it a planned system ? he asked. His experience was that the orders from above were always very fair; the trouble was that individuals sometimes gave way to brutality.

He had plenty of opportunity to talk to his customers. Did they, too, think the gassings were isolated cases I asked him.

His customers never talked about such things. They knew there were bad incidents during the war, but then it happened in every country. Look at his own experience. Look how badly clothed the prisoners came back from Russia. "After all, war is war."

I pressed the point. Did he see no difference between a regime which deliberately murdered millions of human beings and nations who defended themselves against unprovoked aggression?

Again, he hesitated. He knew about the Jews, of course, and that was bad, but then you never knew what was truth and what propaganda.

Did his customers feel that things were better or worse? I asked.

Oh, things were certainly getting worse. Everyone was hungry and few had enough coal during the bitter weather to heat even one room.

Whose fault was that ?

The Russians. They had taken away the machinery and they had removed the people who knew their jobs from all the responsible posts.

But surely the people who had been removed from posts were Nazis?

Yes, that was so and, of course, he was anti-Nazi, but before long they would have to put these people back in their posts. Otherwise they would never recover. You couldn't get on without skilled people, even though they were Nazis.

Now, about this food business. He did realise, I suggested, that there were other nations in Europe as hungry as his zone of Germany. The rations on his card were low, but not starvation level.

Again, he shrugged his shoulders. Germans were not used to such low standards. It was true that you always eventually got what was on your card, but then, supplies were often late and that was very inconvenient.

Why was food so short ?

Mostly it was this land reform. They had broken the land into too small units and they couldn't use machinery as they used to on the big estates.

But was the machinery there now?

Oh no, it had mostly been taken away. Some of the landowners had gone off to the West with their machinery and then, of course, the Russians had taken some. Now the peasants were unable to pay the percentage of crop demanded by the government.

How did he know all this?

He'd just come back from his home town in Mecklenburg, and fortunately he'd been able to bring back a nice bit of potatoes, flour, and a few other things.

So the peasants must have a few reserves after all?

Oh yes, there was a man he met during his visit who was running a lorry to Berlin with foodstuffs. He went twice a week and made 40,000 marks every trip!

Wasn't that sort of thing defeating all the efforts to improve the food situation?

Yes, he supposed it was, but then the Russians never encouraged anyone to show initiative. Why, he heard of a textile factory which proposed to give every one of the workers a piece of cloth and the Russians stopped it.

But surely that was to stop the stuff going in the black market?

He shrugged his shoulders.

What then, I asked, was his remedy for all this.

Of course he was only telling what his customers said. He himself had seen enough of war, but they were saying that the Allies were sure to disagree and then the Americans and the English would come into Eastern Germany.

Did they think things were so much better in the West?

Everybody used to think so, but he'd been hearing a different story just lately. For example, it was amazing how many visitors from the West, during the Leipzig Fair, had said that they were surprised to find that things in the Russian Zone were much better than they'd been led to believe.

Maybe, then, it wouldn't be such a good idea after all for the Allies to start another war?

No, what ought to happen was for all the Allies to agree to send Germany more food and then to restore the frontiers so that all these settlers from Poland could go back. They were really the cause of most of the trouble. He went back to his hair-cutting.

There are millions like him in Germany. Not vicious, but completely impervious to the effects which Hitler's policy inflicted on the world, they are waiting for something to turn up. They would fall to-day, as they fell in the Weimar period, for any demagogue who traded on their hardship and provided them with a scapegoat.

Here is a story of the other people:

The old-established firm of Rudolphe Sack, near Leipzig, was busy making war supplies for Hitler from the beginning of the Nazi rearmament until the collapse in 1945. The owner, Otto Sack, was a prominent Nazi. A certificate from Funk, Nazi Economic Minister, thanking him for his services is still preserved in the shop stewards room. The shop stewards hope this certificate will be asked for by the American Zone, for Otto went away with the Americans and has since written gleefully to say that he expects soon to be cleared by a denazification court.

Otto did not give up without a fight. While the Americans were still in Leipzig, he called together 120 of his workers, including a number of members of the Nazi Party, to try to persuade them to back him. After he had given his address, however, Karl Schindler, an old trade unionist and member of the Social Democratic Party, got up and said that he proposed to resume the job of shop steward which he had held until the Nazis threw him out in 1933.

A few days later Fritz Pfau, a Communist, who had spent some time in concentration camps in the early years of the Nazi regime and who had afterwards been compelled to work under supervision in the most arduous shop in the factory, came back. These two were joined by another old worker who had been in the Social Democratic Party since 1919, and they set to work to organise the factory.

The Americans were persuaded to arrest Sack, but all the other Nazis in the administration were left. Then the Russians came in and the trade union committee promptly turned out all the Nazis.

One director, a Liberal Democrat from pre-Hitler times, who had never had anything to do with the Nazis, was the only director left. He was made general manager. Other posts were filled from the staff. A skilled engineer was made technical director.

Altogether there were only eighty members of the Nazi Party in a staff of 1,200 and no action was taken against the small fry who were known to have taken only a nominal part in Nazi activities.

From that time the shop stewards ran the factory. In May, 1945, they started work. The plant, which had been used for machine gun parts, turned over literally and not figuratively to making plough-shares. It also turned out small agricultural implements and garden tools. Things went ahead very well and by the autumn of 1945 they were short of workers. So the Labour Exchange sent along an assortment of ex-Nazis to help in the foundry. Among them was a doctor, who had so bad a Nazi record that he had been deprived of his medical degree, a lawyer, and a number of teachers.

They were still there in March, 1947, sweating in the foundry. They receive the ordinary trade union rates of pay and live in their own homes, but they are not allowed to leave their jobs in the factory and may not join the trade union.

" We keep an eye on them to see they don't run away," said Fritz Pfau.

By January, 1946, the factory had drawn up an ambitious plan for the year to include production of all sorts of agricultural implements, seed sowing machines, and other articles. Then in March the blow fell. A Russian dismantling squad arrived with orders to take away the machinery. The order came from Moscow and no appeal was possible. Actually, the Russians were within their rights for the undertaking was undoubtedly a war factory. In fact, Hitler's rearmament programme had long ago deprived German agriculture of the machinery which Sack used to provide in the years of the Weimar Republic.

A meeting of the whole staff was called by the shop stewards. The men were angry. The three who had taken over the organisation in the beginning faced the hostile crowd of workers. They told the men that this was the price which had to be paid for Hitler's war, that tens of thousands of Russian factories had been destroyed by German aggression, and that it would still be their task to rebuild after the dismantlement.

They negotiated with the Russian dismantling squad and secured a promise that the shop stewards would retain their rights during the process. For the first few days relations were bad, but the Russians took meticulous care to consult the shop stewards over every question. Thirty-five per cent of capacity was to be left and Russians and Germans jointly decided on the allocation so that at least one machine for every process was left behind. The German staff carried out most of the dismantling, their wages being calculated by the shop stewards and paid by the Russians.

At the time of the dismantling there were 800 workers. None was dismissed and they set to work to re-arrange the machinery that had been left. They retrieved some other machines from bombed-out factories and managed to buy a few more. The job took them two months.

Fritz Pfau patted one of the machines. " If some of your experts saw this, they would laugh their heads off," he said. " But we don't care. It works."

They started work again. With a chuckle they told me how one Russian department encouraged them to clear up and use scrap from bomb sites. Then another department came along and fined them for using metal without authorisation. That sort of thing doesn't happen now as far as the Russians are concerned, since administration has been transferred to the Germans. But there is still plenty of red tape.

In the autumn of 1946 the factory was back in production and promptly received a reparations order, which was far bigger than they could possibly fulfil. They had delivered about a third of it, when early in 1947, Soviet military administration issued the order saying that only a percentage of production in each factory was to go in reparations. So now output was split between reparations and the German market.

What was the reaction of the workers towards making goods for reparations I asked.

Schindler replied that in the main there was far less hostility than might have been expected.

" You see," he said, " this factory was turning out war equipment for years and even in the pre-Nazi times when it was making agricultural implements we had no knowledge of where our products went. Our only concern was to keep our jobs. Now the great thing is that the wheels are turning. The workers feel that something is being rebuilt and that they themselves are responsible for it."

By the time the cold spell arrived in the winter of 1946–7, the number of workers had risen to 1,300 and the factory was turning out some first-class agricultural machinery. The cold meant that for a time only one or two shops could keep going.

" Who owns the factory ? " I asked.

" We don't know," Pfau replied. " Officially it is in the hands of a trustee until its ownership is decided, but we run it.

" Not a single decision is made without the shop stewards taking part. No one can be dismissed and no one taken on without our agreement. Every order and every official document comes in duplicate to us and to the general manager. The manager does not attempt to avoid consultations with us. There are no profits as everything goes back into the business and no one makes much money, for the general manager gets only 900 marks a month (about £60 at pre-war values) and nearly half of that goes in taxes."

Neither the shop stewards nor the manager has any contact with the Russian administration. Apart from the reparation orders, which come to them from the Saxony Government and which are paid for by advance credits, they sell products to agricultural co-operatives and the Peasants Mutual Aid organisation. All questions relating to absenteeism are dealt with by the shop stewards who can recommend the dismissal of persistent offenders, or apply the much more effective penalty of reporting the offender to the Food Office and so depriving him of his extra worker's allocation of rations.

Absenteeism, however, is not a big problem at Sack. I was shown the records and out of a staff of over 1,000 there were never more than between ten and fifteen absent without cause. The sickness rate, however, is as high as ten per cent. Their relations with the peasants enable them to get some extra foodstuffs from the country-side. " We pay control prices," said Pfau, " but the peasants hope to get some machinery out of it when supplies are available."

One of the problems of the Sack factory was an influx of settlers from the territories taken over by Poland. When they arrived the factory formed a committee of aid and collected furniture and clothing for them. " But," said one of the shop stewards, " they are bitter, and unfortunately records have been lost and we have no way of checking who used to be in the Nazi Party."

The factory was practically 100 per cent trade union in 1933 and largely because of the surviving trade union influence never had any substantial Nazi membership. Now it is again nearly 100 per cent organised and in the last elections a number of the officials, who had been in control since 1945, deliberately retired in order to bring in new blood. The factory branch of the Socialist Unity Party is also active and its officials are taken into consultation on all important questions.

I asked about the other two parties. " The fact is, there are no members," was the reply. " When, on instructions from the Government, we were ordered to appoint a tripartite committee consisting of one member of each party to see that denazification had been carried out, we had just one member of the L.D.P. and we had to borrow a C.D.U. member from another factory."

Now let me set down the story of Dresden, certainly the most bombed city in the Soviet Zone, and according to statistics I was given, probably at least as badly damaged as any of the great cities in the West. The story shows how the enthusiasm and determination of just a few men and women overcame apathy and gave to the people of the wrecked city a new sense of hope.

All the destruction was effected in two dreadful nights, February 13th and 14th, 1945. In thirty-six hours, 2,500 high explosive bombs and 600,000 incendiaries were rained on the city by British and American planes. The death roll is estimated at between 25,000 and 35,000. Figures are as vague as that because at the time of the raid the city was packed with refugees and no proper check was possible on the total population in the doomed centre of the city. During the three months between the raids and the collapse, the Nazis did nothing to relieve the agony of the city except to order the dragging out of the bodies, which were piled high and burned in the wrecked streets.

In April, 1945, the Red Army was approaching, and the Americans were halted at Chemnitz, fifty miles away. During the last few days before the Red Army arrived there was a continuous trek of cars and other vehicles from the city to the American lines. Many high Nazis escaped in this way.

In one of Dresden's gaols was the man who, to-day, is the leading figure in the city. Walter Weidauer had been in the German Left Wing movement since 1919. He was first sent to concentration camps in 1933. Freed the next year, he worked illegally until 1935 when he escaped through Czechoslovakia to Denmark. There he was caught, taken to Berlin and sentenced to fifteen years' imprisonment. On May 7th, 1945, the Red Army opened the prison gates. Wandering bewildered through the streets he met a Red Army captain who said: " Why don't you start and tidy things up ? "

Weidauer started collecting volunteers and together they began to organise some sort of order in Strehlen, the part of the city adjoining the prison. At the end of May Weidauer was made District Mayor and a few weeks later placed in charge of personnel for the whole city.

From that moment he led a campaign to mobilise the people of the stricken city for a great rebuilding campaign. In the first weeks the initiative came from the Communist Party to which Weidauer had belonged since its foundation. I saw one of their first posters. It contained the simple slogan: " No bread without work."

The city was a shambles. Half the population was without water. The trams were at a standstill. Gas and electricity were off. The sewage system had at places been penetrated by the bombs and there was grave danger of disease. In the streets there were 1,700 bomb craters, many of them penetrating to the gas and water mains.

By the beginning of July, Weidauer had been made burgomaster and his first move was to call together the Communist and Social Democratic Parties and the Trade Unions which were just beginning to be rebuilt. He said to them quite simply: " This city will never live again unless we mobilise every able-bodied man and woman for the job of reconstruction." The three organisations issued a joint appeal for voluntary workers. Within a few weeks 50,000 had come forward. The voluntary squads got busy clearing the streets, filling in the bomb craters, bringing back a semblance of life to the wrecked city. On Saturday afternoons and Sundays, when the

C

factories were closed, the whole of Dresden was a scene of constant activity. Even during the weekdays, several thousand workers found a few hours' spare time to get on with the work. They went on all through the winter of 1945-6, except for a few breaks when the weather was too bad. The work continued during the week-ends and the long summer evenings, and was only halted by the bitter winter months of 1947. On the Sunday after Easter, 1947, it started again.

The results have been little short of miraculous. The centre of Dresden is still a wilderness. Not a building was left undamaged over an area of seven square miles. Where 117,000 people lived on the night before the first raid, just 890 remained in some sort of accommodation in May, 1945. But to-day there is an uncanny sense of order as you walk or drive through the ghost of what was once one of the most beautiful cities in Europe. From many sites the wreckage has been cleared and the rubble piled in great hills on the banks of the Elbe. On other bomb sites the rubble has been neatly stacked. Not a bomb hole remains in all the miles of streets.

The voluntary work was based on a plan drawn up by Weidauer and endorsed by the leaders of the Social Democratic Party, the Communist Party, the Liberals, the Christian Democrats, and the Trade Unions at a special meeting on January 5th, 1946. Beautifully printed and illustrated the plan was published in book form and gave to the people of Dresden a sense of hope which is so tragically missing in most of Germany.

Weidauer told the meeting:

" Just as we conscious anti-Fascists were in the forefront of the fight against Hitler and war during the last twelve years, in prison, penal servitude, and concentration camps, so to-day we again take the lead, to recreate in the seven square miles of rubble in the centre of our city a new Dresden. Many may shake their heads doubtfully to-day at the boldness of such an undertaking. But we know that we shall do the job."

Weidauer gave the meeting these facts about the reconstruction during the first seven months after the Red Army arrived:

Out of 130,000 damaged dwellings roughly 3,000 had been reconditioned. Hundreds of shops and workrooms had been repaired sufficiently to enable normal work to start again.

The people of Dresden had been supplied with gas, water, and light since August. Two Elbe bridges had been repaired within the first months, with the help of the Red Army. The third bridge was nearly ready.

The number of hospital beds had been increased from 1,670, in May, to about 6,000, by the opening of emergency hospitals.

The number of children's homes had been increased from three to forty-eight. In September, 1945, school meals for children were provided and by November of the same year all the children in the city were included.

" Whatever has been achieved so far—significant as it may be—is only a jumping board for the much bigger tasks waiting for us," Weidauer went on. " The biggest one is the reconstruction of our town. I said earlier that seven square miles of our town are in ruins. We shall and must build a new town. And this new town, our new Dresden, must not be built by our children and grand-children: we ourselves, who are living now, must undertake this tremendous task. That means that to atone for our guilt we must provide this compensation to the coming generation."

The plan for 1946 set out these points: The repair, reconditioning, and the building of 7,600 flats and houses. To make possible the repair and reopening of Dresden University and the accommodation of worker students from the surrounding rural districts. Apart from administrative buildings, police buildings, post offices, railway stations, fire stations, and so on, the rebuilding of a number of theatres and cultural institutions were scheduled. The rebuilding and reconditioning of thirteen hospitals and two outpatient depart-ments to enable the town to return five schools which had been used as ʻemergency hospitals, were also proposed. More than fifty buildings for educational purposes were to be made usable. Repair of bridges, roads and canals, and industrial and commercial buildings was a further item. The last item on the list was the clearing of rubble and here appeared the first credit items—£300,000 to be secured from the sale of reclaimed material. Dresden decided to spend 30 million pounds, at pre-war sterling value, on the plan. Attached to the rebuilding plan was a finance plan. Somehow the money for the enterprise had to be found and only half was put down to direct taxes. Already in 1945, £300,000 had been collected under the slogan " Sacrifice for the rebuilding of Dresden." In 1946, this campaign was extended to bring in a further £300,000. Two lotteries were organised, one for general reconstruction, the other for the rebuilding of the Municipal Theatre. This second lottery was organised by the actors themselves. But the most interesting item was the promise to give the people paying £600 in advance a three-room flat with kitchen and bath when the new blocks of flats were built. Out of 1,000 new flats to be built in one part of the town, 500 were to be reserved for people making this payment in advance. A further share of the new flats was to be given to the building workers taking part in the reconstruction.

Weidauer finally dealt with the problem of building workers, specialists and building materials, and concluded with a word about landowners.

" It is impossible," he declared, " to leave it to the individual to re-build as he wants, when he wants, and where he wants. The town will confiscate all the ground to begin with, start to rebuild and postpone discussions with property owners and mortgagees until later."

So the great plan went ahead and all the time Weidauer was maintaining the enthusiasm of the people with lectures, posters, pamphlets, and press propaganda.

He was particularly successful in the schools, and the boys and girls began to take a personal interest in the work. One day a deputation from the Free German Youth arrived at his office with a decorated brick. It was the millionth which they had collected from the wreckage and cleaned ready for use in rebuilding.

The 1946 plan was not fully completed. Only 6,000 instead of 7,000 dwellings were restored, but more work than scheduled was put into the repair of bridges and factories.

In 1947, the task of the voluntary workers was to clean out and restore Dresden's open spaces and parks. No fewer than 100 were included in the plan. Each organisation took over one or more of the green spots. More than 100,000 trees were to be planted. In a square kilometre of the banks of the Elbe a new Zoological Garden and Botanical Garden was planned. This was the special task of the Free German Youth.

The botanical garden contains plans for ten hot-houses to be owned by the town and to be run as a commercial undertaking. A Park of Culture is included and there is also a home for orphan children which, in addition to living accommodation, will include an elementary and secondary school. This part of the plan was a direct result of the part played by the youngsters in the voluntary drive. They came to Weidauer with the proposal that they should take over and clean up a whole street.

" I felt they ought to have something more constructive if I was to hold their enthusiasm," Weidauer told me. " So I hit on this idea of clearing the open spaces and creating a special youth centre in the new botanical gardens. The youngsters have been consulted about the plans from the beginning and every week I meet their committee. In the city we have about 40,000 youngsters up to twenty-five. About a quarter are in the Free German Youth but many outside this organisation are helping."

The professional gardeners in the city also promised collaboration. When the scheme was launched they were all called to a meeting and decided to form local committees in order to give skilled advice to the voluntary workers. The second part of the 1947 plan was to clear a great barrack square constructed by the Nazis and prepare it for the erection of 12,000 houses. While the area was waiting for building supplies to become available it was being turned into allotments.

While the work of reconstruction was going on, Weidauer was doing a little quiet municipalisation on his own. In those first months, before the new constitutions for the provinces and the towns were adopted, legal formalities were at a minimum. There were many vacant buildings and business establishments from which Nazi owners had fled, and provided the new occupants were anti-Nazis, neither the Russian nor the German authorities bothered very much. Somehow by the time the new Dresden Town Council was elected it had become the owner of ten municipal hotels, a printing works, a large concern for the purchase and sale of building materials, a laundry, and two horticultural undertakings ! Weidauer used the latter to launch a new municipal enterprise for the sale of plants and flowers.

" I made myself pretty unpopular with the Right Wing parties," Weidauer told me. " They believe in leaving these things to private enterprise and are not keen on too much municipal ownership. But I got in quickly and no one dares now to suggest that we should surrender our municipal property. In any case all these undertakings belonged to Nazis."

Altogether Dresden owns about ten per cent of the industry in the town—worth some seven and a half million pounds sterling at pre-war figures, and employing 12,000 workers. Weidauer wants to make them commercially efficient.

" The old idea of municipal ownership was to run them by a committee within the town budget," he said. " I believe we have got to find a way of combining community ownership with the best business brains and the most modern methods."

To secure this object, he drafted a Bill for the Parliament of Saxony, of which he is a member, setting out a constitution for municipally-owned undertakings which would provide for a board of management of nine, three to be nominated by the Town Council, three by the administrative employees of the town, and three elected by the shop stewards.

Dresden was not only the most bombed city in the Zone, it was probably more likely than any other to provide the breeding ground for a pro-Nazi comeback. In the Hitler period a whole series of Nazi organisations were located in the city. During the war Goering built a giant Air Ministry headquarters which, because it was situated on the outskirts, escaped the bombing. It now houses the Saxony administration. The Wehrmacht also had headquarters in Dresden. From all these institutions tens of thousands of employees automatically found themselves thrown out of jobs. In addition, the Dresden town administration discharged 7,500 former Nazi Party members and the Saxony administration 18,000.

On the election register only 531 persons were deprived of the right to vote as proved active Fascists who could not be convicted and imprisoned for active criminal acts. Thus, thousands of Fascist sympathisers were able to record their votes at the polls. What is more, they were free to start whispering campaigns and other forms of opposition.

Life in the city was hard and there was plenty of breeding ground for discontent. Yet somehow the enthusiasm inspired in those first months by Weidauer and his colleagues was maintained through the long hard months.

" When do you reckon to complete the rebuilding of Dresden?" I asked Weidauer. " That," he replied, " depends on what the Allies decide about German economy as a whole. If we are given the chance we could do it in fifteen years."

While this reconstruction drive was being established another anti-Fascist leader was concentrating on a different problem. Max Opitz, a carpenter and an old trade union leader, was arrested in 1933 when the Nazis came to power. He remained behind bars for the whole period of Nazi rule and was released by the Red Army. When he got to Dresden, still bewildered by his new-found liberty, he went to the Red Army and asked what he could do.

A Red Army commander checked over his papers and then said; " You are an anti-Fascist and we have got to have a police force, so you had better get on with forming one." That was in the middle of June, 1945.

" I found that there was nothing left of the old police administration," Opitz told me. " Most of the officers, who were of course Nazis, had disappeared. Some of the staff were still there but there was no organisation and no discipline. The Red Army was performing the necessary police duties."

Opitz's first step was to advertise for everyone with police experience who had been turned out by Hitler. Provided they had a clean sheet, they were at once taken on. Then he started police schools to train selected applicants with a proved anti-Fascist background. In those early months, Dresden's ruins proved a perfect hiding place for criminals and bandits. They easily evaded capture in the labyrinth of cellars underneath the wreckage. The usual stories of crimes by the Red Army went round the city. Finally, at the end of six months, a gang of sixty headed by an officer of the Vlassov army was rounded up. The leader of this gang had shot a Red Army officer and stolen his uniform. A number of Poles and Yugoslavs who were hostile to their own governments had gathered round him.

" Since this gang was liquidated, we have had no serious crime in the city," Opitz said. " There have been plenty of cases of pilfering, an inevitable offence during time of shortage, but no murders, rapes, or other serious offences."

The deputy to Opitz is Hans Esslinger, an old Social Democrat, who spent three years in a Nazi prison. All the officers and men of the old Hitler force are gone.

As the Red Army marched into Dresden on May 7th, 1945, Dr. Franz Lau, Minister of the Evangelical Church of Saxony, was holding a weekday bible-reading service in one of the few undamaged church halls.

" I had to stop after a time because the noise was so great," he told me, " but no one interfered with me or my congregation."

On the next Sunday the bells rang out from the unbombed churches in the suburbs (all the churches in the centre were wrecked). " People were amazed," said Dr. Lau. " They had most of them accepted the Nazi propaganda about the Russians suppressing religion. As it happened, we carried on with our services without any interference at all. The Nazis tried all the time to destroy our church and make it into an instrument for their evil purposes. Now we feel we no longer live under a threat. The allied armies—and the Red Army as much as any of the others—restored freedom of religion to Germany."

Dr. Lau had been thrown out of his church by the Nazis, but had linked up with the Confessional Church with which Niemoeller was associated, and had helped in the illegal education of ministers. He assumed the leadership of the Evangelical Church in Dresden and was soon elected superintendent. At the synod of the Church of Saxony in the summer of 1947, Dr. Lau was due to be elected bishop.

" Our work in Dresden is absolutely free," he told me. " There is no censorship on our services and the Russians do everything they can to help us."

In wrecked Dresden, too, the first theatre was playing to crowded audiences within three weeks of the Nazi collapse. In a score of other ways the life of the great city and its half million inhabitants began to assume an aspect of normality, despite the mountains of wreckage.

You can walk through the streets of Dresden, travel in the crowded tramcars, or stand in the queues, and hear the same sort of talk as all over the Zone. You can hear the same grumbles at the food shortage: " We're short because the Russians take it all," " In the West they get much more than we do," " It's all propaganda what you read in the papers about people in the West being hungry," " They say the Americans and the English are soon coming to drive the Russians out."

But the grumblers and the malcontents are not getting their way in Dresden. Somehow this community activity helped a great number of the people to pull through the dreadful winter of 1946–7. The morale did not drop as in other cities, because they had already started to build. Maybe it was the German tradition of discipline which led so many to disaster behind Hitler, but which this time found a leadership pointing to a new democratic ideal. Whatever the reason, Dresden for all its wreckage and misery is a bright spot in the sombre picture of Germany to-day.

Who is going to win this battle for the soul of defeated, demoralised Germany—the men and women trying to rebuild, or the millions who just wait for something to turn up ? The fight is going on in every zone. In every zone there are German men and women working with the same determination. There are administrators in every zone equally anxious to help in re-creating a democratic Germany. In every zone, too, there are the apathetic or hostile millions and the officials of the occupying forces without interest in the outcome of the battle. My task has been to try to show the course of the battle in the Soviet Zone. It is too early as yet to predict the outcome.

3

THEY HAVE A PLAN

THE first task of the Allies in Germany was set out at Potsdam as the destruction of the German military potential. As far as the Russians are concerned there is no dispute that this duty has been fully carried out. In January, 1947, a Commission representing the four occupying powers carried out an inspection of the Soviet Zone on behalf of the Allied Control Commission. Their report, signed by the British, American, French, and Russian representatives, said that they were satisfied that every plant producing war materials had been destroyed. War machinery, the report added, had either been dismantled or destroyed. Plant and buildings had been treated in the same way, except in cases where empty buildings had been handed to the provincial governments for peaceful purposes as a way of relieving the serious shortage of accommodation.

Figures from Russian sources give a staggering picture of the extent to which the Nazis organised the country for war. No fewer than seventy underground factories were discovered. Scores more war plants were found hidden in the forests. Here the Nazis made flying bombs, poison gas, and a host of other weapons of death. At Ammendorf one can see the ruins of a once great poison gas factory. At Plauen the great tank factory is now a mass of wreckage; the Junker factory at Magdeburg and the Heinkel plant at Rostock have also been completely demolished. The explosives works all over the Zone have been reduced to ruins.

Some 50,000 large and small fortified positions have been blown up. Thousands of war-planes, thousands of flying bombs and rockets, seven thousand guns and 80,000 tons of ammunition were also blown up. No fewer than 25,000 underground air-raid shelters, including almost impregnable hiding places for the Nazi high-ups, have been destroyed. You see the great piles of broken concrete wherever you go. Altogether 30,000 tons of explosives were used in the work of destruction. About eighty-two military aerodromes, in addition to tank training grounds and shooting ranges, were ploughed up and the area included in the land reform. The rocket

stations at Peenemunde, put out of action by the R.A.F. before the
end of the war, have been demolished, but the great electric power
station was given to the Mecklenburg government and has proved
of immense value.

Other investigations by the Russians have shown how completely
Hitler switched over peace production to the purposes of war. Hardly
a plant was left making goods for the population. Everything was
devoted to the manufacture of weapons of war. One interesting
fact, however, emerged—up to the invasion year of Czechoslovakia
in 1938, the Nazis had done no more than prepare for the great
switchover and could count on only a small proportion of the output
of 1941. In other words, if the Eastern areas can be taken as a
standard, they provide complete proof that Hitler was bluffing
at Munich.

While the war factories were being destroyed work began on the
rebuilding of peace industry. As early as July, 1945, Leo
Skrzypzynski, German anti-Fascist released from Sachsenhausen
concentration camp, was given the task of creating a central
administration of industry for the whole Zone. " We left none of
the former organisation," he told me. " I started off with the
principle that we had to have new people in all the leading positions
and new methods of eliminating the bureaucracy which has always
cursed Germany in the past. Above all, we had to ensure real
contact with the workers, and so from the start the trade unions were
brought in on an equal footing."

The economic life of this Eastern Zone is planned by this new
Ministry, in consultation with the democratic governments established
in the five provinces, although nothing like a complete planned
economy has been achieved. Much of the development has been due
to improvisation rather than planning, for raw materials are hope-
lessly short, and transport disorganisation was further aggravated
by the diversion of railway stocks for months in order to shift
refugees from Poland and Czechoslovakia.

Nevertheless, within this framework, the economic life of the
Zone is organised. Raw material and labour are allocated to the
most urgent tasks and a tight control is kept on the ultimate
destination of manufactured goods. In the early months there was
no real check on the proportion going in reparations, but methods
were tightened up so that every item is now carefully checked and
recorded.

The fundamental fact about the Eastern Zone is that it is not,
and never can be, self-supporting. The zonal frontiers have no
economic or political basis. In the various zones frantic attempts

are made to provide substitutes for materials in plentiful supply in another zone. Factories have been divided from their sources of raw material in the most crazy way.

The province of Saxony, in the Soviet Zone, has a much greater weaving than spinning capacity because in pre-war Germany the spinning mills spread over to the area now included in the British Zone. Thus the Saxony spinning machines are working a three-shift system, but still cannot produce enough to keep the weaving machines going. Above all, coal is the central problem and the Achilles heel of the Soviet Zone.

The Zone contains only 14 per cent of the total coal deposits within the new German frontiers, and only 1 per cent of the hard coal. The Western Zones have a capacity of 140 million tons of hard coal and twenty million tons of brown coal; the East can produce only three million tons of hard coal and forty million tons of brown coal. There has been some exchange of Soviet Zone brown coal briquettes for Ruhr hard coal, but the Zone demands an import of hard coal from the Ruhr and Silesia (now in the Polish area) on the pre-war scale of eighteen million tons a year.

This lop-sided economy is extremely wasteful. For example, 500,000 tons of brown coal briquettes are needed to run the railways in the Zone, when the job could be done, with much less strain on the locomotives, with half the amount of hard coal. At the same time districts like Bavaria, which used to burn Saxon brown coal, are taking Ruhr hard coal. Before the war Berlin, which the Eastern Zone has partially to supply, actually imported 15 to 20 per cent of its supplies from Britain through Hamburg.

Everything possible has been done to make the maximum use of these restricted facilities. Production of brown coal reached 96 per cent of the 1938 figures, and hard coal 75 per cent. More than 80,000 miners are at work and receive higher rations than anyone else in the Zone. An extra midday meal is provided and special allocations of soap, cigarettes, and other scarce consumer goods are sent to the mining areas. On the recommendation of the Trade Union and management, workers with a good record receive vouchers entitling them to buy clothing, shoes, bicycles, and other goods. Housing in the mining areas, which in any case was not heavily damaged, has been given priority in regard to repairs.

The President of the Ministry of Fuel for the Zone is Gustav Sobotka, who began work as a miner in the Ruhr in 1900.

When I talked to him he asked me to convey greetings to Will Lawther, Ebby Edwards, and Arthur Horner, British miners' leaders, whom he met at international mineworkers' conferences during pre-Hitler days. A member of the Miners' Trade Union since 1909, Sobotka was one of the union M.P.s in the Prussian Parliament from 1920 to 1933. He was an exile in Paris and during the war in Moscow.

This is what he told me about his work: " Our mines in the Soviet Zone, like yours in England, have been removed from the control of the owners. For us there was no question of compensation, for the coal industrialists were some of the most important backers of the Nazi regime, and in fact most of them fled to the Western Zones before the Red Army came in. One of them, Flick, is on the list of War Criminals drawn up by the Allied Tribunal. The mines in the Zone are administered by the provincial governments through Boards drawn from members of the management staffs with a non-Nazi record and from the workers at the coal face. We have found that the working miner is well able to stand up to administrative responsibility, and in fact, several important coal areas are in the charge of miners nominated by the Union.

" An advisory council consisting of representatives of the trade unions and the provincial government is attached to each Board, and has the right to bring up any question for discussion.

" In the actual pits the trade union has the same right of consultation. Questions of production, appointments, and dismissal of staff, as well as conditions of employment, all come within the province of the unions.

The bitter winter of 1946–7 affected the Soviet Zone miners more than the rest of Germany, because 90 per cent of production is by opencast working. The ground was frozen for weeks to a depth of four to five feet and the machinery could not operate. The miners tried various methods of thawing the ground and dynamiting the seams, and by literally superhuman efforts prevented anything like the decline in output which would normally be expected.

Pre-war figures show that in similar weather conditions production went down by as much as 70 per cent. The figures for the decline in Zone production during the 1946–7 winter was from 30 to 35 per cent.

Slogans like: " Each ton of coal will save a human life " were put up at the pit heads. On the suggestion of the miners themselves special Sunday shifts were worked to secure a special supply for the peoples' homes. This drive from below produced remarkable results.

Output per worker did not entirely reach pre-war standards, but in the winter of 1946–7 it stood at 90 per cent for soft coal and 80 per cent for hard coal—a very much higher figure than in any of the other zones. The failure to reach the pre-war level was due to the fact that machinery is becoming worn out, to the loss of machinery for reparations and to the high age level of the miners. In a propaganda campaign to attract young workers' mining was put over as the key job in the reconstruction of Germany and the miner was proclaimed as the most important link in the new economic drive. Boys entering the pits were not only assured reasonably good food, they were also promised training which would enable them eventually to reach the highest jobs in the industry.

The campaign had secured sufficient recruits by February, 1947. In fact, when I asked the Ministry of Labour for copies of the recruiting posters for the mines, I received the reply: " You can take as many as you like. We are having to withdraw them now for we do not need any more recruits."

Steel is another bottleneck. With only two small steel works in Thuringia and Brandenburg, the industries in the Zone have always depended on supplies from the Ruhr. A great amount of scrap is being used, but this process requires materials only available outside the Zone. Other materials are equally short. Given adequate supplies the Eastern Zone has a wealth of light industry which, even with the loss of factories dismantled for reparations, are capable of replenishing the German market, providing exports in return for raw materials and foodstuffs, and still furnishing a share of reparations from current production.

Much of the progress so far made has been due to the imports of Soviet raw material, including cotton, wool, flax, and leather, without which the factories could not have kept going. The burgomaster of Erfurt in Thuringia, for example, told me that Soviet materials had alone maintained the industrial life of his town. Shortly, he said, the population would see the results in an allocation of stockings sufficient for half the women in the town each to receive a pair. Saxony alone had 50,000 tons of cotton and wool from Russia up to the spring of 1947.

Avoidable absenteeism has, as a general rule, remained extremely low, although there was some sign of a breakdown of morale towards the end of the 1947 winter, and in some factories the absenteeism figures took a sharp rise. On the whole, however, labour discipline has been very good, but sickness has taken a heavy toll.

The economic life of the Zone rests on a number of solid foundations. First, financial control has been taken completely away from the banks, the insurance companies and other financial institutions. One of the early measures of the Soviet administration was to stop all banking accounts. All money deposited up to the time of Hitler's surrender was declared null and void.

It was a drastic measure and some months afterwards was modified to allow people of small means to draw up to 300 marks (about £20 at pre-war rates), but financially it was a completely sound move. The money deposited with the banks had vanished during Hitler's war. The banks, insurance companies, and other financial institutions had been forced to put 90 per cent of their funds into war loans, and to use the rest to finance the repair of damaged war factories. Thus the Soviet decree merely recognised a bankruptcy for which the Nazis and not the occupation was responsible.

The old banks were closed and new ones opened, and rather significantly in view of the chaotic situation, the new banks which are owned by the governments of the provinces, very quickly secured public confidence. Dr. Gaertner, Liberal Democrat, who is President of the Thuringia State Bank, told me that he started his new bank with a credit of £1,500,000 from the Russians and by the spring of 1947, had secured savings deposits to the value of £100,000,000. "There was no other way of dealing with the financial situation," he told me. "We could not possibly have began to replan industry if we had allowed the paper funds held by the banks to flood the Zone."

These community controlled banks provide the financial basis for the economic plan of the Zone.

The bank-stop was by no means a complete method of dealing with the problem. Plenty of loose cash remained in the hands of people who had either refused to trust the Nazi banks or who had drawn out their money before the collapse. There has also been some flow of cash from the Western Zones.

In the main, however, the Soviet administration and the re-formed German authorities were able to rebuild the economy on a comparatively sound monetary basis. Many monied people, who were most likely to be hostile to the regime, were penniless, and had to find a job or flee to the West if they wanted a ration card or the cash to buy their rations. Moreover, an immediate check was placed on the black market. Widespread black market activities developed, it is true, in the Eastern Zone, mainly through leakages of production from the factories, but the cancelling of the bank deposits prevented the black market from dominating and disintegrating the whole economy as it did in the West.

The drastic Allied Control Council order freezing wages and prices at the level of 1944 was made much more effective in the East because the Nazi bank funds had been withdrawn. Had this money been left in the hands of the wealthy the same situation would have developed in the East as in the West, where inflation was prevented in the price-controlled section of the economy but allowed to run riot in the black market. Actually the Nazis controlled prices and the 1944 price is practically that of 1936.

The price and wage stop is applied in the Soviet Zone. Machinery, it is true, is provided for modification of both prices and wages, as in the case of the miners who, in all zones, have received big increases. In the Soviet Zone, too, the principle of equal pay for women and youths doing equal work with men was ordered by the Soviet administration, after consultation with the various German organisations, and meant a substantial increase in the total wage bill. Here, however, it could legitimately be argued that there was no increase in wages but only a conceding of the proper rate to the women. The Russians, in fact, simply cannot understand a wage system making differences, not in respect of work, but in respect of sex.

Generally, however, the wage stop operates and the price stop is varied only if the manufacturer can prove exceptional hardship. Rents are stopped at the 1944 figure, which again means, in effect, the 1936 figure. Compared with England, rent in Germany is a much smaller proportion of the family budget.

Wage agreements are concluded between each of the eighteen industrial unions in the Zone on the one side, and on the other the Ministry of Labour for the Zone, and a special commission of the employers' representatives drawn from newly formed Chambers of Commerce. (The old employers' organisations have all been dissolved.) These agreements, however, must be concluded within the framework of the wage stop, or such modification of the stop as has been agreed by the Allied Control Council.

In addition, taxation is very high, going up to 50 per cent for comparatively moderate incomes and rising more steeply still for the higher salaries. Social insurance takes an additional 10 per cent. The budgets of the provincial governments are having to subsidise foodstuffs otherwise ration prices could not be kept down to the 1944 figure.

With the lack of consumer goods, the average German can live on his wages, for at controlled prices rations cost very little, but he has nothing left to buy at black market prices. Inevitably when goods begin to come on the market, there will be demands for wage increases.

The next basic factor in determining the economic development of the Zone was the confiscation of factories belonging to the war criminals and the war profiteers. Under an order of the Soviet administration, all undertakings suspected of coming in this category were placed in the hands of trustees. Then Saxony took the lead and a plebiscite in June, 1946, declared by a majority of nearly 80 per cent in favour of taking them over. The other provinces followed suit by promulgating a law authorising the confiscation.

Whether owners of factories came under the category of war criminals was decided by special commissions composed of representatives of the three anti-Fascist parties and the trade unions. Decisions of this commission were re-examined and endorsed by a second set of commissions. Any decisions not adopted unanimously by either body were submitted to a special commission.

Here are figures for the five provinces:—

SAXONY.—Out of 4,000 enterprises examined by the commissions, owners of 1,760 factories were found guilty. In 101 cases, only part of the shareholding was found to be in the hands of a guilty party. In these cases the State took over the guilty person's shareholding, the non-guilty shareholders being left in possession.

One thousand and two undertakings were handed to the Government of Saxony. They included all coal and ore mines, all electricity stations, 138 machine tool factories, fifty-six chemical undertakings, 107 weaving mills, sixty-three spinning mills, furniture, and engineering factories, and many other concerns. Local councils in towns and rural districts received 278 enterprises. The co-operatives received seventy-three. A number of small factories were sold to private employers.

SAXONY ANHALT.—Out of 95,000 undertakings in the province, more than 25,000 were examined by the commissions. Just over 10 per cent were finally appropriated. The provincial government received 691, including the mines and electricity works, building material plants, foodstuff factories, sixty-three machine tool factories and eighteen metallurgical plants; local councils received fifty-four enterprises; communal organisations including the co-operatives were given 284 and 706 went to private owners.

THURINGIA.—Out of 3,875 factories originally sequestrated, over 3,000 were handed back to the original owners. Of the rest the provincial government took over 286 factories and the shareholdings of guilty parties in thirty-nine others.

BRANDENBURG.—Out of 38,000 enterprises whose owners were members of the Nazi Party, only 2,000 were certified by the commission as coming under the category of war criminal and of these, on further inquiry, 573 were handed back. The province received 1,371 of the remainder, some were divided between local authorities, co-operatives and trade unions, and the rest sold to private owners.

MECKLENBURG-POMERANIA.—Of 1,192 sequestrated factories 605 were taken over by the province and 451 handed back. One hundred and thirty-six factories whose owners could not be traced were taken by the president of the province in trust.

Some feeling was aroused among anti-Fascist organisations at the number of factories handed back, but it was explained that it was essential to ensure that only those guilty of actual crimes were punished. All factories owned by the trusts and combines were taken over, and as these were the largest units, the proportion of industry coming under state control was much larger than the mere numbers indicate.

Allied holdings in the German trusts have been placed in the hands of the Allied Control Commission. Thus a percentage of the I. G. Farben holdings in the Soviet Zone have been treated in this way because they are claimed by British and American firms. Presumably Woolworths, which is doing a good trade in Leipzig and other cities, comes in the same category.

The new economy of the Soviet Zone must be seen not so much from the viewpoint of its present achievements but in the light of the system which it replaced. In 1927 well over 60 per cent of the capital of all German companies was controlled by the financial and industrial monopolies. The economic crisis of 1930 to 1932 brought more small concerns into the grip of the monopolies. With the triumph of the Nazis, the trusts and combines dominated the whole of German economy. Their hold on finance, coal, iron, chemical industries, and most of the electricity production enabled them to dictate prices and conditions of business in every field. They turned the whole indus-trial might of Germany over to Hitler for rearmament and war.

This is the power which the nationalisation and planned economy of the Soviet Zone has destroyed.

The Russians take the view that this is the only way in which the Potsdam Agreement demanding the breaking up of the over-concen-trated German economic power can be fulfilled and they also claim that it has been carried out by the Germans on the initiative of the anti-Fascist parties.

Once the monopolies were destroyed every encouragement was given to the considerable section of industry still in private hands. Moreover, a growing number of small handicraft shops—cabinet makers, tailors, boot repairers—have come to assume a new importance because of the difficulties of transport and the shortage of raw material. In Germany there are still big reserves of various materials in private hands and many small handicraft shops are doing a flourishing trade making up customers' own cloth, leather, and other goods. How much of this was looted from Europe no-one will ever know.

The private section of industry is compelled to fall in with the

D

economic plan for the Zone, and the administration is able to see that this is done because it owns a good proportion of the essential industries and controls finance, supplies of raw material, and inter-zonal and foreign trade.

Moreover, there is a law forbidding the formation of trusts, so that the private concerns cannot develop towards monopoly. The employers are forbidden to reform their old trade associations. The Co-operative movement, rebuilt on proper democratic co-operative lines, is being encouraged to take an increasing part in the zonal economy and there has also been a big increase in municipal trading.

The third great change in the economy of the Zone was the carrying through of a complete measure of land reform, under which all estates over 250 acres were divided among the peasants. The final economic results of the drastic measure cannot yet be assessed, although by the spring of 1947 there was evidence to show that results had confounded the many critics who prophesied disaster, and the political results have been far-reaching.*

In addition to the state undertakings and those remaining under private enterprise, a number of factories have been taken over by the Russians on reparations account. Most of them take the form of a group of undertakings, each inter-dependent on the other. Each Soviet factory has a Russian general director, but the concerns are run by Germans and German law operates. The undertakings pay taxes just like any German firm and are subject to the normal trade union agreements both in regard to wages and the rights of shop stewards.

The products of these Russian undertakings come within the economic plan of the Zone and not within that of the Soviet Union. Part of the output goes to the U.S.S.R. but it is included in the reparation account in the same way as the output of a German factory. Much of the production, however, stays in Germany. For example, electricity output from Espenhain, the Soviet-owned power station, cannot possibly be used anywhere except in Germany. Some of it, in fact, goes to the Western Zone. The synthetic petroleum remains in Germany and so does the fertiliser output of the great Leuna works.

Under the Allied Control Council agreements, the Russians had the right to dismantle the synthetic petrol works, since manufacture of petrol and of rubber from oil is forbidden to Germany. They could also have taken away the machinery at Buna and Leuna for both were undoubtedly war factories, and in any case were among the properties of the German trusts, scheduled for dissolution in the

---

* See chapter 10

Potsdam Agreement. The German authorities have been given receipts for the value of all property taken over in this way, so that the value can be taken into consideration in all future discussions.

Many Germans I spoke to expressed the view that the taking over of these factories as Soviet concerns was the only way of saving them for German economy. There is a widespread suspicion that the Western Allies imposed the ban on German manufacture of synthetic petrol and rubber, not as a measure against a revival of war industry, but to destroy a competitor of the oil companies. As for the allegation by the American Commander in Berlin that the Russians, while condemning the continuation of trusts in the West, were building their own state trusts in the Eastern Zone, the argument is as old as the controversy over nationalisation. The fact is, of course, that the industrial potential represented by these assets is out of the hands of the private monopolists. It must either be broken up or placed under some form of national control.

At any rate, under Soviet administration these firms will not make cartel agreements with the American and British oil monopolists, as they did in the Weimar and Hitler periods !

There were thus two forms of dismantlement of factories: those which were dealt with because they were built entirely for war purposes and those which the Russians took on reparations account. Sometimes the two types overlapped since large numbers of concerns which were originally used for peace industry were converted into war plants by the Nazis.

Originally a far larger number of factories were ear-marked for reparations but seventy-four were returned to the Germans by order of Marshal Sokolovsky, to date from March 1st, 1947. Where they were formerly the property of war criminals they automatically came into the possession of the provincial governments, but those not in this category went back to their former owners.

Reparations to the Soviet Union and raw materials received from the Soviet Union are all taken into consideration in calculating the economic plan. Each provincial government has to make a provision for reparations in its annual budget. This money is paid into a central fund and from it the Russians pay in cash for all the goods received, both on reparation account and for supplies to the occupation troops and administration. Some of the goods thus supplied are sold in shops catering exclusively for the Russians, who are paid half their salaries in marks and half in roubles.

In the early months of the occupation there were plenty of leakages. The Russians were buying what they wanted and there were many cases of goods being illegally taken from the factories by Russian officials. The Soviet authorities acted as drastically against these offenders as against their own people responsible for other criminal acts, and some offenders were shot.

The German and Soviet authorities got down very early to working out a system as near fool-proof as it could be made in conditions providing the strongest temptation for pilfering. Under this system only three highly placed officials of the Soviet Military Administration are authorised to sign orders for goods. These orders go, not to the factories, but to the Minister of Planning for the provincial government concerned. The factory or other German undertaking can only deliver on the signature of a high official of the German Ministry of Planning. Thus, goods are delivered not to the Russians direct but to the Germans, and factory managements can be severely punished if they part with goods except in the authorised way.

How does the policy of economic planning work out in practice ? You see the picture much more clearly in the provinces than through the eyes of the central administration in Berlin, which has the job of co-ordinating the provincial plans and not deciding day-to-day policy.

Take the story of the Land of Saxony, where the picture of economic planning is typical of the other four provinces. Saxony's state-owned factories represent only about 9 per cent of the total number of industrial enterprises, but nearly 25 per cent of total capacity, and 30 per cent of total value. The province employs 170,000 out of 730,000 industrial workers. All the coal mines were taken over, 50 per cent of paper and cellulose mills, and over 30 per cent of machine tool and textile factories.

" This proportion of industry," Fritz Selbmann, Saxony's Minister of Economic Planning told me, " is enough to give us a directing control over the whole of our economy."

Selbmann began life as a miner in the Ruhr and was a Communist member of the Reichstag until 1933. He spent the whole twelve years of Nazi rule in prison and concentration camp and finally escaped in April, 1945, when being transferred from Dachau to the Tyrol.

" We started planning in Saxony," Selbmann said, " within three or four months of the collapse. Our province, like the rest of Germany, had been drained dry by the Nazis. Saxony's textile industry for example had received practically no capital investments or machinery replacements for ten years. A big proportion of its total capacity had been closed down, and other plant turned over to production of aircraft and other war supplies. Saxony had 300 bridges destroyed. The railways had suffered severe destruction and a big proportion of rolling stock had gone.

" Thus we had to begin with a derelict industry and a disrupted transport system. Added to that, we had the permanent shortage of fuel, which our own efforts could not possibly solve. We made many mistakes but we also recorded steady progress during 1946.

" Our textile industry showed a considerable increase in the year 1946. In the second quarter of 1946 we had a production of 7,900 tons of spinning material, in the third quarter 14,500 tons, and in the fourth quarter 16,800 tons. In the third quarter of 1946 the import of cotton and wool from the Soviet Union began too, and from that date until October, 1946, the number of workers in the spinning industry increased from 33,961 to 40,742 and the number of spindles from 2,194,996 to 2,667,815.

" The production of artificial fabric increased in 1946 from 776 tons to 2,249 tons.

" The production plan for the Saxon paper industry demanded 148,500 tons of pulp for 1946. Production of the first half year was 77,000 tons and the second half year 86,000 tons. That means that we over-fulfilled the plan.

" Planning for us does not mean to produce a system of figures and then trust to luck. Planning means 365 days every year of ceaseless fight on all levels to realise the plan against the difficulties in the way. We know that our work still shows mistakes. There is too much bureaucracy, too many questionnaires and forms. Some of the controls are uneconomic and superfluous. This tendency towards bureaucracy is explained by the fact that the reconstruction of our economy had to be carried through simultaneously with the elimination of the Nazis.

" We realise the difficulties of rebuilding our economy with new and insufficiently trained forces. It is understandable that these new people try to make good their lack of experience by issuing more questionnaires or forms than necessary. They are trying to safeguard themselves by resorting to red tape. But to recognise a mistake means to be able to remedy it.

" An economic plan is not a patent medicine. If our Eastern Zone has a capacity of only three million tons of hard coal, no plan can give us one single ton more. If our Zone has not got sufficient capacity for iron and steel production, then no plan will be able to give us the additional capacity necessary, at least, not for the next few years. But the plan for us is an instrument enabling us to use all economic possibilities at our disposal.

" You should know how we plan in the East. We don't only draw up a general plan. We ascertain the figures of our plan by basing them on the capacity of the individual enterprise, its manpower, and the raw materials at its disposal. Then we find out the figures for the whole plan, co-ordinate them, and finally distribute the production quotas to the factories. Our economic policy and economic measures are directed towards assuring the realisation of the tasks in our plan.

"We in the Eastern Zone consider that economic planning is not only a means of solving our present difficulties but that it will become a permanent element in German economic policy. Economic planning is not completely new. If in former times the international steel combine distributed its production quotas, that was a piece of planning; when the steel trust made the production programme for their many factories, that was planning. The planning was in the hands of monopoly organisations, doing so in the interests of their spheres of influence and markets. Economic planning now will be in the interests of the people as a whole.

"Our principles of planning do not suppress the initiative of the private employer. They call, on the contrary, for maximum initiative. But we do not want the development of private initiative to be directed only towards personal profit.

"Continuous talk is going on about the private initiative of the employers, but in our opinion there is another initiative apart from that, the initiative of the masses of the people.

"I can tell you that 47 per cent of the managing directors of our state-owned factories of Saxony are former workers, the rest consist of former technicians, engineering specialists, and businessmen. The manager of one chain of twenty to twenty-five shoe factories is a former shoemaker."

Selbmann assured me that the economic plan was operated entirely by his own department without interference by the Russians. "At all stages, however," he added, "we have consultations with the economic department of the Soviet Military Administration.

"The Russians working in the economic administration are all technical experts in the particular section with which they are concerned. At one of our recent meetings the manager of a textile factory tried to cover up the use of too much thread. The Russian officer responsible for textiles spotted it at once."

The plans for the five Provinces, all prepared in the same way as Saxony's, are sent to the central administration for economic planning in Berlin. There they are co-ordinated and corrected in the light of the needs of the whole Zone, are passed on for confirmation by the Soviet administration, and then sent back to the provincial governments to be put into operation.

When the production picture is viewed in the towns and factories

it becomes clear that the economic plan is much more an instrument
to overcome a constant series of difficulties than a well-oiled
production machine. Given a constant flow of raw materials, effective
transport, and assured markets, there is no doubt that the planned
system now operating in the Eastern Zone could push German
production in the area to a point it has never yet reached, even in
pre-war years. But none of these elements is present. All the time,
those in charge of production have to live a hand-to-mouth existence,
waging a constant struggle to secure enough raw materials to carry
on. Fuel, electricity, and gas are liable to fail. Transport cannot be
relied upon and the post is subject to long delays. It is in spite of
these difficulties that a remarkable degree of progress has been made.

That was the background to the Leipzig Fair. It showed to the
world that German peace industry is capable of fulfilling a proper
rôle in the economy of Europe, that German technical skill can be
turned to the arts of peace and can provide the basis of a better life
for the German people.

I was in Leipzig during the Fair and there could be no doubt
that it had a tonic effect on the hundreds of thousands who thronged
the great exhibition halls. It was interesting to talk to visitors from
the Western Zones, who had been fed for months with anti-Soviet
propaganda and who were genuinely staggered to find what was
actually happening in the Zone. Business-men from Holland,
Belgium, France, Czechoslovakia, and one or two from Britain, all
agreed that if a basis for proper trading relations could be found,
there would be a ready market for German goods.

I had an interesting conversation with the representative of a
firm making cameras in the British Zone. As soon as he discovered
I was British he at once began to explain to me that he had nothing
to do with the Russians and, in fact, had only come to the Fair just
to show that they could also make things in the British Zone.
"We don't have to give everything for reparations over there,"
he said.

"Your production goes to the Germans?" I asked. "Oh no,"
he replied, "we sell it all to N.A.A.F.I. None of it goes to the
Germans, but we are hoping soon to build up a good export trade
in the dollar countries!"

4

OUSTING THE NAZIS

IN the Soviet Zone, all known Nazis with a record of active support for the Hitler regime are either under lock and key or subject to supervision in one form or another. Plenty of the small fry still hold positions, but rarely where they can exercise any major responsibility.

I discussed denazification with Germans in every field of public life and I am certain this broad statement represents the position in the Zone. Obviously the question can be asked, how a foreign observer, however intimately he is able to see the life in the Zone, can be certain on this point. Officials now loudly proclaiming their anti-Nazi faith may, in fact, have a Nazi history. The foreign investigator cannot know their actual background, but he is entitled to view the situation as a whole and to base his conclusion on the people whom he finds in the leading positions.

And the fact is that, in the Soviet Zone, the key jobs in administration, in the trade unions, and in the other vital sections of public life, are held by men and women who can prove their record of anti-Nazi activity. When you find a police force in charge of men liberated from concentration camps and with a long history of trade union and political activity, you are entitled to accept their assurance that the last Nazi has been cleared out. In the same way the shop stewards' committees, which usually contain several leaders of the underground struggle, carry conviction when they tell you that they have taken the initiative in throwing the Nazis out.

The whole atmosphere among the administrators in the Zone is one of determination to purge public life of Nazi influence, and even if there were a desire on the part of the authorities to reprieve a known Fascist, they would be unable, on the one hand, to stimulate a public demand for denazification, and on the other to resist criticism of tenderness to certain offenders. There have, of course, been mistakes. The authorities are constantly detecting people who have escaped the net. During my visit, for example, Konitzer, the head of the Health Ministry for the whole Zone, was arrested for alleged complicity in experiments on prisoners of war.

Some Nazis have been cleared on assurances from the anti-Fascist parties that they were put there as "under-cover" representatives. Their cases were considered early in the occupation by inquiry committees composed of the trade unionists, the Communists, and the Socialists (who, at that time, had not merged). In the Co-operative movement, which certainly preserved some sort of independent organisation during the Nazi period, and which escaped having its property broken up, there are many officers who could be accused of taking part in the Nazi subsidiary of the Labour Front in which the Co-ops. were incorporated.

In Leipzig, for example, all these cases were considered by a meeting of the Social Democratic Party which decided that some thirty members were compelled to join the Nazi Party as a cover for their anti-Nazi activities, but that their work, with the help of a great proportion of former Co-operative employees, had preserved an anti-Fascist organisation.

Cases of this kind are very difficult to decide, and are always liable to give rise to hostility among sections of the people unaware of the particular circumstances. Moreover, the defence that a particular member of the Nazi Party was an "under-cover" agent is very easy to put forward and difficult to prove or disprove. In one town I was told by reliable anti-Fascists that one man in a prominent position, who had been officially cleared on the ground that he was an "under-cover" agent, was still very much suspect, and that a secret investigation was being made into his past history.

These cases, however, are the exceptions which prove the rule. Official figures give the number dismissed from various jobs in administration, including education, at 307,000. Another 83,000 have been barred from other positions of responsibility. In addition, hundreds of thousands employed in the Nazi Party organisation, and in war activities of various kinds, were automatically thrown out of their jobs.

The main policy has been to clean out the whole administration, not merely as a negative means of punishing those responsible for the Nazi crimes, but also as a positive method of ensuring that authority is placed in the hands, either of proved anti-Fascists or, at least, of men and women who have not been sympathetic to Fascism.

The Russians have been meticulous in ensuring the carrying out of the decrees of the Allied Control Council which stipulate the extent of denazification in public administration, but their main weapon in this work was their mobilisation of the popular forces during the first months after the Nazi collapse. In fact,

denazification from the beginning has been a German and not a
Russian job.

Everywhere in the Zone one hears the same story of spontaneous
action against the Nazis, either before or immediately after the Red
Army came in. In most areas the leadership was taken by the
anti-Fascists, often reinforced by their released comrades from the
concentration camps, but the mass of the population joined in as well.
It may well have been that the anger of many of them was not against
the Nazi system but against the individuals who had lost the war,
but the effect was the same.

In plenty of cases rough justice was meted out on the spot.
The foreign workers, particularly, took a grim vengeance on their
oppressors, but in the main the worst Nazis were rounded up and
handed over to the Russians. In the mines and factories the job
could usually be left safely in the hands of the workers, who weeded
out their own Nazis and filled the vacant jobs as best they could.
In the towns a proved anti-Fascist was usually given the post of
burgomaster and told to carry on with the job of cleaning up.

Once a Nazi was caught, he was kept under supervision. Even
if the case were not considered bad enough to place him under arrest,
he was not allowed, in those first days, to drift away to another town
where his record was not known, but was put to work under the
supervision of anti-Fascists. All those accused of crimes were taken
to prisons and camps to await trial.

How are these arrested Nazis dealt with? The basic principle
is that formulated at the Crimea Conference to divide the offenders
into those brought before the international Tribunal, those who are
tried in the country where their crimes were committed, and those
whose offences were committed against Germans. Most of the big
criminals escaped to the West before the entry of the Red Army.
The second category (those responsible for crimes against foreign
nationals) have been handled by the Russians. Many have been
handed to the Poles, Czechs, and other nations against whom their
major crimes were committed. Offences against foreign workers
were included in this category and particular severity has been shown
to German administrators who operated in the territories occupied
by the German armies. Soviet and military courts of the Allies, to
whom the Russians handed over suspects, have dealt with some
18,000 cases, of which about 300 were acquitted. Those interned
totalled nearly 60,000, of whom over 7,000 have been released,
some by decision of courts and some after preliminary police
investigation.

Responsibility for dealing with the Nazis who committed crimes against Germans has been left to the German courts in accordance with an order of September, 1946, by the Allied Control Council. The law applied to them in the Zone is based on normal German judicial procedure, plus the various decrees of the Allied Control Council. This is how the procedure works in Saxony (in other provinces there are some differences of method) :—

First, there is an investigation by the German police, who decide whether there is a prima facie case, then the offender is handed over to the public prosecutor's department. When the case has been fully investigated, and statements taken from the accused and from witnesses, the offender comes before the court. These courts are open to the Press and public and are bound by the rules of evidence laid down in German law. Defending council can be briefed by the prisoner. If he does not wish to provide his own lawyer one is supplied by the court, or he can conduct his own defence.

The court consists of a chairman and two assessors, all trained lawyers, and six jurors. The method of choosing jurors, which is now applied to ordinary criminal and civil cases as well as the denazification courts, represents a big change from pre-Hitler Germany. The rule has been laid down that only anti-Fascists should be accorded the privilege of jury service. Lists are drawn up by the three parties and a proportion of non-party men and women with an anti-Fascist background are chosen by the anti-Fascist bloc of the three parties. The defence and prosecution both have the right to challenge a jury on the grounds that it is over-weighted by one or other of the political parties. Once selected, a jury sits continuously for four weeks.

These special courts operate in all big centres, and are dealing with cases at an average rate of about three a week. The courts have the right to impose sentences up to life imprisonment or death, but the capital sentence has to be confirmed by the Russians. It is not enough for the court to show that an offender was an active Nazi, it must also prove that he or she committed an individual crime.

New cases are still being reported to the police, particularly of people alleged to have acted as Gestapo informers. Personal malice frequently comes into these accusations, but I was assured by a German lawyer, who spent years in a concentration camp, that meticulous care is taken to sort out the evidence and that a number of cases are dismissed by the police and the public prosecutors' office without coming before the courts.

Punishment of offenders, however, is a comparatively minor phase of denazification; the really big job has been to clean the most important sections of public life. In education, the police, the law, and public administration, the decision has been taken that all Nazis have to be cleared out. This has meant a temporary loss of administrative efficiency, but the speed and energy with which the task of recruiting new staffs has been carried out is one of the most striking aspects of the Soviet Zone. I came across cases where, even in these sections, some Nazis with a nominal record were left, but they were definitely a small minority.

With regard to the law, all Nazis were removed from key posts at the beginning of the occupation, those suspected of individual crimes being arrested and the rest put on other jobs. Former Nazi judges and lawyers are working as labourers on building jobs or in factories and mines.

With the promulgation of the special order in September, 1946, a clean sweep was made. Every former member of the Nazi Party and its subsidiary organisation engaged in the law was ordered to be sacked, with the exception of the German Labour Front, membership of which was compulsory. Even typists who were in the League of German Girls came under the axe.

Right from the beginning steps were taken to fill the gaps. First judges and lawyers who retired from practice before or immediately after the Hitler regime, were brought back. The few surviving Jews or half-Jews were roped in. Then schools for People's Judges (including lawyers as well as " judges " in the English sense) were started. Candidates for these schools are nominated by the three anti-Fascist parties and must include a proportion from the workers. They are given maintenance grants by the Governments. The course takes eight months and is very strenuous—so strenuous in fact that out of 125 students at one of the schools near Dresden, only twenty-five qualified.

Dr. Nymka Kroschal, an anti-Fascist Austrian lawyer who escaped from Vienna when Hitler invaded Austria only to be arrested by the Gestapo in Belgrade in 1941, expressed the opinion to me that the new People's Judges are showing considerable ability. Dr. Kroschal, who remained in a concentration camp until liberated by the Americans, is now the only woman public prosecutor in the Soviet Zone.

" In the Leipzig area," she told me, " we have a former typist, Gerda Schnirring, aged thirty, who is sitting in the juvenile court and is proving not only a brilliant lawyer but a real expert on juvenile delinquency. Three other new judges in the area formerly worked in lawyers' offices. Two prosecutors now in my office were originally plumbers. One of them spent eight years in a concentration camp.

" We are still desperately short of trained people. We need 500 new judges and lawyers to catch up with arrears. The administration of the law in Germany was so completely poisoned by the Nazis that we could never have hoped to eradicate Nazi influence without making a clean sweep."

Dr. Kroschal's one qualification of this statement was in connection with the young people who were formerly in the Nazi organisation. " It is a principle of our law," she said, " that no one is regarded as fully responsible until the age of eighteen. Many of these people joined the Nazis before that age. It is true that they have been undermined by Nazi propaganda but we have got to win them back. Either we do that or we drive them into the ranks of reaction. There is a particular danger that they will get across to the West and form a centre of reaction there."

Dr. Kuelz, Liberal Minister of Justice for Thuringia, also praised the new judges. " There are eleven of them in the Province," he told me, a number due to be increased when the next course for judges ends. " As a professional lawyer," he added, " I am quite prepared to say that these new judges are doing very well, and infusing a very necessary tonic into our judicial system. The idea of having judges without a long training in the law is, after all, operating in a number of democratic countries."

It would be a mistake to imagine that, with denazification and the appointment of new judges, the reactionary influence in the German judicial system has been removed. After denazification, old judges up to eighty years of age were called back. They are not Nazis but their traditions are those of Frederick Wilhelm rather than the new German democracy. Many times Left-Wing members of the provincial parliaments complained to me that all the new legislation has to be examined with meticulous care, since the judges are mostly reactionary and always look for a loophole to allow an offender to escape. Incidentally, an indication of the Russian policy of non-interference with German justice was given me by an important German official. He said that cases occurred of local Russian commanders protesting against verdicts given by the German Courts. When these were brought to the attention of the higher Russian authorities they invariably informed the local commander that there must be no interference.

In the field of education, denazification was no less drastic. The view was taken that, even at the cost of a temporary loss of efficiency, the schools must be cleaned of Nazi influence, and again all available resources were turned on to training new teachers to take the place of those dismissed.*

The other section of public life in which denazification has been carried out most thoroughly is the police. It is true to say that there is now a completely new police force, all trade unionists, schooled in a new tradition of co-operation with the people. To-day the police are the only people wearing uniform. The difference in their attitude from the arrogance one saw among German officials even in pre-Hitler Germany is most marked. Traffic duty is universally performed by police-girls in exceptionally smart uniforms.

The story of Max Opitz, Police Chief of Dresden, told in chapter two, appears to be typical of what happened in most of the big centres of the Zone where the Red Army was the first to take over. The former police were mostly so completely compromised by their association with the Nazi regime that they did not wait to be denazified, while the Red Army carried on initial police duties rather than give any authority to the former guardians of Hitler's regime.

A new sort of war memorial in the main hall of Leipzig police headquarters expresses the atmosphere of the new regime. It records the names of the men and women murdered by the Nazis, and reads: " Leipzig police headquarters honours the victims fallen in the fight against Fascism." Among the names is that of Karl Goerdeler, one of those executed after the abortive revolt of 1944. There is something particularly satisfying in this memorial, for the broad staircase and corridor of this building saw some of the worst atrocities in the eastern part of Germany. In the twelve years of Nazism, this building and the prison adjoining were always packed with victims. It was here that the S.S. conducted a massacre of the prisoners in the last days before the American troops entered the city.

Now three former concentration camp inmates are in the beautifully furnished rooms where the Gestapo tortured their victims. They are Walter Jurich, the police president, Kurt Koehler, the officer in charge of personnel (both released from Buchenwald) and Gustav Kempf, public relations chief, who was liberated from Sachsenhausen.

The force they lead consists of men and women with no former experience of police work. Ninety per cent of them were formerly workers in factories and offices. " They had to learn their jobs as they went along," Jurich told me, " but the fact is that since we cleared out the old gang we have reduced crime figures by 50 per cent."

---

* See chapter 9

When the Americans came into Leipzig they dismissed some 600 members of the police, but a lot were left in office. On July 3rd the Red Army took over and by August 15th 75 per cent of the old force was out.

At first, the new men and women were just brought in and sent to a police school in off-duty periods, but later each recruit was given a four-month, full-time course before taking up duty. The anti-Fascist committee, which was formed in Leipzig during the last days of the Nazis, was at first asked to nominate for the new force and later the names were put forward by the anti-Fascist parties and the factory groups.

" Three quarters of the course for the new police is on professional subjects," Jurich told me, " but the other quarter is political." They learn about the place of the police in a democratic community. Special attention is given to economic questions, particularly the methods of planning production, and then the policeman is able to see the fight against the black market, not so much as a campaign against individual criminals as a struggle against elements which are sabotaging our economic life.

" Above all we seek to impress the idea that the policeman is not apart from the rest of the community but should take every opportunity to work with the people. We have to live down the tradition of the police informer, which was the underlying method of the Nazis, and so we rely for our contacts mainly on the democratic organisations. Our policemen give lectures to the shop stewards on various aspects of their work and we depend on the shop stewards to give us information about the black market, for one of the biggest sources of black market supplies consists of goods diverted from the factories.

" To-day," Jurich went on, " we can say that the democratic section of our people, particularly the workers, can see that the police are their friends and not their enemies."

Politics are encouraged in the Leipzig police force. Jurich himself is a member of the Leipzig Town Council and also the County Council for the Leipzig district. He attends in his capacity as a citizen and not as a police officer, but in the debates he draws on his experience with the force.

The Leipzig force is 95 per cent trade union—a percentage which seems to be fairly general throughout the police forces in the Zone. The police form a group within the public employees' trade union and elect shop stewards in the same way as other workers. A joint committee of the officers and the shop stewards decides all disciplinary cases. Technically the police have the right to strike, but since theirs is an essential service, they must first get the permission, not only of their own union, but also of the F.D.G.B. (the T.U.C. for the Zone). " We should settle matters before it got that far," said Jurich.

The Press and publishing has also been subject to 100 per cent denazification. Here, too, emergency measures had to be taken to secure new staffs. Schools for journalists were opened by the provincial authorities, in addition to the existing courses in the Universities, while the S.E.D. opened a school for its members, most of whom were nominated by the printing trade union. The new journalists, like the new teachers, took up their work with a minimum of technical experience, and this fact is often apparent in the newspapers. But some of the journals have reached a technical efficiency quite equal to that of pre-Nazi Germany.

The school, the law, the police, the Press, and public administration were the main targets of the denazification drive from the first days of the Russian occupation. Where technicians in various departments of industry were concerned, advantage was taken of the inter-allied decision permitting such people to be returned, even though former Nazis. I found factories where this was resented and where the shop stewards had appointed a special committee to keep a watch on the individual concerned and to endorse or veto any decision he took. In fact, in this matter of the employment of Nazi specialists, the Russians seem more inclined to be lenient than the Germans.

In industries and occupations, without a dominant influence on public life, denazification in the Zone has been much less active. For example, former members of the Nazi Party are permitted to appear as actors, though not as producers. Great play was made by the Press in the American Zone because there a complete ban on Nazi actors had been imposed.

Charlotte Kueter, among the most famous actresses in pre-war Hitler Germany, who was one of the first German anti-Fascists to return from England, explained the position to me in this way: " We should much prefer not to use actors with a Nazi past, but the fact was that large numbers of them joined the Nazi Party to keep their job without taking any share in the activities. The alternative to using them was to bring the theatre almost to a standstill. Of course, all active Nazis have been excluded and we keep a close eye on the others."

Dismissed Nazis are obliged to report to the Labour Exchange and are offered such posts as are not excluded by the denazification orders. Some of them fall on their feet. For example, I heard of dismissed judges carrying on quite happily as legal advisers to business firms, or technicians dismissed from public service at once securing re-engagement with privately owned factories. A big proportion, however, were forced to take on unskilled manual work, and in this way tens of thousands of men formerly in comfortable well-paid positions are now working as labourers, miners, foundry workers, and other occupations, receiving the ordinary trade union wage and the normal rations for their class of work.

Actually these ex-Nazis, once out of their jobs, are not treated differently from the rest of the population, but it is revealing to find the sympathy their plight evokes in some quarters. The idea that people who have enjoyed comfort all their lives should now be compelled to accept the conditions under which millions of workers have always existed, seems to horrify many middle-class Germans more than all the crimes of the Nazis. On the other hand, there are many Germans who view this reversal in the fortunes of the ex-Nazis with grim satisfaction.

The position of people who were not guilty of war crimes, yet took an active part in the various Nazi activities, is different from those losing their jobs simply because of their party membership. These active Nazis in the Soviet Zone can be forced to work on reconstruction. In November, 1945, a directive was issued that they must be put on heavy work for thirteen weeks. The method adopted to enforce this order appears to have varied in the different provinces. Mecklenburg, for example, allowed the offenders to do their heavy labour in their free time, while carrying on with their ordinary job. A business-man would leave his office and turn out for rubble clearing in the evenings and at the week-ends. They were paid in the ordinary way, but where they were also drawing salaries from their ordinary work, the extra money had to be turned over to men and women released from concentration camps. Altogether, in Mecklenburg, these ex-Nazis put in 3,270,000 hours of work and turned over about £50,000 to the victims of Fascism organisation.

More serious offenders are sent to the Labour Exchange with a notification that they must be employed on manual work for six months, after which their case goes to a denazification commission to decide whether they shall continue or be allowed to take up other work. When a Nazi who has served a prison sentence comes out— and quite a number are now reappearing—the Labour Exchange is told whether or not he is to be allowed to take up responsible work. Some are barred from everything except manual work, but others are offered training in skilled trades.

Anyone capable of working who refuses to do so can be prosecuted and imprisoned by order of the Allied Control Commission. Practice

E

varies among the provinces of the Soviet Zone. Saxony, for example,
brings offenders before a special commission which has power to
order them to camps, where they live and sleep while going out to
work in the ordinary way. Only if they continue to refuse to work
do they go to gaol. Mecklenburg and Thuringia put a law before
their Parliaments in the spring of 1947 giving their governments
power to open camps from which any person undergoing a prison
sentence can be put on productive work outside the prison. Wages
are to be at trade union rates and are paid over to the man's family,
minus the cost of upkeep. Single men would collect the balance
at the end of the sentence.

The final stage of denazification was supposed to have been
reached in January, 1946, with the issue of directive 24 by the
Allied Control Council, entitled "Elimination of National Socialists
and persons hostile to the policy of the Allies from offices and
responsible posts."

This directive, which is binding on the four occupying powers,
demands the dismissal of all Germans who were more than nominal
members of Nazi organisations and all who are hostile to the Allied
objectives, from public and semi-public offices and from responsible
posts in important private enterprises. They are to be replaced by
persons considered capable of furthering the development of genuine
democratic institutions. A long and detailed definition of the
difference between a nominal and an active Nazi is given, and a
further check is ordered on persons retained in public posts and
on those newly appointed.

A careful check is also ordered on a whole range of people,
including those who gave the Nazi Party financial assistance, and
all who held important posts in industry, commerce, finance, or
agriculture.

Although this directive was the most detailed of any issued by
the Allies, its effectiveness depended very largely on the way it was
operated, especially as in many cases discretion is left to the local
commander.

In the Soviet Zone, the duty of applying it was in the hands of
262 Denazification Committees drawn from the three parties and
the trade unions. Some of these committees are operating on far
too crude and drastic a scale, without apparently reading the carefully drawn distinction between the active and the nominal Nazi.
I came across a hospital for example where an order had to be
countermanded for the dismissal of a number of nurses who had
joined the Nazi Party, but had no record of activity. Their departure
would have dislocated the whole hospital administration.

In fact, as far as the Soviet Zone was concerned, the directive conveyed orders for Nazi dismissals which in the main had already been carried out. Its chief importance lay rather in the check ordered on people remaining in office, for in many cases new details had come to light since the original purge.

The two big remaining problems for the Soviet Zone are the replacement of all the dismissed Nazis by genuine democrats, and the drawing into the democratic life of the community of hundreds of thousands of nominal Nazis. These two problems are linked, for until both are accomplished there remain the twin dangers of the anti-Fascist leadership being isolated from the mass of the people, and of the dismissed Nazis drawing the mass into a new reactionary movement.

There is no doubt that the anti-Fascists do tend to form a community of their own. To spend an evening with a group of them is an inspiration, for one realises that however much the Germans as a whole failed to fight the Nazis, there were Germans whose record of courage and self-sacrifice ranks with that of any other people. These are the men and women who are bearing the main burden of rehabilitation in the Soviet Zone. All over the Zone I met personal friends who had played their part in the Free German Movement and the Free German League of Culture in Britain, who are now occupying important positions. I met Ludwig Renn, the famous author, and Anna Seghers, the author of the *Seventh Cross*, both of whom had returned from Mexico, and a considerable number of others who spent the war years in Moscow. All these returning refugees are seized upon immediately and swept into the work of the Zone.

Many of them find it difficult to get back fully into the life of a people whose whole mentality is coloured by years of life under Fascism, and it is understandable that they tend to form into separate groups. They were away during the critical years, and never lost touch with democratic forms, consequently they were able to see the whole picture of the struggle of the free nations against Nazism, which the anti-Fascists who remained still do not fully understand.

Then there are the men and women released from the prisons and concentration camps, and those with a record of struggle against Hitler, who emerged to take their place in the anti-Fascist committees which were formed as the Red Army marched in. All over the Zone you find them, and you marvel that the human spirit could have survived through such years of torment. Men and women who spent up to a dozen years in Hitler's gaols, who suffered every conceivable humiliation from the Nazis, are active in every sphere.

Not all the victims of the Nazi terror survived the ordeal. Some were broken; some, it must be confessed, were corrupted by years of torture. Of those who came through, sickness has already taken a heavy toll. Too many threw themselves into the tasks of reconstruction while still undermined by their experiences, and have either died or become victims of chronic ill-health.

The other important section of anti-Fascists are those who joined the opposition during the war. There is evidence to show that the revolt of 1944 was more than the plot of a few generals. A small but by no means negligible section of the people took part and hundreds suffered death and imprisonment as a result. In many parts of the Zone there are members of the Free German Committee founded in Moscow by German prisoners of war. I met one who went over to the Russians at Stalingrad. He crossed the line when a plot to arrest Paulus, the German C.-in-C., in which he and others took part, had failed. His story seems to show that the Free German Committee was more than a mere propaganda move. Members were given plenty of opportunity to show their genuineness by risking their lives in active work at the front. On one occasion a group penetrated a hundred miles behind the German lines and scattered leaflets among German soldiers in a cinema. Selected members of the Free German Committee were given a three months' course at a special school and the best students went on to a further eight months' course. Many of these former prisoners now occupy important positions. I also met a German from England who was dropped by parachute by the Americans and was able to play a valuable part in the last period of the war.

Then there are those who did not have the courage to stand out against the Nazis but were bold enough to listen to the foreign radio. Scores of times I was asked whether I knew Lindley Fraser and Hugh Carlton Green, the two commentators in the B.B.C. German programme, whose following during the later war years must have been enormous. (Incidentally, few who listened during the war now appear to make any attempt to tune in to London.)

These elements form the nucleus round which the new democratic life is being built, but the gap between them and the rest of the population has yet to be bridged. That is why the question of bringing back the little Nazis is assuming such importance. Something like a third of the population was in one way or another associated with the Nazi machine. Hardly a family, even those containing anti-Fascist fighters, but had some member in a Nazi organisation. Thus, denazification has touched almost the whole population and has reversed the social position of many. The need now is for some degree of stability.

All the organisations in the Zone are agreed on a youth amnesty for non-active Nazis born after January 1st, 1919, but such a decision can be taken only by the Allied Control Commission.

In February, 1947, the three anti-Fascist parties submitted a resolution to the Soviet administration stating that good results had already been achieved in the Eastern Zone by allowing nominal Nazis to prove themselves in the work of reconstruction. It expressed the view that to carry through Directive 24 mechanically, as was being done in many cases, would eliminate many experts from the administration.

That the Russians apparently accept their viewpoint was shown in an article in the Soviet-owned Berlin paper *Taegliche Rundschau*, which declared on February 13th, 1947: "A system making responsible many millions of human beings without considering whether they are criminals or not, and necessitating denazification commissions having to examine tons of formal questionnaires of various sorts, cannot guarantee fair administration of justice. Almost necessarily such a system leads to the real criminals' avoiding responsibility, while people who had nothing to do with the crimes are suffering. . . . We stress that denazification policy must not and cannot consist in persecuting without discrimination all former members of the Nazi Party and its affiliated organisations.

"Such a course would not be right, and the Soviet Military Administration will not allow itself to be provoked into following it. Any deviation from this principle would be a violation of the policy laid down by the Allies at the Berlin Conference. Beyond that, it is in the interest of the speedy reconstruction of a peaceful economy and a peaceful life in Germany to draw the former Nazi Party members into reconstruction, particularly those coming from the working strata of the population. These former nominal Nazis must be easy in their minds and convinced that they will find full support in their efforts to come back to the right way and to free themselves of their former errors and mistakes. There must not be any obscurity or extremism about this question."

When I called at the headquarters of the Saxony Government in Dresden, the building was placarded with a notice issued by the public employees' trade union on which was this slogan: "Hang the big ones and let the little ones run." That, generally speaking, is the policy towards the Nazis in the Soviet Zone.

5

REBUILDING DEMOCRACY

DENAZIFICATION in itself is no more than a negative measure against a revival of Fascist activity. The positive phase is the rebuilding of democracy.

How far is there political freedom and democracy in the Soviet Zone ? Any answer to that question must be qualified by the facts set out in previous chapters. There can never be complete freedom and there can never be complete democracy in a country occupied and administered by foreign powers. What must be assessed in an analysis of the position in any zone of Germany is the progress made towards an agreed objective which has never before been attempted— the military occupation of a country not for the purpose of holding down an alien population and not primarily to secure restitution, but to assist a conquered people back to a democratic life and a place among the free nations.

In their relations with the German people, the Russians have always stressed the basic aims of their administration—to ensure themselves and Europe against any renewal of German aggression, to assure reparations for the damage caused to their country and their Allies and to assist the German people to transform their land into a peace-loving nation which, while utilising its peaceful industrial and agricultural potential to the full, will be deprived of the economic and military possibility of aggression.

The Russians believe that the rebuilding of democratic institutions in Germany is the best way of achieving these aims, but they have no illusions about the difficulties of this task. I discussed the question with scores of Russians in responsible positions. They all agreed that there had been substantial progress since 1945, but that the Germans had a very long way to go before it could be said that they were free from the influence of Nazi and Fascist ideology. If openly reactionary parties were allowed in Germany, the hardships of the moment and such questions as the frontiers and the burden of reparations would provide just the material for a revival of aggressive nationalism and fascism.

The Russians, and indeed all the Allies, with varying interpretations, have met this situation by insisting that only anti-Fascist parties have the right to use the democratic machinery which is being created in Germany.

Marshal Zhukov, the first head of the Soviet administration in Germany, took very swift action. On June 10th, 1945, only five weeks after the Red Army occupied Berlin, he issued an order authorising the creation of democratic parties " whose declared aims are to eliminate the remnants of Fascism, secure democracy and civil liberties, and to further the initiative of the population in these tasks."

At the same time the formation of free trade unions and organisations for mutual aid, culture, and education were permitted. Organisations had to submit their programme of policy and work to the control of the Soviet administration within the framework of the orders of the Allied occupation authorities.

Four parties quickly issued their programmes and their appeals to the German people. The Communists, on June 11th, came out with demands for the property of war criminals and Nazi leaders to be expropriated and handed to municipal and provincial administration, the distribution of the big estates to landless peasants, and the nationalisation of transport, gas, electricity, and other services. They declared that they were not pressing for Socialism in Germany because the situation demanded unity of all progressive forces. The Social Democrats followed with a programme calling for nationalisation of banks, insurance companies, and mines, the taking over of the big estates and heavy industry. They also declared that a strong bloc of the anti-Fascist parties must be formed.

The Christian Democrats Union declared for the " rebuilding of Germany on the moral and spiritual forces of the Christian faith." They accepted nationalisation of the sources of raw material, and monopoly-controlled industry, and expressed agreement with a land reform safeguarding the economic position of the peasants.

The Liberal Democrats stressed the need for an economy based on private property, but accepted public control of undertakings where the public well-being demanded it, and also agreed to the taking over of " agricultural enterprises of exaggerated size."

On July 14th the four parties came together on this joint five-point programme :—

Purge of German Nazism and the rebuilding of the country on an anti-Fascist, democratic basis.

Reconstruction of German economy to provide work, bread, clothing, and housing.

The rule of law within the democratic state and freedom of conscience and religion.

A policy directed towards regaining the respect of other peoples, prevention of race hatred, and sincere co-operation with the occupation authorities and recognition of Germany's duty to make restitution.

It was agreed to set up a permanent committee and a special office to facilitate discussion on all matters of policy. That was the beginning of the " bloc of the anti-Fascist parties " on which political life in the Soviet Zone is based.

The " bloc " is not a coalition. The Five-Point Programme represented the basic principles on which all were agreed, but in all matters of day-to-day policy each party reserved the right to its individual viewpoint. The supporters of this policy—and they are found in all the parties—explain that in the present political conditions in Germany, the only way to get things done is to hammer out agreed decisions.

The committee representing the three parties sits at regular intervals. No votes are taken on this body. Thus, decisions have to achieve virtual unanimity, and it is surprising how often agreement is reached.

From the beginning, the Soviet authorities recognised the " bloc " and a mass of orders and regulations brings it into the administration of the Zone. The same recognition is accorded to the Free German Trade Union Association (F.D.G.B.), which for the first time in German history has created a united trade union movement for all the organised workers irrespective of political and religious beliefs.*

It was after the four parties had been operating the " bloc " policy for some months that the movement began for the merging of the Communist and Social Democratic Parties. It began in Thuringia and Saxony, where the tradition of a united working class went back to the early years after the first world war, when joint Communist-Socialist provincial governments were established in both areas and dissolved with the use of troops by Ebert and the other Right Wing Socialists in the central government.

Conferences in the five Lands and Provinces decided on the merger and the final decision was taken by separate conferences of the two parties in Berlin, which then merged into a joint conference to form the Socialist Unity Party. The first anniversary of the S.E.D. was being celebrated all over the Zone during my visit, and again and again speakers emphasized the point that in those twelve

---

See Chapter 6.

months it had become a single organisation and had drawn into its ranks hundreds of thousands of new members who were not in either of the old parties and to whom the previous differences meant nothing at all.

It is not my task here to go over the story of the quarrel between the S.E.D. in the East and the S.P.D. (Socialist Party) in the West, nor to analyse the factors present in the Berlin elections when the S.P.D. fought and won on an anti-Russian, rather than a Socialist, programme.

I think the most important factor in the situation at the beginning was the spontaneous unity between former Social Democrats and Communists which grew up during and immediately after the collapse. In the towns and villages I heard the same story of anti-Fascist committees coming into being, taking over various administrative tasks and bringing into their ranks men and women opposed to the Nazis, irrespective of their political views.

In those early days—and this clearly applied equally in all parts of Germany—there were no ideological differences between Communists and Socialists. The memories of the old, bitter struggles had been softened in the illegal struggle and in the concentration camps. The complete achievement of Socialism was too remote and the circumstances of occupation too strange, for differences of method to cause a split between the parties. The programmes put forward by the two sides for the immediate tasks confronting them had no essential differences. In these circumstances a move from below to secure joint working was an inevitable development.

Moreover, the memory that the split among the workers had been one of the primary reasons for the triumph of Hitler had a very real influence on the German Left Wing during the Nazi period, and over a period of years spokesmen from both sides had declared that they would not make the same mistake again. Had these factors been given a free rein, I do not think there can be any doubt that unity of Socialists and Communists would have been achieved all over Germany. What unfortunately happened was that the conflicts between the Allies transferred themselves to Germany, so that the S.P.D. tended in the West to become the spokesman, not of Socialists, but of the West against the East, and to some extent, though in my view by no means so completely, the S.E.D. sponsored the East against the West.

In the Eastern Zone there could clearly be no mass basis for a Socialist Party leaning on the Western powers. Although there were many reactionary elements only too ready to cash in on a policy of hostility to the occupation and particularly to the Russians, such a party could certainly not hope to gain the support of the working class.

The Russians do not disguise their satisfaction that the two former working class parties have come together, but they insist that the S.E.D. was started by the Germans and was in no sense a Russian-sponsored party. Certainly, the documentary evidence is there to show that the various conferences which accepted the merger were called constitutionally and with democratically elected delegates.

Are the Social Democrats within the S.E.D. subject to pressure and intimidation by the Russians and the Communists as is constantly alleged in the West? I met and talked to scores of former Social Democrats. They are in important posts, sharing administrative responsibility and all profess their satisfaction at the achievements of the party. Far from being deprived of the important offices, the former Social Democrats are better placed than the Communists to achieve promotion, for in all key positions in the party and to a large extent in administration, the principle of duality applies. That means that in these positions a former Communist and former Social Democrat have equal status. I was told of many instances where former Communists were barred from promotion because this would alter the balance between the two former parties.

Take Bruno Boettge, President of the Saxony Anhalt Parliament and a member of the S.E.D. He founded the Socialist Youth Movement in Saxony in 1906 and joined the Social Democratic Party in 1908. Arrested after the Reichstag Fire, he spent a long period in prison. Then in 1945 he reformed the Social Democratic Party in Saxony Anhalt. In the Saxony Anhalt Parliament the S.E.D. has fifty-four members against fifty-five representing the C.D.U. and the L.D.P. Boettge gave me a long and vivid description of the meeting of the anti-Fascist "bloc" which he had just attended, prior to the session of Parliament the following day. The Liberals had alleged that there was undue preference for the Co-ops. and had demanded concessions to the private trader. The C.D.U. had weighed in with complaints about high-handed methods during the land reform. Apparently, the meeting had been extremely lively, but in the end general agreement was reached.

I asked Boettge, "Do you have many disagreements with the Communists?" "We have differences in the S.E.D. of course," he replied, "but the divisions of opinion seldom, if ever, follow the previous Party line-up."

"Do the Russians favour the Communists?"

"The Russians," he replied, "have very few dealings with the parties as such, but they take the greatest care to treat all parties equally. They certainly do not distinguish between the former Communists and Socialists in the S.E.D."

" Are you subjected to pressure as a former Social Democrat ? "

" Hitler tried to do that to me. Do you think the S.E.D. or the Russians would succeed?"

I put the same questions to August Froelich, Social Democratic President of the Thuringian Parliament, who was in the Social Democratic Party from 1923. He said: " The Nazis took me to Berlin handcuffed to Theodore Neubauer, one of our Communist comrades who was afterwards murdered. I said to myself then: ' Why did it need the Nazis to bring us together?' and I determined that I would never help to split the workers again."

These men, and many other former Social Democrats who answered in the same vein, struck me as being completely sincere. They are men who, on their record, are entitled to be believed.

The S.E.D. is far more in evidence in the Zone than the other political parties, although there are plenty of posters by the L.D.P. and the C.D.U., mostly left over from the election. The S.E.D., however, conducts a ceaseless campaign for increased production, against the black market, for increased efforts on the land, and many other immediate tasks. It also gives terrific prominence to the demand for the economic and political unity of Germany, a policy on which the other two parties agree. S.E.D. Party headquarters in the various towns—some former Nazi Party buildings—are always decorated with banners bearing slogans. The pictures of Thaelmann, the murdered Communist leader, and Breitscheid, the murdered Socialist leader, are everywhere, and many streets have been renamed after them.

The main difficulty of the Party appears to be not the former Communist-Socialist clashes, but the lack of political knowledge among the membership. To meet this need, the Party is carrying out an ambitious educational plan. Each branch is expected to meet fortnightly to discuss some political problem which is suggested by Party headquarters and accompanied by a booklet analysing the various issues. The branches report the result of their debates to headquarters and the conclusions are examined as the basis for further discussion. Party schools have been set up in various parts of the Zone with a fourteen days' course covering theoretical and topical questions. These schools are scheduled to turn out 130,000 students yearly, the best of whom go on to provincial schools for a three months' course. The cream of these students are sent for six months to a Party High School.

About 2,500 take the district course each year and 400 the high school training. In this way the Party aims to satisfy, mainly

from the ranks of the workers, the desperate demand for people
able to take on the highest administrative tasks. The Party owns
a publishing house which turns out a flood of literature at a speed,
and over a range of subjects which no political party in Britain can
equal. It also owns newspapers all over the Zone.

It is concentrating, too, on a drive to bring the little Nazis back
into the democratic life of the community. The task is not easy.

Here is a report given to me of an open evening of the S.E.D.
in Leipzig, to which former " little Nazis " were invited:—

" Three Party members were present and the rest were there
mainly because, as Nazis, they had been turned out of their jobs
and were working as building labourers. They were aiming to be
admitted to the Party in the hope of getting their former jobs back.
They were just waiting for the discussion to start to begin grumbling.

" They talked a great deal about individual freedom and one
declared that the people were better off under Hitler. The amazing
thing was the way in which the S.E.D. members quietly argued
with them. The Party members pointed out that far from being
' slave labourers ' as so many were under Hitler, they were getting
the proper rate of pay for the job and received a heavy worker's
ration card.

" One former Nazi who used to have a job as a railway official
complained that his old chief wanted him back but that he was refused
permission to go. When the facts were elicited in the discussion,
it was found that it was the shop stewards' committee on his building
site which had refused permission—as they are entitled to do by
law—because of the urgency of building work.

" This particular ex-Nazi shouted that he was being robbed of
individual freedom and subjected to intolerable suppression."

As many as thirty visitors, all with more or less a Nazi background,
will come to such meetings organised by local branches of the Party,
and in many cases begin to see the political situation in a new light.
And inevitably it is with such material as this that the campaign
for political education has to be carried on. Conditions, however,
vary. For example, I was told that in strong working class areas,
Nazis would be frightened to expose themselves so openly.

Despite many mistakes and faults due to inexperience, there is
a vitality and enthusiasm in the Socialist Unity Party and a genuine
upsurge from below, showing itself in a democratic machine
extending from the branches to the annual conference. There are
only individual members and no affiliations or block votes. There
is also plenty of red-tape and a real danger of corruption and·
careerism, for there are tens of thousands of important jobs to be

filled and clearly membership of the S.E.D., and indeed of any of the political parties, offers exceptionally good opportunities.

When the two parties merged they had 1,200,000 members. By the end of the first year (March, 1947) membership had increased to 1,700,000, so that half a million men and women have been brought in who were not even associated with the old quarrels between the two wings. That is a big achievement when one considers the exceptionally difficult conditions, the disillusionment caused by shortages, and the discontent caused by dismantlement, reparations, and the flood of refugees from the Polish and Czech areas.

Wilhem Pieck, former member of the Communist Party, and Otto Grotewohl, former Socialist, are joint secretaries of the S.E.D. I met them together at their headquarters at Berlin, which formerly housed the Hitler Youth Organisation. Each leader joined in the conversation and Grotewohl, in particular, emphasized the complete unity of purpose between the former Communists and Socialists. " We don't recognise these differences any more," he told me. " We are all members of a single working class party."

I asked whether the S.E.D. feared the result if the Social Democratic Party were allowed to operate in the Soviet Zone.

" We are not in the least afraid," Pieck replied. " We are only anxious to prevent Party quarrels interfering with our work of rebuilding. We are anxious for negotiations with Schumacher (leader of the West Zone Social Democrats) on the question of a united programme for the unity of Germany. In the Western Zones there is a strong tendency for the formation of working committees between the S.E.D. and the Communists, and we believe that the desire for unity is far stronger than the forces aimed at perpetuating the divisions."

In the Zone the general view is that the Social Democrats from the West, led by Schumacher, would receive support from some former members of the Social Democratic Party, from discontented elements in the S.E.D., and from anti-Russian elements among all parties, but it would not seriously split the S.E.D.

It could formulate a negative policy of opposition to the S.E.D. and the Communists, but it would certainly not be able to offer an alternative to the land reform, nationalisation, and planned economy which are the real basis on which the Zone is going forward and on which the " bloc " of the anti-Fascists parties is operating.

Leaders of the C.D.U. and the L.D.P. discussed the political situation with me with equal frankness. Professor Huebener, economist and playwright, and the Liberal Prime Minister of Saxony Anhalt, emphasized his Liberal principles in a way that

Gladstone could not have bettered. " I've been a Liberal all my
life and no one is going to change me," he told me. He asserted his
belief in private enterprise and private initiative and complained
that taxation was simply destroying both these virtues.

He went on to tell me about mistakes made during the land reform
and to criticise the policy of denazification.

" I think too little was done in the British and American Zones
and too much here," he said. " I don't like the business of putting
men of sixty, who've worked in offices all their lives, on to manual
work. Some of these former members of the Nazi Party are perfectly
decent and useful people, and some of the people pressing for more
and more denazification are pretty near to Pharisees."

A Russian officer dropped in to make an inquiry during our
talk. His presence did not make Huebener any the less outspoken.
The fact that he was so ready to express his views so forcibly made his
comments on the general situation in the Zone all the more convincing.

I asked him how, with his views on private enterprise, he managed
to preside over a government which had taken over a considerable
proportion of industry. " There is no doubt," he said, " that a big
section of economy was ripe for national control—banks, transport,
insurance, and electricity for example. We also had to take out of
private hands the industries that had been used under the Nazis for
war production. But beyond that we've got a large number of small
and medium enterprises which are far better in private hands."
The professor, incidentally, ardently supports the trade unions,
particularly because he thinks they have just as hard a fight to protect
the interests of their members in state-owned factories as in private
firms.

Dr. Kuelz, Minister of Justice for Thuringia, who in the spring of
1947 attended an international Liberal Conference in Oxford,
expressed almost similar views on the " bloc " policy. " Perhaps," he
said, " the best proof that there is freedom of opinion within the ' bloc '
is the fact that there is no marked tendency at all for professional men
to try to get to other zones. That would hardly happen if we were
being overwhelmed by a Communist dictatorship."

Georg Schneider, Secretary of the C.D.U. in Thuringia, told me
that co-operation between the Parties was better in the government of
the province than in the local councils where clashes sometimes
occurred. In his province he had 36,000 members and 514 branches,
all operating with democratically elected officials.

" Does your Party get equal treatment with the S.E.D.?" I asked.

" The S.E.D.," he replied, " is preferred by the occupying power here just as the S.D.P. is preferred in the British Zone, but there is no obvious discrimination."

" Do you find it difficult to work with Communists ? "

" We have many rows.   For example, the S.E.D. is only too ready to christen something we do as Fascist, although our people were also driven out by Hitler.   I myself was dismissed by the Nazis.   But we have our scenes in our private meetings and we usually reach agreement, although there are occasions when we go to a vote in Parliament and the S.E.D. only gets its way because it has a narrow majority."

" Do you find religion interfered with ? "

" There is no interference and religion is free.   Church services are not subjected to any regulations and the Catholics and Evangelicals can organise their processions.   We have to keep a watch to see that the law allowing churches to give religious instruction in the schools is obeyed.   Some S.E.D. mayors in the villages try to make it difficult. In some villages, however, we have a majority—up to 80 per cent in the Catholic area."

" Does the S.E.D. dominate the trade unions ? "

" They are much more active there than we are, but we have now appointed special officers to organise our people in the unions."

Dr. Ruland, a Judge in the Saxony Courts and leader of the C.D.U. for Leipzig, said that his Party had a number of clashes with the S.E.D. during the taking over of war criminals' property, " when things were done in the interests of one party and not of all."

He agreed that religion was free and that church feasts, including Reformation Day on October 31st, were declared holidays by law. He said he would like the church given the right to form its own youth organisations and that perhaps that would come when the zonal barriers were broken down.   Meanwhile the job of the C.D.U. in the Free German Youth movement was to safeguard the young people from coming under Communist influence.

" Do the Russians give preference to the S.E.D.?"

" Undoubtedly they sympathise with the S.E.D.'s economic and political aims.   I cannot say there is any deliberate preference shown, but I can say there is sympathy.   The Communists in the S.E.D. who have been to Russia speak Russian and are able to get much closer to the Soviet administration.   But I must say that whenever we approach the Russians they always listen to us and the general atmosphere is one of confidence.   The S.E.D. certainly have an advantage in regard to the Press."

Judge Ruland explained the policy of his Party as " Socialism on Christian principles."

" We oppose the S.E.D.," he said, " because they are Marxists and the Liberals because they are capitalists.

He was certain that " bloc " policy was the only way in which the work of reconstruction could go on.

Here is another comment by a leading Liberal, Dr. Alphons Gaertner, Vice-Chairman of the Thuringia Parliament and President of the Thuringia State Bank:—

" Our democracy here is based on the ideas of western and not eastern democracy. We have three parties, all with the right to propagate their policy and to appeal for support from the population. I know there is a danger in the method of reaching agreement between the parties in private discussion and then presenting a common policy in public.

" It is likely to give the impression that we are just staging a play in Parliament. But you must remember that Germany is not yet a democratic country. We have not got your British traditions of democracy, but we are trying to learn them.

" To-day, if we do disagree in Parliament, we fight out our differences in a much more decent way than in the years of the Weimar Republic.

" I am a Liberal and I want the world organised in one way. The Communists want to go another way, but we both agree that we must get the walls of our new house built before we start disagreeing on what the roof should look like. We had thirty-six Parties in Weimar Germany. Now we have got three and we find that is quite enough."

The three Parties organise combined demonstrations on various questions—as, for example, one I attended during the Leipzig Fair, at which representatives of the Parties spoke and 3,000 people in a hall packed to suffocation declared in favour of a resolution demanding economic and political unity for Germany and a Central German Government.

I found the evidence of democratic development in the Zone conclusive. The alternative is to believe that thousands of men and women who were not afraid to defy Hitler are acquiescing in a gigantic bluff and doing so with no obvious signs of pressure. That to me just doesn't make sense.

6

TRADE UNIONS AND CO-OPS

NEXT to the political parties, the trade union movement has the biggest influence in the Soviet Zone. Of some 7,000,000 organised trade unionists in post-war Germany nearly 4,000,000 are in the East. The trade unions are represented through the whole range of economic activity, from the planning administration of the Zone to the management of the smallest factory, and are taken into consultation on every important question. In every undertaking I visited the shop stewards' committee was treated on an equal footing with the management. In some factories, particularly those in the possession of trustees because the owners had run away, the shop stewards were running the concern.

This revolutionary change has been made possible not by any unilateral decisions of the Soviet authorities but by a joint decision of the four occupying powers giving to the trade union movement responsibilities far wider than they have enjoyed at any previous stage of German history. This law, laying down the duties and rights of shop stewards and factory committees within the framework of the trade unions, was issued under the signatures of the four Allied Commanders in April, 1946. It provides for the election of shop stewards' committees by secret ballot vote and guarantees to these committees rights which many trade unions in the Western countries have not yet won. For example, in addition to the duty of seeing that collective agreements are carried out, the shop stewards may negotiate machinery for dealing with dismissals and the remedying of grievances. They are entitled to take part in ensuring that de-militarisation and denazification are properly carried out. They have full rights of access to the management and, in the words of the law, "the employer has to submit to the shop stewards' committee at regular intervals all documents necessary for the execution of its fundamental tasks." The right of the shop stewards to submit proposals for improving production and preventing unemployment is also guaranteed.

It is further laid down that, in order to reach agreement on the contents of such reports, the presence of representatives of the shop stewards' committee at meetings of the management, for information purposes, may be necessary. Shop stewards are obliged to report to all the workers at least once every three months. All German laws contradicting these rights were formally abolished by the Allied decree. The only rôle of military government in its operation was a clause giving the occupying power the right to dissolve any shop stewards' committee whose activities were opposed to the general aims of the occupying powers or if it failed to carry out its duties as laid down by the Allied order.

The laws relating to the duties of shop stewards in the Weimar Republic were formulated in a much more specific way, and did not prove sufficiently flexible to meet the many difficult problems facing the trade union movement. The first use of arms against the workers by the Weimar Republic was during a demonstration demanding greater responsibility for shop stewards. The Allied law sought to provide a general basis on which the trade unions themselves could build, and thus the first task of the newly formed German trade unions was to force employers to conclude agreements permitting the shop stewards to operate in an efficient way. Significantly, the first strikes in both the British and Soviet Zones were on this issue. Those in the Soviet Zone took place at a timber works at Leipzig, twenty-one building sites in Merane, a machine-tool factory in Raebeul and six furniture factories in Rabenau. In most cases the workers won payment for lost time as well as an agreement. Inevitably, however, this method meant that the interpretation of the limit of responsibility allowed to the shop stewards depended on the attitude of the occupying power. Russia has come down heavily on the side of the trade unions. The right of the shop stewards to advise on production and to attend meetings of the boards of management has been carried to the point where in many cases they actually share in the administration.

The trade union movement in the Eastern Zone was reborn in Berlin in the first weeks of liberation. Eight German anti-Fascists, all victims of the Hitler terror, came together in Berlin to issue a manifesto calling for the re-creation of a free German trade union movement: the signatures were Otto Brass (Socialist), Bernhard Goering (Socialist), Hermann Schlimme (Socialist), Paul Walter (Communist), Roman Chwalek (Communist), Ernst Lemmer (Christian Democrat), Jacob Kaiser (Christian Democrat), and Hans Jendretzky (Communist).

" After the destruction of the German Trade Unions by the Hitler tyranny," the manifesto declared, " a number of men joined hands to take an active part in the fight against Hitler Fascism. Many of them fell victims to the Gestapo executioners. Among the fighters for liberty on July 20th, 1944 (the Generals' revolt), who were trying to destroy Hitlerism, responsible leaders of the former trade unions took part; only a few escaped the hangman."

The movement grew with striking speed and in February, 1946, the first Congress of the Free German Trade Unions (the F.D.G.B.) of the Soviet Zone was held in Berlin. Twelve hundred delegates attended from factories and from town and village organisations. All had been duly elected. Fraternal delegates attended from the other zones, and from the four anti-Fascist Parties (at that time the Socialists and Communists were still separate). A representative of the Soviet Military Administration, Colonel Tulpanow, greeted the delegates as " representatives of the German working-class who for the first time after twelve years of Hitler slavery have the opportunity to organise the creative strength of the working class and of the people."

The Congress adopted a constitution declaring that the trade unions were open to all workers and professional employees, irrespective of sex, race, party, political belief, or religion. It called for the right of the trade unions and factory committees to have a voice in questions of economic planning and in questions of production. It guaranteed full democratic rights to all members and declared for the industrial form of organisation, i.e., one industry, one union.

The immediate programme adopted by the Congress included removal of Nazis and active supporters of the Hitler regime from all executive positions, and the expropriation of the Junkers and great land-owners. " The German working class and the German people must never forget that the armament industrialists, the bankers, and the landlords brought Hitler to power. The trusts and cartels as well as the great land-owners were responsible for the policy of aggressive war." Only by mobilising the initiative of the trade unions and factory committees, the Congress stated, would economic reconstruction improve the well-being of the people instead of strengthening the power of capitalism. To achieve this, positions of responsibility must be given to proved anti-Fascists and full participation ensured for the trade unions. Factory committees should have a voice in what is produced as well as in the administration of the factories. It determined to fight for collective wage agreements, for the right of association in all industries and professions, and for a forty-eight-hour week and equal pay for equal work. Unified insurances to cover sickness, accident, old-age and incapacity to work were also called for.

Finally, it noted the unequal development of trade union activity in the various zones, and " in the interest of free German trade unionism" decided to call a conference of all the German Zones. It greeted the World Federation of Trade Unions and pledged itself to work to gain the confidence of the workers of the world so that it might be accepted into the ranks of the world federation.

There is certainly nothing in the programme which would not command the backing of trade unionists anywhere in the world. How is it carried out in practice ? I talked to trade union leaders, to shop stewards, and to rank-and-file workers all over the Zone and I do not think any unprejudiced observer 'could deny that the trade union machinery is being operated in a democratic way, without interference by the Russians, and that the workers themselves are beginning to assume a new status as they see for themselves the authority enjoyed by their unions.* It is true that the Socialist Unity Party is much more in evidence in the factories than the Liberals or the Christian Democrats, but the position is no different from a British factory where the most active trade unionists are normally members of the Labour Party, and, in some cases, the Communist Party.

In several factories I was told quite bluntly by the shop stewards' committees " nothing happens here without our consent." I saw plenty to prove that this was no empty claim. Questions of employment and dismissal were always decided in conjunction with the shop stewards. Copies of documents relating to supply of raw materials, and to the destination of output were going in duplicate to the shop stewards and to the managements. The books were open to shop stewards' inspection, and they were using their right to protest to the government department concerned if profits were too high or if there were evidence of improper methods.

This new authority is breeding confidence. Where a genuinely progressive shop stewards' committee has been elected, one finds that apathy and disillusionment are being replaced by the idea that in the long run the workers are in a position to organise the betterment of their material conditions. This development has had many setbacks. In particular, the dismantlement of factories for reparation caused bitter disappointment and led to a very definite increase in hostility towards the Russians. Some shop stewards came out boldly with a reminder that the Soviet Union had suffered far greater devastation than Germany and was entitled to take whatever was necessary for her own reconstruction. Very often, however, shop stewards and rank-and-file members alike watched the Russian dismantlement teams with a sense of dumb frustration. The long, hard winter of

---

* The report of the delegation to Germany from the World Federation of Trade Unions which was presented to the General Council of the W.F.T.U. at Prague in June, 1947, confirms this broad conclusion.

1947, with the widespread hold-up in production owing to coal shortage, made the tasks of the progressive trade unionists even more difficult. Nevertheless, progress has been made and an increasing number of workers are being drawn into genuine trade union activity.

Probably because of the memories of the compulsory membership of the Nazi Labour Front the question of the " closed shop " has never arisen. There is definitely no official pressure either by the union or the management to force men and women into the unions. Yet membership everywhere ranges between 60 and 95 per cent. How far is this a genuine membership ? The question is a pertinent one, particularly when one takes into account the very low political level of a big proportion of the population. One Russian director of a Soviet-owned factory said that in his view the German workers had a long way to go before they arrived at a real sense of trade union consciousness, and that the main incentive was the knowledge that improved conditions and, in particular, increased food was only obtainable by harder work. Many other Russians and most of the German shop stewards were more optimistic. They agreed that a considerable number of members were coming into the unions because it was the popular thing to do, but they expressed the view that increasing numbers of workers were realising that the trade union was in reality an organisation which belonged to them and in which they were free to express themselves.

Certainly there can be no doubt at all that the average worker feels himself free to voice his viewpoint. I talked to scores of them and they were perfectly ready to express themselves with a frankness which would have landed them in gaol in the Nazi period. One evening I attended a party given to the staff of a small tailor's shop. A Russian officer who could speak German had been specially invited. He was sitting between me and one of the women workers, and with complete abandon she delivered herself of the view that Germany was " kaput," that things were better in the West because Britain and America were rich and Russia was poor and that the Russians were taking away so much that Germany could not recover !

The elections for union posts in March, 1947, were carried out in a completely democratic way. In fact, some of the politically-conscious shop stewards expressed the fear to me that the workers were not yet ready for such complete democracy and might fall for the sort of demagogue who would merely cash in on their present sufferings in much the same way as the Nazis. The procedure is for the workers in each factory to elect a preparatory commission to supervise the election of the shop stewards' committee. This commission consists of three to fifteen members according to the size of the enterprise and must include representatives of the manual workers, the technicians and clerks, and the women. If a shop stewards' committee already exists it calls the meeting. In cases where elections are held for the first time, the industrial union concerned supervises the meeting. Union officials either from headquarters or from the district committee attend the meeting, make suggestions and ensure that procedure is democratic. All workers and employees over eighteen who have been at the undertaking for at least three months have a vote, except managers with the right to engage and dismiss employees. Former officials of the Nazi Labour Front and non-active members of other Nazi organisations may vote but are not eligible for election.

Nominations for election come from the floor, from the F.D.G.B., and from the Industrial Union, and the election is carried out by direct secret ballot. Union nominees have first to be publicly submitted to the full meeting of workers for endorsement. The actual list of voters is made up by the preparatory commission, which has access to official documents in order to determine which workers were former Nazi officials. Anyone has the right to register an objection to the list before the actual vote is taken, the decision of the commission being final. Detailed provisions are laid down for the locking of the ballot box and the counting of votes. Those heading the list are automatically elected with one important proviso. This lays down that the completed committee must include one woman and one representative of the employees, i.e., the supervisory and clerical staffs. If these representatives fail to secure election, then those polling most votes replace the manual workers who are at the foot of the elected list. Protests against the validity of the election may be lodged within a fortnight, with either the Ministry of Labour or with the appropriate department of the provincial government, and in the event of proof being given of breaches of democratic procedure, the election can be declared invalid. Not only mines, factories, and railways, but offices of public administration, schools, hospitals, police stations, and all sorts of other undertakings elect their shop stewards in the same way.

I also checked up at all levels on the election of branch officers and delegates to regional, provincial, and zonal trade union conferences, and again there can be no doubt that the machinery is democratic. Each of the eighteen industrial unions decides policy at an annual conference. These eighteen unions cover building, clothing, mining, chemicals, printing, wood, railways, postal services, transport, land and forestry, leather, metal, textiles, food, public administration, clerical and supervisory staffs, theatrical and cultural posts and teachers.* The F.D.G.B. has organisations in each Land and Province. Delegates are first elected to local conferences from factory groups. The local conferences in turn choose delegates for district conferences from which the delegates to the conferences of the provinces or the Zone are elected. All elections are by secret ballot. Each provincial organisation has an elected executive with the addition of representatives from each of the eighteen industrial unions. There is a rule, however, that if the F.D.G.B. delegate conference is not satisfied with an industrial union nominee it can call on the organisation concerned to nominate someone else. At the F.D.G.B. conferences voting is by delegates and not by the block votes of unions.

Each industrial union is autonomous except for matters affecting the trade union movement as a whole. Strikes can be sanctioned by a single union except where essential services are concerned, in which case the endorsement of the F.D.G.B. is necessary.

The Annual Conference of the Saxony F.D.G.B. was held at Chemnitz during my stay in the Zone, and the Standing Orders Committee had to contend with 1,090 resolutions, all duly submitted through factory groups and local and district conferences. Proposed new rules for the F.D.G.B. were the subject of 250 amendments. The motions covered the widest possible range of questions and included some complaining bitterly of too much red tape in union administration.

This network of trade union activity is becoming one of the most prominent features in the life of the Zone, and although it has by no means broken down the apathy and even hostility still existing among sections of the workers, it is making steady headway. Factory meetings and trade union meetings are better attended than in most British unions; even during the bitter winter weather attendances were generally about 60 per cent. All the time, the propaganda of the unions is directed towards convincing the rank-and-file worker that democracy gives him a right to share in the running of his country. On the few occasions when a Russian speaker is invited to a union function, he invariably voices the suggestion that organised workers must take the responsibility for rebuilding a democratic Germany. A document broadcast all over the Zone by the F.D.G.B. on the right to strike declared bluntly that " the strike weapon, used when all other means are exhausted, is one of the decisive, fundamental rights

---

* The union covering clerical and supervisory staffs (known as employees), is not on an industrial basis, members being spread over all industries. Within this union itself there is a demand for its abolition with the incorporation of its members in the union organising their place of employment.

of the organised workers," and that the decision to strike must be taken by the workers themselves " according to the principles of democratic self-determination."

The sort of argument being used in the West of Germany, which compares the trade unions in the Soviet Zone with the Nazi Labour Front, presumably because Communists play a leading part (as they do to-day in every free trade union movement in the world), seems to me to be completely destroyed by an examination of this picture. There are no doubt plenty of cases where officials attempt to over-ride democratic decisions or where corruption enters into the trade union organisation. I have yet to find a trade union movement free from these dangers. What can be said is that elected officials in the Soviet Zone are much more subject to the control of the members than in many other trade union movements and that the rank-and-file members are being constantly urged to make full use of their democratic rights.

The big difficulty of the trade unions, like every other organisation in Germany is the shortage of trained personnel and a drive is being made to remedy the deficiency. In 1946 no fewer than 13,000 shop stewards attended courses at special schools. 509 of them went on for a further seven weeks to another school, and thirty-three of this number continued their studies at a central training college. During the year, too, 2,683 trade union officials, including 523 women, took a month's course in trade union organisation. The Saxony branch of the F.D.G.B. has introduced a part-time school for shop stewards at which they spend six hours a week for six months. The curriculum is significant, including such subjects as " The tasks of the trade unions in economic planning," " What the shop steward must know about balance sheets," and " Calculation of industrial costs." Employers must give time off for these courses. When I was in Leipzig a strike was threatened because the employer refused to take back an employee who had left to train for a judge but who decided, after two months, that the course was too difficult.

I talked in Berlin to Jendretzky and Goering, two of the chairmen of the F.D.G.B. (the third is Lemmer of the C.D.U.). They both agreed that the watch kept by the shop stewards on the use of raw materials, the costing of jobs, and the factory accounts were some of the most important factors in getting the economic life of the Zone going. They told me, too, that the watch of the trade unionists on denazification had prevented many attempts by factory managements to smuggle Nazis back into important positions.

The Trade Union movement in the Soviet Zone contains officials from all four anti-Fascist parties, and it quite openly fights on a political as well as an industrial programme. " We work for the

complete democratisation of the German economy," Goering told me.
" We are fighting for a united Germany and for the right to be heard at
the peace conference. On this platform, I, as a former Social Democrat, Jendretzky, a former Communist, and Kaiser, Christian Democrat member of the Trade Union Central Committee, have all spoken
in unity. Kaiser, at an inter-zonal trade union conference, went
further and declared for a Socialist economy in Germany."

Jendretzky and Goering both have a long record of struggle against
the Nazis. Jendretzky was a member of the Metal Workers' Union
from 1912 to 1919. He was in the Independent Labour Party in 1919
and was a founder member of the German Communist Party in 1920.
He sat as Communist deputy in the Prussian Parliament until Hitler
came to power. He spent seven years in a concentration camp and
was then in and out of prison until arrested for the last time for his
part in the abortive revolt of 1944. Shackled for a year in a "solitary"
cell at Nuremberg, he was finally liberated by the Americans and
walked to Berlin.

Goering was an active worker in the Trade Union movement and
Socialist Party, and from 1922 to 1933 was general secretary of the
Federation of Clerical Workers. After the Nazis came to power he
helped to keep an illegal clerical trade union alive, and attended secret
conferences with foreign trade unions in Amsterdam and Copenhagen.
In 1937 he was arrested and imprisoned for high treason. Released
early in the war, he kept in touch with sixty centres of anti-Nazi
activity until 1944, when further work became impossible.

I put this direct question to Goering: " Are you satisfied that
former Social Democrats have full rights within the trade unions and
in the Socialist Unity Party?" This is his reply: "The experience of
several months' work with my Communist friends and the common
struggle during twelve years of Fascism have convinced me that to
rebuild the Trade Union movement we must have unity. There are
no outstanding questions on which there is not complete agreement
between us."

I asked: " Have you been subjected to any pressure by the
Russians to join with the Communists?" Goering replied: "We
did this by ourselves and for ourselves. Most of us resisted Hitler and
certainly neither the Russians, nor the British, nor the Americans
would induce me to do anything against my convictions. The facts
have proved that the Russians respect the opinion of Germans on
matters affecting German conditions."

The alternative to this co-operation is to return to the old pre-
Hitler conditions when the German Trade Union movement was torn
and weakened by political and religious divisions. Nothing could be

more disastrous in the difficult conditions of Germany to-day. The big aim of the Soviet Zone trade unions is to secure the creation of a single democratic movement for the whole of Germany.*

The re-creation of the Co-operative movement in the Zone did not begin officially until December, 1945, when Marshal Zhukov issued an order returning the co-operative property taken over by the Nazi Labour Front. In this, the Soviet Commander stressed the importance of the movement in the development of normal trade and called for the rebuilding of co-operative societies throughout the Zone. Local authorities were instructed to hand over the co-operative property as soon as societies and co-operative federations for each Land and Province had been reformed.

Elections for both societies and federations were ordered to be carried through by March, 1946, former members of Nazi organisations being excluded from all official posts. The rights of the co-operative organisations to buy and produce goods and to purchase land for development were all laid down in the order and a constitution was set out ensuring democratic control and the payment of dividend on the basis of purchases. Under this constitution co-operative employees are accorded two representatives on the board of directors of nine, but are not otherwise eligible for office. The directors are elected by secret ballot at the members' annual general meeting and hold office for twelve months. This meeting has the right to elect a commission of members to check the yearly accounts and examine any documents.

By December, 1946, twelve months after Marshal Zhukov's Order, co-operative membership in the Zone had passed the figure of the pre-Hitler period. It totalled 1,298,616, against 938,086 in 1932. The number of societies was 237, against 349, and the total of shops 5,831, compared with 3,556. The tendency to reduce the number of societies by amalgamation is still going on.

Trade turnover is difficult to assess owing to the difference in prices and the present high taxation on certain goods, but is estimated to be double that of 1933 and to cover nearly a third of the population. Employees totalled 29,000, of whom 18,000 were engaged in retail shops. Development went forward rapidly in all provinces of the Zone.

I saw the movement in action in Leipzig, a co-operative stronghold in pre-Nazi times and once the scene of the International Co-operative Congress. There can be no doubt at all that the Leipzig Society (and

---

* This demand has now been backed by the World Federation of Trade Unions, which has agreed to accept the affiliation of the German Trade Unions when they achieve a democratic organisation for all Germany.

my inquiries in other parts of the Zone convinced me that it is typical)
is organised on the normal democratic co-operative basis. As soon as
the movement was free to reorganise, the nucleus of co-operators
remaining in the town, together with proved anti-Fascists from other
sections of the city's life, began to recruit members. Activity started
in April, 1945, when the Americans entered the city and the employees
in the former co-op. shops heralded the event by dismissing the Nazis
who had been pushed in by the Labour Front. After the Zhukov
Order, recruiting was carried out on an organised basis and by August,
1946, it was possible to hold the first general meeting. The members
in the various retail districts elected between three and four delegates
to the general meeting. Wilhelm Fischer, a former Social Democrat
and old co-operator, was elected president. His vice-president was
Hans Hummel, former Communist and victim of Buchenwald.

These two men told me about their movement. Both now belong
to the Socialist Unity Party and both declared that as far as they
personally were concerned the former political differences had been
swept away in the common tasks of reconstruction. It was again
the sort of assurance that I received from Socialists and Communists
all over the Zone. Membership of the society in February, 1947,
was 75,000, compared with 60,000 in 1933. In order to calculate
dividend purchases are entered on a card up to twenty marks and then
cancelled in favour of a twenty-mark stamp which is gummed into the
membership book. The first dividend will be paid on eighteen months'
purchases at the end of 1947, and the society hopes to achieve its
pre-war dividend figure of 5 per cent.

The society deals in all rationed goods, including clothing, which
is only obtainable on special vouchers granted in cases of need. It
also runs a mill, bakeries, and slaughterhouse. " We receive exactly
equal treatment with the private traders, who dislike our co-operative
principles just as much as they did in the pre-Hitler times." Fischer
explained to me. " The difference to-day," he added, " is that
whereas in the old days we were cold-shouldered by the authorities,
we are now shown the utmost friendliness." (I should add here that
I heard complaints from private traders that preference was being
shown to the co-ops., while people registered with private shops
alleged that the co-ops. were getting a better selection of rationed
goods.)

Work in education both for the staff and members was begun very
soon after the formation of the society under the supervision of a special
official and at the time of my visit a special committee was working
out a syllabus for the education of members.

Every co-op. employee is expected to be a member of his trade
union—in this case the industrial union for food and distributive
workers. " Does that mean you impose a closed shop? " I asked.
" There is no compulsion," Fischer replied, " but we ask for a trade
union card before taking on new workers and our workers usually see
that no non-unionist comes in." This is very much the same procedure as in Britain.

Representatives of the shop stewards, in accordance with the Trade
Union agreement, are entitled to be present at management meetings
and every three months report back to a trade union meeting of the
staff. Officially the co-operatives have no relations with the Socialist
Unity Party, but in fact there is quite a close contact and an unofficial
observer from the Party is present at board meetings.

No Russian is ever present at co-operative meetings. The only
contact, as far as Leipzig is concerned, is maintained through a Russian
liaison officer in Dresden, who has the job of seeing that the Zhukov
order is fulfilled and that no difficulties are placed in the way of co-
operative development. " We always find him extremely helpful,"
Fischer told me.

The Leipzig Society forms part of a Co-operative Federation for
Saxony which in addition to retail societies owns fifteen factories. Nine
were formerly the property of the German Co-operative Wholesale
Society at Hamburg, and the rest were handed over by the Saxony
Government as compensation for co-operative concerns turned into
war factories by the Nazis.

I visited one co-operative match factory which provides supplies
for the whole Zone. I found that though Marshal Zhukov's order
restored the property taken by the Nazis, it did not release the grip
of the international match monopoly. In 1929, Kruger, the Swedish
match king who had a monopoly of match-making machinery, made
a loan to the German Government in return for control of the German
match market. The co-operative matches had to carry the label of
the German monopoly and pay a levy on each box. To-day out of every
case of matches costing 165 marks to produce, the monopoly claims
54 marks. This money is being paid into a Berlin bank until the claims
of Sweden for compensation are considered by the Allied Control
Commission.

In addition to the revival of the consumer co-operatives, agricultural co-operatives are developing in the rural areas. The first inter-
zonal co-operative conference was held at Hamburg in March, 1947.
Like the trade unions, the co-operatives in the Soviet Zone are
pressing for a single unified German movement.

7

THE GERMANS TAKE OVER

ON the basis of the democratic development described in the previous chapters, elections were held in the Soviet Zone during the autumn of 1946. Polling was held separately for the various bodies, ranging from the Gemeinderat—the local council for towns and villages of under a hundred thousand inhabitants—to the Kreistag—the County Council with authority over fifty or so Gemeinderats—the Stadt Verordneten Versammlung—the Council for towns over a hundred thousand—and finally the Parliaments for the Lands and Provinces.

Voting was by party lists, and any recognised party was entitled to put forward lists. That meant that, in addition to the three main parties, the Peasants Mutual Aid organisation, the Women's Anti-Fascist Committees, and the Cultural League all put forward candidates. The result on the over-all picture was a victory for the S.E.D. who secured round about half the total seats in the provinces and between 40 and 60 per cent in the towns.

On every elected body, the principles of the "bloc" policy were carried out. Offices in the administration were divided according to the proportion of votes cast, and an all-party organisation set up to formulate policy.

The main task of the Soviet administration when these bodies were set up was to transfer to them as much authority as possible and to integrate them with the mixture of military and civil government which had grown up since the occupation.

In the first days the nucleus of German administration was created haphazard out of any anti-Fascists who happened to be available. Political prisoners released from the concentration camps would begin to organise their own supplies and would be left to get on with the job by the local Red Army commander. In the towns and villages a Russian officer would call the population together and ask for the names of anti-Fascists, and one would be promptly appointed burgomaster and told to start forming a local administration.

Some towns the Red Army by-passed, and there the German anti-Fascists took over without any support from the Russians.

This happened in Riesa, Saxony, where an anti-Fascist committee, formed by Richard Wunderlich, an old trade unionist, set about rounding up the Nazis without waiting for orders from anyone. The population started looting, but the anti-Fascist committee got the situation in hand and, as mentioned in Chapter 1, Wunderlich saved the Co-operative store from the mob. The Nazis, including the Burgomaster, most of the police, managers of factories, and teachers prominent in the Nazi Party, were put to work under supervision, and anti-Fascists put into all administrative posts. All this was done without arms. When the Russians arrived they checked up on what had been done, made one additional arrest, and handed over the flats of the Nazis to concentration camp victims who were already coming into the liberated towns. In this spontaneous way German local administrations came into being all over the Zone, parallel with that set up by the local Red Army commander. In the main, the early stages of this joint work consisted of orders by the Russians to the German officials, but as confidence grew up between the two more authority was transferred to the Germans. In the provinces, provisional administrations were appointed rather more formally from the available anti-Fascists, and finally central administrative offices for the whole Zone were set up to take charge of Health, Education, Labour, Economy, Agriculture, the Mines, and so on. The general principle was to select officials for their reliability as anti-Fascists, even though they might be lacking in experience, and many rank-and-file workers found themselves in high office. In the early days, too, a good many Nazis escaped scrutiny.

These German bodies were all operating within a few weeks of the collapse of the Nazis, and got into their stride with surprising speed. All of them worked under Russian supervision, and each head of a department, whether in the central department or the provinces, would have a Russian opposite number with whom ultimate authority rested. In the first months there were many urgent matters in which the Russians issued peremptory orders to the Germans to get on with specific tasks, but gradually there grew up a mutual respect, and most decisions were taken in consultation.

The central departments still exist but with the election of the various democratic bodies, much of their authority is being taken over. They do, however, still act as a co-ordinating authority for the five Lands and Provinces and stand in the position of a central German government. Above them and the elected German authorities is the Soviet Military Administration which enforces all decisions of the Allied Central Commission, the supreme body in Germany, and which retains the over-riding authority to ensure that the purpose of the occupation—the demilitarisation and denazification of Germany—is carried out. That means, for example, that security measures against any pro-Nazi activity remains in the hands of the N.K.V.D., the Soviet security organisation, and that the Russian administrators are consulted on all important measures by the German authorities.

The method is unique, but it works, and while the over-riding military authority is there, the work of administering Germany is being carried out increasingly by the Germans. Within this framework, the actual constitutional machinery in the Soviet Zone is far more democratic than at any period in German history. It places full power in the hands of the electorate and gives Parliament complete authority over Ministers, unlike the Weimar Republic which was weighted on the side of the President and the Executive. In the local councils, the same democratic rule applies, and thus a clean break has been made with the old German tradition which gave authority to local officials answerable to the central government and always provided a powerful weapon in the hands of a reactionary central administration.

The five Lands and Provinces formulated new constitutions in the last months of 1946 and early in 1947. Certain points are common to them all. They all make anti-Semitism and propagation of racial hatred and militarism, punishable. In varying form they lay down the duty of the state to plan economy in the interests of the people, and register certain basic rights of every citizen. Parliament in each case is the supreme authority, drawing its power from the electorate and with the power to dismiss Ministers. All guarantee freedom of religion. They also reinforce the land reform by limiting the size of landed estates to 250 acres.

Thuringia was first in the field, and the document hammered out by the anti-Fascist parties was adopted by the Parliament of the Province on December 20th, 1946. In the Parliament were fifty S.E.D. members, twenty C.D.U., twenty-eight L.D.P., and two representatives of the Peasants Mutual Aid. The first part of the constitution declares that Thuringia is a Land (province) within the framework of the German democratic republic and, in words paralleling Abraham Lincoln, declares that " power comes from the people, is exercised by the people, and has to serve the welfare of the people." The method by which the people govern is laid down as the election of their representatives by universal franchise and secret ballot to the provincial Parliament and the Parliaments for the towns, districts, and villages. Punishment for any expression of national, religious, and racial hatred is laid down in a special article which adds that persons propagating or supporting militarist or national-socialist ideas shall be expelled from public office.

The constitution defines the rights of the Parliament, the supreme body in the province, to elect the Prime Minister and confirm the measures he proposes. Moreover, to enable every citizen to perform his rights, elections are to be held on Sundays or public holidays. Decisions in Parliament are taken by simple ballot unless differently laid down by the constitution. Parliament and its commissions sit in public. The public can only be excluded by a two-thirds majority of the M.P.s present, and from commissions by a simple majority. No M.P. can be arrested or limited in his or her freedom of movement because of an offence while Parliament is sitting, unless caught red-handed or if Parliament has agreed to detention by a two-thirds majority. Parliament can be dissolved before the end of the election period by its own decision or by a plebiscite of the electorate.

The constitution also defines the right of Parliament to dismiss any minister not retaining its confidence. The Prime Minister and all ministers are responsible to Parliament and bound to conduct their offices according to the principles laid down by Parliament. Laws are adopted either by Parliament or by plebiscite. The constitution can be altered by a two-thirds majority of all members of the Parliament or by plebiscite with a simple majority of all the electorate (not just those voting).

A special section devoted to economy states that "economic freedom of the individual is guaranteed only within the limits of sound justice and the right of every human being to a full life." The duty of the Government to plan economy is specifically laid down.

The new peasants who received their land under the law on land reform from September 10th, 1945, are confirmed in their rights, and the state-owned factories are declared national property as long as Parliament does not decide otherwise.

The section dealing with education assures equal rights for all citizens and the establishment of the same type of school for all. A further section guarantees freedom of religion.

The Parliament of Saxony Anhalt adopted their constitution on January 10th, 1947. All the main points contained in the constitution of Thuringia are included, but there is one additional section dealing with the rights and duties of the citizen. Habeus corpus is proclaimed in the following words: " Persons who have been deprived of their freedom must be told at the latest the following day, which authority ordered the arrest and on what grounds; they must be immediately given the opportunity to protest against their arrest." Included in this part of the Saxony Anhalt constitution are the right to work, to holidays and recreation, the right to be cared for during illness and old age. Under this constitution the province has to adopt a unified and all-embracing law for social insurance on the basis of administration by the insured.

The right to form trade unions and other organisations and the right to elect shop stewards is safeguarded. Equality of the sexes and equal pay for equal work for men, women, and young people are also guaranteed.

The parts dealing with parliament, government, administration, legislation, finance, education, and religion are essentially the same as in the Thuringia constitution. The same is true of the part dealing with economy, but here the Saxony Anhalt constitution contains an article going much further. Article 73 states: " All private monopoly organisations, like cartels, syndicates, trusts, combines, and similar organisations aimed at increase of profits by production, price or sale agreements are forbidden."

The Land of Saxony adopted its constitution on February 28th, 1947. Fundamentally it is the same as those of Thuringia and Saxony-Anhalt but goes further in its formulation of some of the main principles. The right of the workers, civil, manual, and professional, to an equal share in the development of production is specifically affirmed. Marriage is set down as a state in which there is equality for both sexes. The duty of the State to accord special care to mothers is put on record with complete equality for the unmarried with the married. Work for children is declared illegal and night work is banned for children under sixteen. Articles setting out the right of the citizen may be altered only by a two-thirds majority. The constitution recognises that a number of the basic freedoms may be limited by laws issued since the collapse to meet the situation left by the Nazis but it imposes on Parliament the right to decide by the end of 1950 whether these measures should continue.

Saxony's constitution is probably the only one, besides that of the Soviet Union, which guarantees sanctuary to political refugees. It accords this right to refugees from countries whose law " is in contradiction to the civil rights formulated in this constitution." The right of Parliament, if necessary, to take over the means of production for the increase of production or to prevent misuse of resources, is laid down.

Mecklenburg vor Pommern, until 1945 the most reactionary province of Germany, passed its constitution on January 7th, 1947. Rights of the citizen are laid down in a separate section, one of which declares the " right of every citizen to work in a profession of his choice and the duty of the Government to provide work for all by directing the economy." " Freedom from want," it adds, " is the right of every citizen." The 1st of May is included in the guaranteed public holidays. Equality of women is guaranteed and the constitution goes further by specifically abolishing all laws contrary to this right—a clause of outstanding importance when it is remembered how much behind other countries Germany has always been in its attitude to the rights of women. The rights of young people to work, equal pay, recreation, and cultural entertainment are also stated.

Mecklenburg has instituted a check on immediate operation of laws passed by Parliament. A waiting period of fourteen days after the first reading is decreed, during which a postponement for a month may be ordered on the demand of one-third of Parliament. During this month one-fifth of the electorate, or parties and organisations representing one-fifth, may demand a plebiscite. A majority of the whole electorate is again necessary to ensure the passage or rejection of a law. A section on finance declares that taxation on inherited property must be diverted towards preventing the accumulation of inherited fortunes. Mecklenburg has also attempted to prevent reaction, using the democratic machinery in order to destroy democracy. In a final article the constitution declares:—

"All endeavours to abolish or curtail democracy or the principal rights of the citizen are contrary to the constitution and are punishable as acts against the constitution and actions contradictory to the constitution do not become legal by using methods contained in the constitution."

Brandenburg's constitution, adopted on February 6th, is signed by the President, Frederick Ebert, a member of the S.E.D. and son of the first President of the Weimar Republic. The clause dealing with the rights of the individual also lays down his duty to resist laws contrary to morals and humanity, while the section on the judiciary stipulates the right of the democratic parties to nominate lay judges.

All Parliaments adopted constitutions for the villages, county areas, and towns. These bodies have the duty to carry out tasks laid down by the constitution and by the Parliament of the province, but they have specific powers of their own and their decisions on a wide variety of questions cannot be over-ridden by the higher authorities. Provision is made for the election of mayors and other officers, all of whom can be dismissed at the will of the elected body.

I saw two Parliaments in action—Thuringia's, which sits in Weimar, and that of Saxony Anhalt which has its headquarters in Halle. Members sit in Party groups and speakers are announced as representing one or other of the Party factions. There is a complete absence of ceremonial and, in contrast to every previous German Parliament, not a uniform was in sight. When proposed laws or resolutions have been previously agreed by the all-party bloc, this fact is normally announced when the matter is first introduced. Debates inevitably tend to deal only with detail and not with principle. There are occasions, however, when party feeling flares up. This was particularly the case in Thuringia over an S.E.D. proposal to introduce the death penalty for black market offences. On this question, prior consultations had failed to reach agreement and the question was left to debate in Parliament. The L.D.P. and the C.D.U. both opposed, and eventually the question was referred to a committee. In the Saxony (Land) Parliament the same proposal by the S.E.D. was forced to a vote and narrowly defeated.*

Laws go through a first reading, a committee stage when each clause is examined on the English system by a smaller committee formed on the same Party basis as the Parliament, and a third reading at which committee amendments are considered. Non-controversial measures, however, can be pushed through at lightning speed. I saw, for example, the Thuringia Parliament pass a Bill through all its stages in a quarter of an hour, appointing a deputy Prime Minister to take the place of the Prime Minister who was seriously ill. Once the third reading was passed the President signed the Bill and immediately it became the law of Thuringia.

Saxony Anhalt Parliament was discussing the annual budget at the time of my visit. The nature of their tasks can be seen from some of the sums allocated. Education was estimated to cost £600,000, health and social service about the same, the police £225,000, but training of craftsmen and the establishment of new small handicraft businesses was scheduled to absorb £1,200,000, and the care of the refugees from the areas now under Polish and Czech rule amounted to £4,500,000.

Members of Parliament receive £15 a month, expenses, and free travel. The Prime Minister's salary is £1,800 a year, of which, at present rates, at least half goes in taxes. At the black market rates ruling in Berlin this yearly salary in terms of marks would buy luxury meals for about a week.

The democratisation of local government has brought the biggest constitutional revolution. Germany, since 1870, has tended towards a strong central government with a firm hold on the local administrations. Under the new constitutions in the Soviet Zone, very considerable powers are left in the hands of the local authorities from the village council upwards.

---

* A Bill was subsequently passed in the summer of 1947 providing for the death penalty for the most serious black market cases.

I saw this new democracy being born in the Kreistag of Leipzig,
the body responsible for a population of 170,000 and an area of sixty-
five towns and villages in the Leipzig area, excluding the town itself
which has its own Town Council. Until the new Kreistag was elected,
the man in charge was Erich Boehme, a trade unionist since 1926 who
was sent to a concentration camp in 1936 for organising a Society for
Friendship with the Soviet Union. The Americans were the first to
occupy the area and they gave Boehme the task of rounding up
members of the Gestapo and the S.S.

After two months the Americans left, and the Russians came in.
The changeover meant the sacking of 125 more Nazis out of 210
officials in charge of the local administration. Boehme was appointed
Landrat, an official who combines the authority of our mayor and
town clerk. He worked under the direct control of the local Soviet
Command. His job was to recreate German organs of administration,
to encourage activity by the three parties, to assist in carrying through
the taking over of factories owned by war criminals, and the land reform.
In addition, he had to help in the fight against the black market and
in the re-creation of cultural and similar activities. The Russians had
every confidence in him and were anxious for him to continue in his
job, but with the creation of a democratic County Council they had
no power to keep him in office. As it happened, he held his job by
one vote. In the Kreistag, the S.E.D., to which Boehme belongs,
has twenty-seven members, the L.D.P. sixteen, and the C.D.U. ten.
On the week-end before the critical council meeting, the S.E.D. were
making desperate efforts to see that all their members turned up
even though some were sick.

Some 150 members of the public were present long before the
proceedings opened. There was a complete absence of ceremony.
At one point the chairman was interrupted by a reporter at the press
table, and asked to repeat a list of figures. As in the case of the two
Parliaments I visited, no Russian was present during the proceedings.
When the chairman called for nominations Boehme was nominated
by the S.E.D. I learned afterwards that in the previous meeting of
the anti-Fascist bloc, the two Right Wing Parties with whom Boehme's
activities were not at all popular, had agreed not to put forward their
own candidate, but had not promised to vote. If the S.E.D. failed to
turn out in strength there was still a possibility of his defeat.

The nominations having been taken, the chairman ruled that it
must go to a ballot vote even though no other candidate was in the
field. The ballot box was handed round and opened by the scru-
tineers in the presence of the Council. When the vote was disclosed
it was found Boehme had polled his full party strength. The other

two parties had put in blank papers. Boehme was declared elected by 27 to 25—one C.D.U. member being absent.

Boehme, giving thanks for his election, reminded the members that their meeting marked a new phase in the reconstruction of Germany. From that day the imposed rule of the occupation authorities had been replaced by the rule of a democratic body. He promised to do his best to win the confidence of those who had not voted for him, and urged that the unity of the democratic parties in the common work of reconstruction must be preserved. Finally, he gave a pledge to remember always that he was the servant and not the master of the Kreistag.

The formal work over, the members turned to subjects dominating every German home—coal, food, and clothing. The S.E.D. moved a resolution, approved by the other two parties, asking for an additional allocation of clothing to boys and girls leaving school, particularly those going into the professions. The leader of the L.D.P. joined in to demand real soap and not ersatz for chimney sweeps. Then an S.E.D. member got up to ask what were the prospects for the third hundredweight of potatoes promised for the following May, and when deliveries of coal could be expected. Boehme announced that the potatoes in store had been ruined by the intense frost and that the rationing position depended on Karlshorst (the Soviet administration). The position of fodder for cattle was very nearly catastrophic, while the fuel shortage had been intensified because so many mines were rendered idle by the cold. Wood had been secured by the local administration, and despite transport difficulties 1,000 tons had been delivered to homes in most desperate need. The C.D.U. leader closed the debate with a warning that there were already families without potatoes, and a call for consultation on the question with the Soviet military authorities. The resolution was adopted and with a brief word from the chairman the Kreistag adjourned.

The constitution of the Kreistag is very similar to that of an English local authority. The Administrative Committee, rather like the General Purposes Committee in an English Council, is responsible for the general administrative work. The Economic Committee implements the economic planning drawn up by the Provincial Government but has far wider powers than an English Council in regard to the building and siting of factories, the provision of raw material, the fight against the black market, and other economic questions. The Personnel Committee deals with the appointment of staff and negotiates with the trade unions on wages and conditions. Another committee is responsible for relationships with the rural and town councils within the area. Every committee is composed of members of the three parties in the same proportion as the Council, and has power to co-opt people of special experience, giving them the right to take part in discussions but not to vote. Chairmen have a full-time job and are paid.

I have given this detailed picture of the rebirth of local government in the Zone because my observations convinced me that here will come the real testing ground for the new democratic developments in Germany. In the provincial governments it is comparatively easy to ensure sufficient anti-Fascists to fill administrative posts and to push forward with progressive measures. The political parties have no great difficulty in securing Parliamentary candidates with some basic conception of democratic procedure. But in the local authorities, particularly those serving the small towns and the villages, the conceptions of democracy have got to be re-created. Moreover, it is in these areas that reaction is more inclined to come to the forefront.

Because of these dangers I think the Soviet authorities acted wisely in permitting only candidates nominated by the three anti-Fascist parties to go to the polls. The sanctioning of independents, who emerged in such numbers in the Western Zone elections for the local councils, is dangerous in a country which has yet to learn democracy. A Party can be tested on the basis of its declared policy, but the term independent can be used as the cloak for the worst type of reactionary—as indeed it often is in Britain. There are many pro-Nazis in the Soviet Zone who would welcome such an opportunity. The organisation of local administration on the basis of the bloc of the three parties has certainly given an opportunity for the evolution of an effective democratic system. During the early months of 1947, when this new system was slowly coming into being, many questions had still to be sorted out. Even the officials were not quite clear on the division of authority between the Provincial Parliament, the County Councils, the Town Councils, and the Rural and Urban Councils. The extent of the powers in the hands of the elected bodies and the questions still reserved by the Soviet administration had not been precisely formulated, and much depended on the local Soviet Command.

Certain factors became clear, however, very early. The decentralisation carried out by making local officials entirely dependent on retaining the confidence of the elected body was instilling the idea of democratic control into the people in a very striking way. In many parts of the Zone I heard of protests and appeals being organised to the Council or to the Mayor—a clear indication that the public was beginning to understand that its rulers were subject to public pressure. On the whole, the principle of an agreed programme in which the three parties could co-operate was maintained, although bloc policy sometimes became very strained with the majority party taking every advantage of its position.

The Russians very quickly began to hand over a considerable amount of administrative responsibility. Before the elections, the Landrat or Mayor would receive peremptory instructions from the local Soviet Command to carry out certain work. He would be told, for example, to organise supplies of essential food, or to ensure assistance to the peasants at critical periods. In most cases of failure to do his job a local official could be removed by the Soviet Command. The procedure was altered immediately the elected Council took over and statements were issued by the Soviet authorities in each area, telling the elected officials that their new task must be to see that self-government was made to work.

How far, in fact, do the Parliaments and the local authorities act independently of the Russians? Theoretically they can pass any legislation and carry out any executive act which does not conflict with the over-riding authority of the Allied Control Council. In practice, there is consultation on all major questions. Before a Bill is put before Parliament, the responsible Minister would ascertain the views of the Soviet administration. The same is true regarding the general work of the democratic bodies. Each official knows where to find the Soviet official handling his particular aspect of administration and a close consultation is maintained. This method means that the Russian administration by no means washes its hands of the German problems once power has been transferred, and at the Russian Central Administration in Berlin statistics and other information are collected from both German and Soviet authorities in the Zone so that a clear picture is always available.

If an elected authority takes careful steps to ensure thorough denazification in all spheres of its activity, the Russians would leave all such questions in its hands. If, on the other hand, known Nazi sympathisers were given jobs, the Russians would interfere because under the Potsdam Agreement they are pledged to denazify Germany. The observance of the price and wages stop is enforced by the Russians on both trade unions and employers because the decision was taken at quadripartite level, but other orders affecting conditions of employment are issued by the German Central Administration for the Zone and enforced by the local authorities. The set-up in the Zone is, in fact, moving towards the position which the Russians visualise when they demand a united Germany and a central German Government. If that goal is attained the state would be run by Germans under democratically formulated German laws and the occupying powers would merely have the duty of seeing that the country remained demilitarised and denazified and that it fulfilled its obligations in regard to reparations.

On the Russian side I heard complaints, not of Germans assuming too much authority, but of their taking too little. The tradition of obedience to a higher authority is still deeply engrained in the German people and many cases were reported to me of Germans going to the Russians for orders about some phase of administration and being told that they must make the decisions and do the job themselves. There, perhaps, lies the most urgent and fundamental task in Germany to-day—to make democracy-conscious a people who are only just beginning to regain the art of democracy. In the Soviet Zone the machinery has been provided, but there is a long battle ahead before democracy becomes an effective instrument.

I met a German woman who had spent several years in America. " Democracy ! " she exclaimed wearily, " the things they do to-day in your name." She told me that one of her main difficulties was to explain to her fellow-citizens that democracy was not synonymous with anarchy. Millions of Germans, particularly those under thirty, have never experienced the working of democratic machinery. And many of them consider it means the right of everybody to do exactly as he likes. It is often extremely difficult to run a meeting, because there is no tradition of respect for the chair. Majority decisions are not regarded as binding by the minority. An Executive Committee will take a decision and at the next meeting members will get up and ask for matters already discussed to be reopened because " We have got democracy now." Another difficulty is in making the rank-and-file member take an active share in proceedings. From the trade unions, the co-operatives, and the political parties alike, I heard the same story of meetings where men and women influenced by years of Nazi propaganda were still ready to say " Yes " automatically to proposals put by their elected officials.

I saw many efforts being made to encourage the people to take a real share in democratic life. At a Berlin theatre in the Soviet sector of the city a play by Friedrich Wolf, author of *Professor Mamlock*, was produced for an audience of Berlin University students, and was followed by an open discussion. The play, *Sailors of Cattaro*, told of a meeting of the crew in an Austrian rebel ship in 1918 which failed to act swiftly in an emergency and as a result had to surrender. When the play was over, Wolf appeared on the platform with four students representing the S.D.P. (which operates in Berlin), the S.E.D., the L.D.P., and the C.D.U. First, Wolf stated his view of the play. He intended to portray, he said, the difference between formal and fighting democracy. One of the students on the platform asked whether the moral of the play was not that democracy defeated its own ends. Another defended the action of the sailors in surrendering because the alternative would be suffering for themselves and their families.

At this point the audience took over the show. The students on the platform were given no further opportunity to join in the discussion and the chairman sat helplessly listening to the cross-talk from all sides of the crowded theatre. Here is a sample of the debate:—

Boy of about eighteen: " Oliver Cromwell had to destroy Parliament as the only way of saving democracy. If we in Germany had over-ridden the formal democracy of Weimar we wouldn't be in our present plight."

Girl from the gallery: " Wasn't Oliver Cromwell a dictator and not a democrat ?"

Another girl: " Every Berliner is thinking about food and shortage of coal. Only a few take any interest in democracy."

Boy in the stalls: " For twelve years we heard that democracy was false, and now we are told it is the only way of life. This play is dangerous to-day because it points out the weakness of democracy."

Girl (very nervously): " This play is no use to-day because there is nothing now to prevent us having a proper democracy."

Someone shouted " What about Witzleben," and the audience rocked with laughter. (Witzleben is a director of Sieman's factory and a former high official of the Nazi economic organisation in Berlin who had just been " cleared " by a German denazification committee.)

Boy: " Countries are different. In Germany nothing would have stopped a man in Churchill's position winning an election after leading a victorious war."

Some of the actors joined in the discussion and finally Wolf concluded the proceedings with a speech in which he reaffirmed his view that the play merely pointed out the necessity for democracy to be prepared to take decisions in moments of emergency. The confusion of that student audience is the confusion of Germany to-day. What can be said is that in the Soviet Zone the facilities are there to create not only a formal but a fighting democracy.

8

SELF HELP AND CULTURE

DEMOCRATIC life in Russian-occupied Germany does not rest only on the political parties, trade unions, and co-operatives; there are, in addition, a number of mass organisations which are having a striking influence on the general develop 1ent of the Zone. These are the Peasants' Mutual Aid,* a movement which has grown out of the land reform, People's Solidarity, the Democratic Women's League, the Free German Youth, the German Cultural League, and the Victims of Fascism Organisation. With the exception of the Victims of Fascism, which is restricted to those who can prove their claim to have resisted the Nazi regime, the other bodies are open to all parties, and former Nazis without a criminal record are entitled to apply for admission.

The aim of all these organisations is to create single bodies for the whole of Germany, but they have met with opposition because in the Western Zones the tendency has been to sanction a number of separate bodies rather than a single organisation. The Victims of Fascism Organisation held an all-zonal conference at Frankfurt in the spring of 1947, but from the reports made by delegates, it is clear that the fighters against the Nazi regime are not regarded in the same light in the west as in the east. According to the speech of one delegate, some minor official in the British Zone actually issued a directive to the radio stations that it was " not advisable " to use the words " anti-Fascist " in broadcasts !

People's Solidarity epitomises, perhaps more than any other development in the Soviet Zone, the beginning of a new atmosphere of hope and a genuine struggle against difficulties. Created in October, 1945, on the initiative of the Communist and Socialist Parties of Saxony, it spread to all five provinces and soon incorporated within its ranks all progressive bodies in the Zone. All its activities are based on the principle that the difficulties facing Germany call for the co-operation of every section of the people, and in this spirit it

* See Chapter 10.

has waged a consistent fight for higher production in both industry and agriculture, and for a clean-up of the corruption and black market activities which threatened to torpedo all the efforts to put the country on its feet.

I talked to the leaders of the Saxony branch of People's Solidarity in a spacious mansion on the outskirts of Dresden, which was presented to them by the town council. (The former owner had two houses, so one was confiscated.) They were employed full time and had been nominated for their jobs by the various organisations. The nominees of the Trade Unions, the C.D.U., the Free German Youth, and the L.D.P. were all present at my talk. The S.E.D. representative was away at a conference. " We believe we are making history," the woman representing the L.D.P. said to me. " We are building up a new democratic way of life based on co-operation of all sections. It is a way of progress which has been born out of our common suffering." Maybe that statement was a little too optimistic and a little too sweeping, but certainly People's Solidarity has got nearer to such an ideal than any other organisation which I saw in Germany.

When it first started in the grim autumn of 1945 the difficulties facing the Zone must have seemed almost insuperable. Vast areas had been devastated by the fighting. The danger of epidemic diseases was not over. The Nazis had left industry and agriculture on the verge of collapse by their failure to renew or repair machinery, and the situation had been intensified by deliberate destruction of a considerable amount of plant, and by looting on the part of the German population as well as by the foreign workers and elements among the Russian troops. In addition, many Germans fled to the west long before the Red Army reached German soil, taking movable property, livestock, machinery, and other assets with them.

The first manifesto of People's Solidarity was issued jointly by the Communists and Socialists in Saxony, and called for the instant mobilisation of all popular forces to get industry restarted and agricultural machinery repaired, and to relieve the worst cases of distress. The movement spread rapidly. Other provinces in the Zone which had already begun to form similar *ad hoc* organisations linked up. Then the Trade Unions and the other two Parties joined in, until finally every organisation in the Zone was represented. The Churches, Protestant and Catholic, co-operate with People's Solidarity, although their own charity organisations continue to be run separately.

During the winter of 1945-6, the organisation got into its stride. Factories worked overtime, the employees giving voluntary labour and the employers raw material, to make goods to be distributed by People's Solidarity. Considerable quantities of foodstuff were collected from the peasants and given to the children, the aged, and the towns where the food shortage was most acute. Special voluntary squads of skilled workers were organised to repair machinery. They went round the villages to put the farm implements in order, and helped to restart the shops for small handicraft workers—tailors, cobblers, and so on. Material for house repairs was collected from the bombed towns and first-aid work carried out on houses and factories. Homes were opened for children, convalescents, and expectant mothers. Volunteers were organised to assist the peasants to bring in the harvest.

Considerable sums of money were also collected to aid the re-settlers from the Polish and Czech areas, prisoners of war, and others in need, and here very careful measures were taken to stress that every gift was voluntary—for the tradition of the forced levies for Hitler's Winter Help had to be lived down. Audited accounts, showing the very small percentage taken in expenses, are published. The movement produced a focal point for any tasks arising out of recon-struction. When the fuel shortage became acute, the miners worked voluntarily on Sundays and passed the proceeds on to People's Solidarity. The drive to persuade peasants to sell their surplus to the factory canteens, the schools, and the hospitals, was undertaken by People's Solidarity in conjunction with Peasants' Mutual Aid. In the search for the parents of orphan children a booklet containing 116 photographs was issued, and resulted in forty parents' being found, twenty-five of them from the Western Zones.

During the summer of 1946, 300,000 children were sent on holiday to peasants' families in the country, and 500,000 were given organised recreation near their homes. For 1947, a far bigger scheme to include holidays in the seaside towns was carried through. Thirty thousand orphaned children in the Zone are under the care of People's Solidarity. In the first year if its existence 500,000 extra tons of coal were distri-buted in Saxony alone as a result of voluntary work by the miners, while the peasants gave two tons of butter and two tons of cheese to T.B. sanatoria. The peasants of Rochlitz, a district in Saxony, pre-sented a quarter of a pound of butter each to 53,000 people in Chem-nitz. People's Solidarity has no individual membership but is a loose federation of all the organisations taking part in the work. The executive is composed of nominees from the organisations and the paid officials are also representatives of the various bodies. There are branches, formed in the same way, in all the towns and country districts.

The land reform in the Eastern Zone provided a windfall for the various organisations, all of whom shared in the division of the castles and mansions taken over from the great landowners. People's Solidarity are using their castles as children's homes, convalescent homes, and hostels for the resettlers from the Polish areas.

When the provincial governments of the local authorities want a job done, they go almost automatically to People's Solidarity for advice and help. If the organisation wants to consult with the Russians, it can always approach the official whose department deals with the particular question under discussion. Apart from that, however, there is little contact with the Soviet administration.

* * * *

Organisations of women in the Soviet Zone also began in the early weeks after the Nazi collapse. In Berlin and other bombed towns, the women set up loose committees and began to organise collective activities to relieve distress. They took over bomb clearance, the care of the children, and so on. Early in 1946 these Women's Anti-Fascist Committees were given an official place in local administration by order of the Soviet administration—an arrangement which developed into the creation of a special women's department by each provincial government.

By the beginning of 1947 there were 7,000 women's committees in the Zone, with a membership running into several hundred thousand. It was this organisation which took the initiative in calling a conference in Berlin in March, 1947, to create a Democratic Women's League of Germany. The proposal was resisted by the Berlin Social Democrats, and for the first time one of the Parties of the anti-Fascist bloc was induced to boycott the conference; the C.D.U., whose women members had taken a prominent part in the preparations, instructed its members not to attend. Nevertheless, the conference went ahead, and elected as officers women universally respected in Germany. The executive is composed of women from all walks of life, including housewives, youth, shop stewards, and the peasants. One thousand four hundred delegates representing 250,000 women were present, and the conference was greeted by the Soviet and American administrations and by the International Democratic Federation of Women.

Of all the problems facing Germany to-day those of the women are most urgent. The figures for the loss of man-power are so terrifying that it becomes clearer every day that only if the women take a full part can there be any hope of reconstructing Germany. According to the census of December, 1945, in the Soviet Zone, there are two men to every seven women in the age groups between twenty and twenty-five, and just over one to three in the group between thirty and forty. This proportion has been made worse by the influx of refugees, among whom are very few young men. The figures mean that millions of women must be brought into industry or some other form of productive activity. The first step in the Zone was the adoption of the principle of equal pay for equal work, but apart from the Women's Anti-Fascist Committees only a minority of women have been drawn into the political and social organisations. The tradition of Kinder und Kueche (children and the kitchen) is still very strong among German women, and a big proportion of men, even in the Left-Wing organisations, still fight shy of the idea of women's equality. Elections for the Parliaments, the local administrations, the trade unions, and the political organisations, produce only a very small proportion of women.

Yet millions of women can never hope to have a normal family life, a situation which cannot go on being ignored. Already it is showing itself in a sharp increase in the divorce rate. As a minister in one of the provincial governments said to me: " It may not be a good solution, but separations and divorces are having the effect of giving more women the chance to have children, for it means in effect the man raises more than one family. The illegitimate birth rate is rising, and some of the provincial governments have carried legislation, against the opposition of the C.D.U., giving completely equal status to the children, whether legitimate or illegitimate."

*　*　*　*

The Victims of Fascism Organisation, like the others in the Zone, grew rapidly from the first days of Hitler's collapse. Local committees were set up to provide food, clothing, and accommodation for the stream of fighters against the Nazi regime coming from the prisons and concentration camps. Very early these committees were brought into the work of administration. From the outset the Soviet authorities gave them recognition and special concessions. " It is well that the German people as a whole should have a constant reminder that the free world makes a distinction between those who resisted Hitler and those who acquiesced in his crimes," a Russian explained to me. The committee of the three Parties, each member of which must himself be a victim of Fascism, examines the claims of each applicant for membership.

The comradeship of the concentration camps is a very real thing in post-Nazi Germany. It is an inspiring experience to spend an evening with these men and women who have come back to rebuild their country after their years of suffering. They played their part all over the world in the fight against Fascism. Some went over to the Maquis in France and helped to equip the French patriots with arms taken from the German soldiers. Others fought with Tito in Jugoslavia and with the Greek patriot armies. A number who served in the German division of the International Brigade hold important positions in the Zone. Very often Russians join in such gatherings, but they come not as representatives of the occupying force but as friends. The victims of Fascism are given priority for the meagre supplies of clothing and other goods, but they usually remain worse off in this respect than the rest of the population, for they lost everything during their imprisonment, whereas the average German family which escaped bombing still retains a full wardrobe.

The Victims of Fascism Organisation has received some of the landowners' mansions for use as convalescent and rest homes. They have also been given the luxurious mansion near Dresden, built at a cost of £1,250,000 by Mutschmann, Gauleiter of Saxony. Mutschmann, who had been posing as a refugee, was arrested as a war criminal in April, 1947. In the halls where he used to entertain Hitler, Himmler, and Goering, and where he built up a cellar of 30,000 bottles of the choicest wine, the victims of the Nazi tyranny are being given facilities for a return to health.

* * * *

Every Sunday for several weeks during 1946, a group of former Nazis well known to the local population were turned out to clean up the Dresden Jewish cemetery. They were in charge of Leo Loewenkopf, who survived the murder camp at Maidanek and returned to his native town to become head of the Dresden Jewish community. Loewenkopf is also a member of the Jewish Committee for all Germany which is trying to work out proposals for the restitution of Jewish property taken by the Nazis. These are the most pathetic of all the victims of Hitler's torturers.

Loewenkopf gave me the figures quoted in Chapter 1—133 Dresden Jews left of the 5,800 who lived there before the Nazi regime. Of 800 children only fourteen are left, and of that number four were rescued from concentration camps. Similar ghastly details could be given for almost every town in Germany.

One of the first acts of the Allies was to restore to the Jews all the rights taken from them under Nazi laws. In the Soviet Zone property owned by the Jewish communities has been returned, but the question of the Jews' personal property taken by the Nazis or bought by Germans at bargain prices has still to be considered. Saxony has decided to restore all Jewish cemeteries, while Dresden Town Council has agreed to set up a memorial to murdered Jews on the site of the synagogue wrecked during one of the Nazi-organised pogroms.

The persecution of the Jews is the one crime of the Nazis which the Germans do not attempt to deny. They take the first opportunity to assure any foreign visitor that they were against the pogroms. Jewish Germans who have returned are always overwhelmed with inquiries from Germans asking anxiously about Jewish friends who disappeared during the terror. To some extent this feeling of shame at the crimes against the Jews is genuine. I heard of a number of instances where Germans risked their lives to try to help Jewish friends or to try to preserve their property. Dresden fire service sent a delegation to Loewenkopf to present him with the Star of David which they had saved from the burning synagogue and had hidden from the Nazis. A non-Jewish German worker called at his office with a parchment roll of the Book of Moses which he had saved from the fire and preserved in his house for several years.

Nevertheless, the indisputable fact is that the great masses of the population either took part in the persecutions or made no attempt to resist them, and the gulf between the few surviving Jews and the rest of the people is very wide. Jewish Socialists and Communists, many of whom have returned from emigration, are working in responsible positions and are anxious to play their part as Germans in the reconstruction of their country, but the non-political Jew is aloof and often hostile to the rest of the community. Most of them would emigrate if the opportunity were there. Traces of anti-Semitism still exist, although the evil is not so apparent as in certain parts of Britain. Moreover, the German authorities are determined to make full use of the laws against race hatred, and anti-Semites are careful not to come into the open. I was told of two cases where action was taken. A councillor for a suburb of Dresden (a member of the S.E.D.) called a half-Jew a " Jewish scoundrel " and was promptly charged. He was awaiting trial at the time of my visit. An evangelical minister in charge of cemeteries wrote a letter before Hitler's collapse in which he said that he could not reconcile it with his conscience that Jewish Christians and executed Communists should lie side by side with Protestants in the same graveyard. The letter was discovered and he was promptly dismissed from his post, but the legal department of the Saxony Government decided that he could not be prosecuted retrospectively under the race-hatred law.

* * * *

In Wiemar, Thuringia, I was called to the telephone early one morning to receive a frantic appeal from the Free German Youth. They had organised a great demonstration to celebrate International Youth Week and were expecting delegates of the French Youth movement as the chief guests. But the delegation was still somewhere between Dresden and Weimar and they were desperately anxious for some word of welcome from a foreign visitor. Since I was the only citizen of Western Europe in Thuringia, they pleaded with me to say a few words. Erfurt had taken an afternoon off to celebrate the occasion. Some 7,000 marched in procession to the Olympia type-writer factory and there the speeches were made from a platform flanked with the British, Russian, French, and American flags. The Soviet Commander of Erfurt sat unobtrusively among the crowd on one of the wooden benches.

When I was called upon I told them how youth organisations of the countries under Hitler's oppression, as well as the German anti-Fascist Youth movement found refuge in Britain during the war, and I assured them that progressive people all over the world looked to German youth to play its part in rebuilding a peaceful German democracy. Like all the organisations in Eastern Germany, they are pathetically anxious for contact and encouragement from the West and they cannot understand why their attempts to make contact are so often cold-shouldered.

The Free German Youth has played a great part in mobilising the people for the work of reconstruction. In the factories it has formed youth groups to aid the production drive. In the villages it has co-operated with Peasants' Mutual Aid in helping to solve the problems of the new peasants. Its campaign for the spring of 1947 was to give every assistance to the spring sowing and to ensure that every available plot of land was cultivated. Schools are held in the big houses which came to the Free German Youth as their share in the land reform. Sometimes the enthusiasm of the youngsters goes too far, as when they decided to ask the school children to clean up the streets when the schools were closed for lack of coal in March, 1947. A Russian professor who is in charge of the Soviet side of education in Thuringia told me about this. " I stepped in and put a stop to that," he said. " The children had lost quite enough schooling, and I didn't want them all in bed with colds."

All three Parties take part in the Free German Youth. The S.E.D. has the biggest membership, but in some of the smaller towns and villages the C.D.U. has the majority.

*   *   *   *

In one aspect of administration, at least, the Russians have won the reluctant respect of their critics; that is in the field of cultural activity. Here it is also true that the Russian influence has been very definitely applied. The view of the Soviet administration is that

in present circumstances it is impossible to tackle all the tasks necessary to provide normal living conditions for the mass of the people,
but that at any rate they can be given the opportunity to enjoy plays,
music, and other forms of cultural entertainment.

Each provincial government has its special department for
cultural activity, and there is also a responsible department in the
central administration for the Zone. In charge at the central administration is Herbert Volkmann, who worked as a journalist for the
United Press of America until America entered the war, and later took
part in a Berlin resistance group. His job is to encourage the theatre,
music, painting, literature, and every other cultural activity. When
I talked to him he was very proud of having secured, for the use of
authors, one of the castles taken over during the land reform. It is
Wiepersdorf in Brandenburg and was formally handed over on May 1st,
1947. " We are doing everything we can to encourage new German
authors," Volkmann told me, " but how can you expect people to do
decent work in the sort of overcrowded conditions most of them
have to endure? So I put up the idea that we should have this castle
where we can provide peace and quiet for anyone engaged on
creative writing."

In the Zone, seventy-six theatres, either municipally or privately
owned, are playing, while a large number of repertory companies
are also putting on shows. The administration gives them financial
help. In every town you see posters advertising the shows of the
week.

Ninety publishing firms operate in the Zone and have already
produced more than 250 titles, with a total print of about 4,000,000
volumes. There are about 200 periodicals and sixty newspapers.
Practically every government department issues a technical weekly
journal.

The Cultural League works in close collaboration with the German
authorities and with the department of the Soviet administration
responsible for cultural activities. Formed in Berlin in July, 1945, it
was immediately given full facilities to organise in the Soviet Zone.
The French followed with permission to set up local groups without
application to the central office. The British Zone permitted a
restricted organisation in January, 1946, and the Americans in August,
1946. In the British Zone particularly, despite handicaps, considerable progress is being made. The League, however, has not yet been
allowed to set up a single organisation for the whole of Germany, and
the most intensive activity is still confined to the East. There it has
a paying membership of 65,000, and 450 branches, all run by elected
voluntary officials. Until the spring of 1947 little Nazis were barred,

but the rules were then altered to permit them to submit their applications to the local committees.

The influence which the League is beginning to exert on the life of the people is apparent to the most casual visitor. In the villages particularly it is providing a focal point for communal life which has never before been present in Germany. Local branches are organising concerts, amateur dramatics, rambles, and various other outdoor activities. During the winter they arrange evenings for the children —often in the only heated premises in the locality. Debates are held between representatives of the three Parties. In the towns the League forms a link between the municipal and private activities which are continually going on in the cultural field. These activities are striking when one considers the difficulties which have to be overcome. Here are figures for Saxony, which are typical of the other five provinces: by December, 1946, thirty-three theatres were giving daily performances; twenty repertory companies were touring; forty-four puppet theatres were giving children's shows, and, in addition, there were a large number of variety shows and concerts. The weekly attendance was 700,000 adults and 255,000 children. Shakespeare, Shaw, Moliere, and Chekov, as well as German authors, were included in the repertoire.

In Dresden, the most bombed city in the Zone, where every theatre and concert hall was destroyed, the Saxony State Orchestra and the Dresden Philharmonic Orchestra were performing, and the first theatres had started within three weeks of the Red Army's occupying the town. By the beginning of 1946 entertainment was quite up to the level of the Weimar period. There were two opera houses, three theatres for straight plays, two for musical comedy, one for light opera, and two variety halls. In Dresden, too, began the revival of the Volksbuehne—a peoples' theatre based on the trade unions which was extremely popular before Hitler. Charlotte Kueter and her husband, Paul Levitt, both well known on the German stage before the Nazi triumph, took charge immediately on their return from England. In March, 1946, they gave their first show in a former dance hall. It was *Professor Mamlock* the famous anti-Nazi play by Frederick Wolf. They kept the performances going through the summer and most of the bitter winter of 1946–7. " Even when we had no fuel at all and the temperature was many degrees below zero, the theatre would still be packed," Charlotte Kueter told me. " The audience would sit huddled in overcoats and rugs, oblivious of everything except the show. For those of us on the stage it was even more difficult. I think acting, when every inch of your body cries out with cold, is the most devastating experience I have had since I came back to Germany."

Actors are given worker's ration cards, but those taking leading parts and the producers secure the extra heavy worker's rations.

The censorship of plays, designed to prevent any Nazi or militarist propaganda, is carried out by the German Ministry of Culture, doubtful points being submitted to the local Soviet official responsible for cultural activities. Jokes about the Red Army, so Herbert Gute, Saxony Minister for Culture, told me, would be permitted provided they were not calculated to stir up bad feeling between the Germans and the occupying forces.

Perhaps the most fascinating experiment in the cultural field was going on at Weimar, where the famous National Theatre was being rebuilt with material supplied by the Soviet administration, ready for opening in the summer of 1947. Here the High School for Actors, a branch of the Weimar School of Music, is making an ambitious attempt to scour the whole Zone for talent and to train them for the theatre in a new way. Professor Maxim Valentin, the principal, and his two colleagues, Otto Fritz Gaillard and Otto Lang, formulated a plan to create a new school of acting in Germany based on the methods pioneered by Stanislavski in Russia. Valentin and Gaillard published a joint work on the subject entitled the *German Stanislavski Book* which was published early in 1946.

They started their new school in October, 1945, with the backing of the government of Thuringia, and Valentin and his colleagues began their talent hunt in the Zone. The students came from factories, offices, and mines, chosen on the sole test of ability, irrespective of social class, political party, or any other consideration. Out of 500 applicants interviewed, thirty were chosen to start the course in December, 1945. I saw their first play in March, 1947. They had chosen Cervantes' *Miraculous Puppet Show*, a piece calculated to tax the most experienced cast. To equip themselves for the performance the students had made a detailed study of Spain in Cervantes' time, the Spanish theatre up to the sixteenth century when Cervantes wrote, and the social implications which the author intended to portray. To secure the costumes the school had organised collections of all sorts of material and had made them up on the basis of a careful study of the period. Performed as part of a programme arranged for Youth Week, the show had a tumultuous reception. One felt that this young company offered something new in the re-awakening of Germany, offering big possibilities for the future.

The students receive a grant from the State and, although they qualify for only the lowest ration category, the Soviet authorities made

special arrangements for them to have an allowance of additional food
during rehearsals. When they end their course in December, 1948,
they will tour Germany, aiming to bring the new conception of the
theatre to the whole country. Already their fame has spread through
the country, and up to the time of my visit forty would-be students
had smuggled themselves across the frontiers from the other zones in
the hope of being able to join the school. Unfortunately, only four
reached the required standard.

* * * *

In October, 1945, Alfred Lindemann, a former movie cameraman
who was thrown out by the Nazis in 1933, together with six assistants
set out to rebuild the German film industry. To-day the firm Defa
has two studios, employs 15,000 workers, and has already produced
films for which a number of countries are clamouring.

Their first film, *Murderers Among Us*, tells the story of a
German factory-owner who comes back from the war to make
patronising speeches to his employees about the need to collaborate
in rebuilding a democratic Germany. But a young doctor, whose
mental health has been almost broken by the sufferings of the war
years, knew this benevolent factory-owner as an officer in the occupied
territory who, during one war-time Christmas, ordered several
hundred men, women and children to be shot. The film was made
amid the ruins of Berlin and reaches its climax as the young doctor
sets out to shoot the factory-owner while he is making a Christmas
speech to his employees. The brutal realism of the story, including
one brilliant scene when the doctor operates to save a girl dying from
diphtheria in a bomb-wrecked room, strikes a new note in the post-war
cinema.

The film has been shown to 5,000,000 in the Soviet Zone. It
has been allowed in the French Zone, but is banned by the British
and Americans. Copies have reached Switzerland, Denmark, France,
Sweden, Rumania, Bulgaria, Persia, and a number of South American
countries, and all of them have asked for permission to show the film.
One American producer who saw it in Berlin expressed the view
that it achieves a realism which Hollywood had never reached, and
is trying to secure permission to show it throughout the U.S.A.

So far, however, there is no Allied agreement on the export of
German films, and a valuable source of revenue for the Soviet Zone
is being lost. Part of the difficulty is caused by disagreements over
the showing of British and American films in the Eastern Zone. The
viewpoint of the Russian Zone is that some quota must be imposed,
otherwise the young German film industry will be wiped out by the

flood of pictures from abroad, and there is a general suspicion that, although some licences for film production have been issued in the West, Hollywood is determined to secure as near a monopoly as possible of the German market.

" We can take 250 new films a year," Lindemann told me, " so there are no grounds at all for the suggestion that we want to bar films from the west. Russian pictures are coming into the Zone, but we estimate that only between twenty and forty are likely to appeal to German audiences. Thus it should be possible to reach an agreement providing us with British and American films, while at the same time protecting our own industry."

The Defa company has made a full-length news-reel every week since April, 1946, providing a valuable record which, so far, few outside the Zone have been allowed to see. Altogether, the company had produced six full-length films and a number of documentaries by April, 1947. It planned to make twenty films and forty documentaries by 1949. The Russians have nothing to do with the production, except that, like the other Allies, they have the final right of censorship.

One tragi-comedy marked the production of *Murderers Among Us*. Borchardy, who brilliantly played the part of the young doctor, had been acting in the American sector of Berlin before joining Defa. There is proof that he was actively co-operating with anti-Nazi groups during the last years of the Nazi regime. His relatives perished at the hands of the Gestapo. Nevertheless, after he had made the film, the Americans discovered that he had been a nominal member of the Nazi Party in the early days. He was alleged to have concealed this fact, and the Americans promptly arrested him and sent him to gaol for three months.

9

NEW TEACHERS, NEW BOOKS

FOURTEEN million new school text books had been printed in the Soviet Zone up to the spring of 1947 and the presses were then still hard at work turning out more. Since the autumn of 1945 no fewer than 40,000 new teachers have been trained and are now at work.

These are perhaps the most striking achievements in the Russian-occupied area, and in the long run may prove the most decisive in the rebuilding of Germany. Right from the beginning the clean-up of the schools has been regarded as the most positive side of denazification and the task has been given priority over everything else. Sixty per cent of available paper was allocated to the printing of school books and the officials of the Ministry for Education, together with a committee of the Teachers' Trade Union, worked night and day getting out the new texts.

Up to May, 1947, German text books were printed to a total of 7,100,000. Russian books numbered 170,000 and English 300,000. Arithmetic books totalled 3,760,000. The biggest job has been to prepare new history books and up to May, 1947, only skeleton schedules for teachers had been resumed. I was given samples of the new books to bring home—volumes ranging from elementary reading books to advanced texts on Greek, Latin, mathematics and chemistry. The foolish ban on the sale of books across the zonal frontiers, which has now ended, meant that texts of Sophocles, Virgil, Goethe, Dean Swift, Shakespeare and a host of other classics were all formally banned from the West.

Every new text book issued by the Nazis was automatically withdrawn, for it was found that even in mathematical or scientific problems various forms of Hitler propaganda had been introduced. Many of the books from the Weimar Republic were little better, for despite the democratic forms introduced after 1918, the German educational system was still soaked in the Prussian militarist and imperialist traditions. In the words of Paul Wandel, head of the Education Ministry for the Zone: "The schools ought to have been purged after 1918 but there was no yard-stick with which to assess the reactionary influences. To-day we have the means. Our aim is to remove every trace of Nazi influence and to rebuild the whole educational system on a new democratic basis. That is a positive and not a negative policy."

I talked to Dr. Gertrud Rosenow, a former school inspector, and daughter of a village school teacher, thrown out of her job by the Nazis, who was responsible for training the new teachers. " We started," she said, " in September, 1945, with a three months' course. We secured the students from factories, from universities—anyone likely to prove at all efficient was roped in. But the schools were opened in October, 1945, and we had to carry on somehow until the first of the new teachers were ready. To bridge the gap we brought back teachers from retirement, students who had been unable to complete their training because of the war.

In January, 1946, the proper course of nine months began, and by 1947 it became possible to prolong the training period to twelve months. Early in 1948 this phase will have ended and teachers will undergo a normal three years' course at the universities—a standard comparing favourably with pre-war Germany which was satisfied with training colleges for elementary school teachers ending at the age of twenty. In the spring of 1947 no fewer than 1,300 were training at the universities.

Dr. Rosenow explained that the new teachers' training does not stop when they are appointed to schools. They are obliged to go on learning while teaching. A definite curriculum, lasting two to three years, has to be carried through, the new teachers attending lectures and submitting written work. To ensure adequate time for study they are forbidden to take on any other work during the holidays.

The political parties helped in the selection of the new teachers and all were interviewed. It was too much to hope to secure so large a number of proved anti-Fascists, but at least every possible step was taken to prevent the re-admission of people likely to re-instil Fascist or militarist ideas into the German children.

Figures for the Soviet Zone, which presumably compare with those for the other zones, showed that out of 39,000 teachers, 28,000 were members of the Nazi Party. Some 3,000 to 4,000 of these Nazi Party members, who have shown that they played no active rôle in the Party, had been allowed to remain but they are all liable to be re-investigated as more teachers are trained. The decision on whether Nazis should go or stay was taken by special commissions composed of the three Parties and the trade unions, particularly the teachers' union. The school administration was purged in the same way.

Not only have the teachers and the books been changed; there has also been a complete reform of the whole educational system. For the first time in Germany, education from the elementary schools to the universities has been made dependent on ability and not on wealth. After 1918 an attempt was made to introduce reforms, but only the first four years of elementary education were made universal, after which, children whose parents could afford to pay went on to the secondary schools, the rest remaining for another four years at the elementary school. There was a system of scholarships, but only a fraction of the poorer children was able to benefit.

The new system is based on one single system of education from pre-school age up to university. Only merit decides on admission to any of the higher schools. Although fees for sons and daughters of well-to-do people have not been abolished, money cannot secure a place at a higher school and the children of the poorer families receive grants.

To give an equal opportunity to the countryside a programme for the enlargement of village schools has been begun despite the shortage of material, and, where necessary hostels for children living in the distant villages are being built. The trade schools provide part-time instruction during working hours for young people between fourteen and eighteen who are engaged in a given trade. Professional schools give full-time instruction and include not only subjects like architecture and accountancy, but printing, engineering, and similar technical courses. Students from these schools can go on to the universities. Secondary school lasts for four years and is the normal stepping stone to the universities.

The new school law for the Zone decrees that education is exclusively the concern of the State. All private schools are abolished on the grounds that if they are allowed to operate a loophole would be created in the system of equal opportunity for everybody. Religious schools, always formerly a feature of German life, have been abolished.

The question of the religious schools led to a bitter fight between the Socialist Unity Party and Christian Democratic Union, with the Liberal Democrats standing somewhere in between. Eventually a compromise was reached under which the churches are allowed to use the schools for religious instruction out of normal school hours. The churches provide their own teachers and parents have to " contract in " for religious instruction. In other words, parents now have to say they want their children to attend religious classes, whereas under the old pre-Hitler system they had to say they did not wish the children to attend. Teachers are paid by the church and

Catholics and the Evangelical church have equal rights. I talked to many leaders of the Christian Democratic Union and all appeared satisfied that there was no interference with religious instruction. Dr. Ruland, leader of the Christian Democrats in Leipzig, told me that in some small towns and villages obstacles were sometimes put in the way by headmasters antipathetic to the idea of religious instruction.

" But," he said, " when these cases are taken up with the higher authorities they are always put right. During the Nazi period every possible effort was made to wipe out any genuine religious teaching. My Party believes in the integration of religion with the life of the people and we naturally tried to get a bigger place in the schools for the churches in the new system. Nevertheless, something like 90 per cent of parents in Saxony are asking for religious instruction, so we have no need to be discouraged."

The curriculum for the schools was drawn up by the central and provincial administration and the Teachers' Trade Union in consultation with the Soviet administration.

In addition to the normal educational system, "People's High Schools " for adult education, which existed in Weimar and Nazi Germany, are run by the town councils on new lines. The schools are open to everybody and a special drive is going on to bring in students from the factories. Special courses are included at the People's High Schools for workers wishing to go on to the universities. In Saxony, for example, 800 students recommended by the factories took a course from March to September, 1946. About 500 qualified and went on to the university, backed by state grants and a fund of 2,000,000 marks raised by the trade unions.

How does the new education work out in practice ? There is no doubt that the drastic clean-out of qualified teachers had a serious effect on the general efficiency of the education system. Moreover, among the parents, particularly in the villages where the dismissed Nazi teachers were well known and in some cases respected, there was a widespread hostility and even contempt for the new teachers. Some amusing contradictions arose, as, for instance, where a woman teacher, dismissed as a nominal Nazi Party member, was immediately enlisted by the church as a religious instructor, with the result that instead of teaching the children in one school she was going round to a whole series of schools.*

In one village the parents, anxious to discredit the new teacher, sent their children armed with the most difficult questions they could

---

* I was told at Central Administration for Education that this was a breach of the regulations.

find. In this case the teacher won. He dealt with the questions and made the children copy down the answers. Then he told them: " To-morrow I will put a special form at the back of the class and all your parents who seem so anxious to learn can come along too."

The policy of bringing back the teachers retired before 1933 also aroused amusement among pupils and parents. " It was just like listening to ghosts from the past seeing my old teachers, all of them over seventy, trying to do their jobs again," was the comment made to me by one German who looked in at his old school.

These problems are still very real, but on the other hand there is plenty of evidence of progress. I met in Weimar a Russian Professor of Pedagogy with a wealth of knowledge on the educational systems in many countries, who is in charge of the Russian side of education for the province of Thuringia. He admitted the difficulties of the situation: " But," he said, " we had to start at the beginning. We may lose ground in the first years, but there can never be a hope of destroying the militarist tradition in Germany unless we cleanse the schools of this reactionary influence which has existed in them ever since Germany became a nation."

I saw the new education in action in the village school of Tannroda, near Weimar. The children were aged six to fourteen. The headmaster, Carl Diesel, was a teacher up to 1933 when he was dismissed by the Nazis and had spent the intervening years drifting from one job to another, always maintaining some sort of opposition to the regime. Four Nazi teachers had been dismissed from the school. His new teachers were formerly a merchant, a railway clerk, a tailor, a girl who had just left secondary school, and a girl who had previously lived at home with her parents. Some of them were on leave, taking a course in history. English is the first language in the school and Russian the second.

The two qualified teachers were the headmaster and Frau Olga Orsel, a teacher from the new Polish areas. " Until I came back to teaching I did not realise how great were the effects of the Nazi methods on the youngsters," the headmaster told me. " The children were all dried up. They were simply incapable of solving any problem requiring initiative, but if you asked them to learn something by heart they suddenly came to life and absorbed the stuff with remark-able speed. I have found it fairly easy to break down those relics of Nazi ideology among the children, but the parents are far more difficult. Nearly every day I have a parent coming to see me and saying ' if you would beat them you would get much better results.' " (Corporal punishment in the schools, abolished under Weimar, was re-introduced in the later years of the Republic and actively encouraged by the Nazis. It is now illegal in the Soviet Zone, and a number of teachers caught giving corporal punishment have been instantly dismissed.)

The headmaster, Herr Diesel, was meeting with opposition from his local council, in which the Liberal Democrats are the strongest Party, as well as from the parents. " Partly," he said, " hostility arises out of opposition to the new teachers and partly from the simple fact that Nazi sympathies coupled, of course, with antipathy to the occupation are still quite prevalent." Nevertheless, Herr Diesel and his colleagues are developing original methods of teaching the children practical democracy. For example, I watched Frau Orsel teaching literature to a mixed class of children aged ten and eleven. First of all she read a poem, the children obediently chanting it after her. Then she asked which line best expressed the meaning of the poem. Some half-dozen answers were given and then the whole class was asked to vote on which was the best answer. Next, pupils were picked out to read the poem. When each sat down the rest of the class was asked for comments on the way the poem had been presented. It was not long before the whole class was engaged in a lively discussion.

Next, I sat in at a meeting between the class captains and the headmaster. These representatives (two from each class) are elected by ballot vote by the children between ten and fourteen, and they are encouraged to meet and discuss school problems. Each week the headmaster selects a slogan and presents it for discussion to the class representatives. For the week of my visit he had selected the sentence from Sophocles, " Not to hate, but to love, I am here." I went through the slogans for previous weeks. None had any propaganda slant. The agenda for this particular meeting was to receive a report of an inspection of the school organised by the children themselves.

Here is the report. (" A year ago we could not possibly have had such a display of initiative," the headmaster told me.)

SCHOOL INSPECTION

On March 18th, 1947, the pupils' representatives inspected their school, the new and the old building as well. The result was saddening. In each classroom something was at fault.

In class 6 the blackboard has to be replaced as it spoils the look of the whole room with its broken glass. The missing wall socket must be fixed. The two broken window panes should be replaced, too. Inkpots, as well as lampshades and electric bulbs, are missing. The door knob is broken and should be renewed. There is no arrangement to hang up maps. The classroom ought to be repainted as well. The man who was to do the job has told us there is no distemper.

In class 3 it is particularly necessary to distemper the ceiling. It is covered with soot and does not look homely. Electric bulbs are missing here too. The door of the stove is broken and has got to be repaired.

Class 8 must have three new window panes. Electric bulbs and an arrangement to hang up maps are missing here too. In the desks the broken bottoms of the sockets for the inkpots should be renewed. The classroom has no decent decoration.

In class 4 there are big holes in the sink and in one of the window panes. Both ought to be repaired. Apart from that, two electric bulbs are missing.

Class 7 could not be investigated because a piano was standing in front of the door.

All classrooms and the staircase must be thoroughly cleaned. In all schoolrooms the electric wiring has to be put in order, but when we wrote to the electricity works at Kranichfeld they said that they have no material and the central works at Gispersleben did not reply to our letter.

The doors to the toilets should be repaired. Window panes are missing. The utmost cleanliness must be demanded here.

In the interest of the children, as well as the neighbouring farm, it is about time the wooden fence between the courtyard of the old school and the farm is put up again. The burgomaster says there are no nails. We suggest we make a collection as we did last autumn when the fence around the school grounds was built.

It would be desirable that at least part of the drainage be repaired. We are sure that it is possible. We children are supposed to be brought up to be tidy. That is right, but then a good example must be given.

The pupils' representatives of the elementary school,
TANNRODA.

The report having been read, the children went on to talk about what should be done. The headmaster joined in but did not attempt to lead or dominate the discussion. Now and again he chimed in to say " That is for you to arrange, not for me."

At one point someone suggested that the children should set to work to clean the school. An earnest little boy expressed the opinion that it was not healthy for children to " get in all that dirt." Then a small girl wanted to know if the school cleaners were properly paid because if they were they ought to be made to do their work properly.

In the end they decided to organise their collection of nails and to try to do some of the decorations themselves. When I left, they were discussing the first issue of a wall newspaper.

The hostility to the new teachers among parents is by no means universal. In some areas " Friends of the New Schools " committees are being formed. Parents and teachers meet at these committees to discuss educational problems and to give practical help. In Mecklenburg a number of such groups have promised to devote a number of hours a week to help the school rebuilding programme, while other committees are making straw-soled slippers for children unable to attend school because of lack of shoes.

The tasks in the elementary schools were simple compared with the secondary schools and the universities, for, in both, reaction was entrenched among students and teachers alike. It was impossible to train teachers for the secondary schools in three months, so they had to be brought in from other jobs. Engineering technicians were brought in to teach mathematics, people with a good knowledge of a foreign language were recruited and given a short training in teaching practice. And thus, although in the words of one educationalist, "the situation for a time was catastrophic," the schools were kept going.

The universities provided the most difficult problem of all. There, all the worst traditions of German nationalism had been given free rein ever since Germany emerged as a state. Anti-Fascist professors and lecturers were simply not available and whole faculties were so lacking in staff that they had to be temporarily suspended. Many professors disappeared to the west before the Red Army arrived and others have been getting over the zonal frontiers during the Russian occupation.

In the universities one sees how little the mere negative act of denazification does to solve the real problem. Large numbers of university professors were not Nazis; they were simply reactionary, steeped in the traditions of German militarism and perfectly oblivious to the Nazi crimes. Now they remain in office because they do not fall in the denazification categories, but they obstinately resist the new trends of policy and threaten to move to the west when they do not get their way. In Leipzig a number of professors threatened to resign when a Communist dental surgeon was appointed lecturer.

The shortage of professors is one that cannot be remedied quickly and both the German and the Russian administrations, who are equally keen on preserving the prestige of the universities in the Eastern Zone, have to make the best of the available material. Men like Professor Juergen Kuczynski and Professor Meusel, who returned to Germany from England, have proved invaluable. Rather significantly, however, early in 1947 the universities began to receive applications from professors in the west and in exile in various countries. About half a dozen including Professor Lieb, a leading theologian, arrived from Switzerland, and others announced their intention of coming back from America, Persia, and Turkey. Eight leading professors crossed over from the British and American Zones.

A big effort is being made to get the children of workers and peasants to the universities. Special pre-university courses have been established for those with only elementary and middle school education and results so far have been encouraging. A new faculty has been started in Leipzig designed to train men and women for leading administrative posts in all branches of the national life. All these students are over twenty-five and must have had at least one year's experience either in the State service or in one of the democratic organisations. Active Nazis were expelled from all universities and students turned out by the Nazis were given an opportunity to resume their studies.

In general, however, the students are still very far from accepting or understanding the new democratic developments and are proving malleable material in the hands of the Right Wing professors. Much propaganda is made in the universities about the frontier question and already the slogan is going round that Germany was defeated by bad leadership—the 1945 parallel to Hitler's assertion that the German army was stabbed in the back in 1918. Several cases have been discovered of Nazi students' getting in with faked papers.

Purging of pro-Nazi books was carried out in the universities on the basis of an official list in which all known Nazi publications were indexed and by a special commission made of the three anti-Fascist parties. This commission had to decide in all doubtful cases—for example apparently technical books on biology published under Hitler would be found to be twisted to prove the Nazi race theories, or mathematical text books would contain problems couched in Nazi terms. Except in flagrant cases the tendency appears to have been to preserve any books likely to be of use during the period of shortage. University libraries are allowed to keep one copy of each suppressed book for reference. Printing of text books for higher education began in the Zone in 1947.

When I visited Jena University eight of the professors, including Professor Zucker the Rector, turned out to see me. Their main anxiety is the lack of books and the isolation which they feel because they are cut off from the technical literature published in other countries. Books are available in Switzerland, but the university has no means of securing them. One professor trembled with indignation when he told me that he was unable to receive a copy of the English scientific journal *Nature*. (This is the result of red-tape on the part of either the Russian authorities or the Control Commission which ought to be remedied. It arises not from any censorship but because letters from England to the Soviet Zone are restricted to one ounce).

In Jena lectures continued all through the bitter winter. When the university's buildings were too cold the students gathered in the hospital, one of the few warm buildings in the town. The division of students between the various faculties is as follows: Theology 27, Economics and Law 484, Medical 724, Philosophy 398, Mathematics and Science 547, and teaching 237.

The curriculum is drawn up by the senate of the university in consultation with the Soviet and German authorities and the teaching of history, which was subjected to the closest scrutiny, did not start again until the summer of 1946.

The political parties are active in Jena, as in all the universities in the Zone. The S.E.D. has the biggest membership—705 against 281 in the L.D.P. and 167 in the C.D.U., but the biggest group, totalling 1,133, do not profess any Party allegiance. Only a very small percentage of the women students are enrolled in the political parties.

Among the university students in the Zone, however, an interesting form of local patriotism has grown up. It arose very largely because the universities have been the target of the most fantastic propaganda stories in the Press of the Western Zone—stories which are so nonsensical that even the Right Wing students are indignant.

10

END OF THE JUNKERS

HANGING in a place of honour in hundreds of thousands of homes all over the Soviet Zone is a framed certificate, with a picture of a peasant toiling in the fields in the light of the rising sun. At the foot is the signature of the President of the Land or Province in which the farm is situated. Those certificates are a symbol of a new era and the death warrant—at least in the east—of the Junker class, which always nurtured and sustained German militarism. Each bears the name of the peasant owner of a farm carved out of the great estates, and assures him that his name is entered in the official records and that he is guaranteed the permanent possession of his land. There are 483,737 of these new peasant holdings in the Russian Zone, representing a family population of nearly 2,000,000.

Altogether more than 7,000,000 acres of land were confiscated. Some were retained for State farms and other large-scale units, but the great proportion was split up into peasant holdings of between fifteen and seventeen acres. The great landowners, representing half of one per cent of the population, owned 40 per cent of the land. Branches of the Hohenzollern family had been left in undisturbed possession of nearly 500,000 acres. The Von Arnim family counted 292,000 acres, and the Prince Stolberg family 180,000. To-day their power in the east has been broken and their ancestral homes are being enjoyed by the common people. I saw many of these great houses in the hands of their new owners. There may be some sentimentalists who would feel depressed to see a score of peasant families and their children playing on the magnificent lawns and among the flower beds which once marked the stately splendour of Germany's great landowning class. To those who remember the role of the Junkers, it is one of the happiest sights in post-Hitler Germany.

There are landlords who write from safe havens in the Western Zones to tell their former tenants that soon they will come back to resume possession of their lands. Never was there a more forlorn hope. Whatever decisions may eventually be taken about Germany's future this great programme of land reform will never be undone.

There was a period when the new peasants were affected by this propaganda. I found some in Doebeln, Saxony, who became so perturbed at the constant letters from their former landlord telling them that they were only temporary tenants in his house, that they set to work to pull down the big house, using the material to build separate houses on their own plots. Neither the Germans nor the Soviet authorities prevented them. Now, however, the peasants have gathered in their own harvests. They will proudly show you the first cow which they have bred themselves. This primeval pride of the peasant in his land is one of the biggest factors in the stability of the Zone.

The great argument used against the land reform, both in and outside Germany, is that the plots are too small to permit efficient cultivation. How far is this true? After only a short period it is difficult to give a full assessment but there is abundant evidence to show that in the particular circumstances of the moment far from leading to a decline the land reform has increased production. Tests taken in Thuringia of the yield per acre of the land under peasant cultivation compared with the same land under the landlord's control gave remarkable results. Sample figures showed an increase of between 10 and 60 per cent for wheat, 10 to 50 per cent for rye. In some cases, barley and oats did not reach the previous yield, but in others it was up by 25 to 60 per cent. Potatoes showed a general increase while sugar-beet and roots for cattle were particularly successful, in some cases rising as high as 300 per cent. Breeding of livestock has certainly risen at a steeper rate owing to the individual care of the animals by the peasant farmers.

Mecklenburg, the province where the Junkers were most deeply entrenched, made another test. Officials analysed the output of the big State farms, where large-scale farming is carried out on the best possible lines within the limits of the existing shortages, with that of the small farms and the peasant holdings. The State-farm figure was 7 per cent lower than the average for the farms of between 125 and 250 acres, which in turn were 2 per cent lower than the average of the peasant farmer with his seventeen-acre plot. The over-all harvest per acre is below pre-war level but every expert agrees that this is due to the lack of fertilisers coupled with the neglect of the war years.

It should also be remembered that although each peasant works his own plot he has the use of all available heavy agricultural machinery, which is owned by Peasants' Mutual Aid and hired out at almost a nominal fee. In fact, the machines worked every daylight hour during critical periods. In addition, operations like draining, which must include more than a single holding, are being carried out collectively by agricultural co-operatives.

But it is necessary not only to grow food: methods have to be found to ensure that it reaches the community. That is where land reform has proved the most effective weapon of all in the Eastern Zone. Had the landlords remained they would have been hostile to both the German and the Soviet administration. Sabotage of food supplies could have brought the life of the Zone to a standstill, for Russia, at any rate, could not have afforded to bring in foodstuffs to make good the depredations of the black marketeers.

There have been mistakes and setbacks but the situation has been kept in hand. Not only has the Soviet Zone fed its own population and the millions of refugees from the eastern areas; it was possible to raise the lowest rations during the winter of 1947 and to schedule some 210,000 tons of grain for export to the west up to the 1947 harvest. When I was in Mecklenburg potatoes were being loaded for export to the Western Zones, although there had been heavy losses in the Zone during the frost.

Another statement which is constantly appearing in the western Press is that the Eastern Zone has the majority of Germany's agricultural areas. The statement is patently untrue. In terms of agricultural area per head of population the Soviet Zone is only a little better off than the combined American-British Zones, although it is in a more favourable position than the British Zone on its own.* Moreover, the countryside in the East suffered heavier damage in the fighting and it lost many herds of cattle and considerable quantities of machinery, which were taken to the West ahead of the Red Army.

The difference in the East is that all the popular forces are mobilised to stimulate the peasant to greater production and to persuade him to deliver his produce to the community rather than the black market. On the Sunday before Easter, 1947, I toured some of the villages of Mecklenburg with Johannes Warnke, Vice President of the Province, and Minister of Planning. On that Sunday every member of the government was out in the countryside to stimulate the spring sowing campaign. The late spring had seriously endangered the harvest and super-human efforts had to be made. A government order was issued saying that work was to go on from 6 a.m. until 8 p.m. and that there must be no break on Sundays, or even on May Day. Everyone knew that it was useless to try to ensure obedience to the

---

* With 26 per cent of the population, the area comprised in the Soviet Zone produced before the war 39 per cent of the wheat crop, 21 per cent of the potatoes, and 20 per cent of the oats.

order by threats, so a great campaign to encourage the peasants was launched.

Warnke called on the burgomaster in each village and asked to see the plan of campaign. He went over it point by point. How much of the winter corn had been lost ? How much land remained to be ploughed ? Were there sufficient horses ? How many machines were out of action and how quickly could they be repaired ? For hour after hour he was at it, bullying, cajoling, flattering, listening patiently to complaints but all the time communicating his own sense of urgency. Until the late evening the men, the horses, and the tractors were busy in the fields.

During the first year of the land reform there were plenty of mistakes. Assessments of the proportion of the harvest each peasant was called upon to deliver were frequently arrived at by rule of thumb, without proper regard to the difficulties or to the nature of the soil. As a result, there were many peasants who simply could not pay up. Local authorities, and in a number of cases, local Red Army commands acted ruthlessly and foolishly and peasants were promptly gaoled. The Russians, however, realised their mistakes and Marshal Soko- lowski issued an order cancelling all punishments except for cases where there was complete proof of sabotage. For the 1947 harvest much more careful methods were worked out to ensure a correct assessment and to encourage genuine co-operation by the peasants.

Here is a picture of how land reform worked out in Thuringia, a miniature of the procedure all over the Zone. Just under 500 big estates with a total area of 375,000 acres were broken up. In addition, 22,000 acres belonging to war criminals and 30,000 acres belonging to the State were made available for distribution. Nine thousand new peasants received holdings. Fifteen thousand peasants, whose plots were not sufficient to maintain a family, were given additional land. More than 16,000 non-agricultural workers received allotment land up to about an acre. Some 1,100 rural councils were given an area of forest and grassland for the breeding of stocks, while the provincial government retained a number of estates for experimental work and for breeding. Each peasant received from fifteen to $17\frac{1}{2}$ acres, but in most cases about a quarter was forest land. Nearly 3,000 resettlers from the territories taken over by Poland were among those who benefited.

The farm implements from the big estates were dealt with in two ways. Smaller tools, ploughs, barrows, and the like, were distributed among the new peasants, but the bigger implements—tractors, thresh- ing machines, and so on—were handed over to the Peasants' Mutual Aid. The peasant is not prohibited from employing labour, but the general rule is that the holding should be worked by himself and his family. If he were to employ labour to farm his land while himself concentrating on some other work, action would be taken against him. The land can be inherited, but it cannot be sold. In cases of deliberate neglect a peasant can lose his land but the case has to be proved by a judicial inquiry. If the accusation is established there must be a special order of the land department of the provincial government depriving the offender of his title deeds. Holdings under $12\frac{1}{2}$ acres may not be divided.

For the 1947 harvest Thuringia, in common with the other provincial governments, planned much more carefully than was possible the previous year. In the autumn of 1946 the agricultural department made a census of what the peasants wanted to grow. These figures were collated and compared with the actual needs of the population as assessed by the central administration for the Zone in consultation with the Russian administration. As a result certain alterations had to be made. For example, the peasants, who had been doing well out of live-stock, were planning to grow too much cattle food at the expense of potatoes and oil crops which the town badly needed.

An amended plan incorporating these needs was sent to the district councils on whom the responsibility was placed for consulting with the village councils, who in turn discussed the question with the individual peasants. Thus, the peasants themselves, in most cases through Peasants' Mutual Aid, decided how the necessary crop could best be produced and what adjustment each must make in his original scheme.

In this way the authorities avoided the mistakes of 1946 when orders were sent out from the top, with the result that in many cases peasants were ordered to grow crops for which their soil was totally unsuited. In the main a surprisingly high degree of genuine co-opera-tion was reported, but in the event of a show-down the State retains the whip hand, since seed and fertilisers are allocated to each area on the basis of the production plan.

The district and village councils have also been given the task of assessing the contribution to the State which each peasant must pay. This is again designed to remedy the mistakes of 1946, when the assessment was made from above, more or less by rule of thumb. The local people know the nature of the soil and are thus in a far better position to act fairly, but again the provincial administration can keep a tight control since it knows the total which can be expected from a given area. The peasant knows in advance his total commit-ments and has a guarantee that he will be able to sell everything over this limit in the open market. Thus he genuinely feels that he is working for himself. The total State levy amounts on the average to half a normal harvest, so that a very big margin is left to encourage hard work and initiative.

When the harvest has been brought in the peasant is allowed to sell at controlled prices (those ruling in 1944) either to private firms or to the agricultural co-operatives. He produces receipts to his local Mayor and only when these total his scheduled contribution is he free to sell privately. Contributions of livestock for meat and eggs and milk are based on the same system (for a hen the peasant pays forty eggs a year). Although the administrative work is done by the local authorities there is again a close check by the agricultural department of the provincial government. Under a law for the safeguarding of the people's food, peasants refusing to pay up can be fined or imprisoned.

Thuringia has organised various departments for the encouragement of agriculture. State research stations are selecting the best seed varieties and intensive work is going on to improve breeding stock. Bulls and other stud animals are owned by the Peasants' Mutual Aid, while horse breeding, in which artificial insemination is used, is being developed by the Thuringia government. A model seventeen-acre holding at Jena University is designed to show exactly what can be done with a farm of this size.

There is still something of a clash between the new peasants and the middle farmers who retained their farms up to 250 acres. These bigger farms employ labour; the workers are organised in their trade union and have a forty-eight hour week averaged over the year. But the landless farm-worker is getting better pay than before the war and is encouraged to join Peasants' Mutual Aid while the middle farmer, although his allocation to the State is bigger, is probably better off than anybody else in the Zone. He may grumble, but he certainly is not going to quarrel with land reform.

New peasants pay 200 to 300 marks for their land (forty English cigarettes at Berlin black market prices) and can spread it over a period of years. They pay nothing for the animals and can take a State loan to pay for new buildings.

Here is a picture of a typical colony of new peasants at Nieder Rossla, near Weimar:—

The former estate was over 1,000 acres and was taken over as State land from the Grand Duke of Weimar after 1918. But the State did not farm the land. It was merely rented out to a tenant who acted no differently from the owners of other big estates. Eighteen peasants shared in the distribution of the land. Fifteen were workers on the estate; three already had tiny holdings, which were not sufficient to maintain a family. The land was first of all surveyed and each recipient got some good land and some bad, so that their holdings were not in a single piece. Two estate gardeners shared the hot-houses and so had less land. The shepherd received a bigger proportion of the sheep and less of the other livestock. Eighty-six workers employed in the nearby town of Apolda got allotment plots of about half an acre.

This division took place immediately the law for the distribution of land came out and was carried out by a land reform committee of the village, without intervention from outside either by Russians or Germans. At the meeting called to settle the matter a committee of seven was elected. Walter Albrecht, the village carpenter, who was known to have carried out some illegal anti-Fascist propaganda during the Nazi period, was elected chairman. The former tenant of the estate, who was seventy-six years of age, moved to a large house nearby, where he continues to live undisturbed. Enough small equipment was available to give each new peasant some essential implements while the tractor and the thresher were kept for communal use. Small animals like pigs and sheep were simply divided out, but for the horses and cows, which varied considerably in value, the peasants drew lots. Each peasant had seven sheep, four pigs, a horse, two cows, and a calf. Those with reasonably good accommodation in the village went on living there. Seven families divided up the big house—an historic old building dating from the twelfth century in which Goethe once stayed. The stables, barns, and other farm buildings were also divided up.

All this was done by the peasants in co-operation with the village parish council from which the old pro-Nazis had been thrown out. Arthur Zeunert, who was well known and respected in the village and had returned from a period as a prisoner of war in the American Zone, became mayor. Nieder-Rossla, incidentally, was one of the best villages I saw from the anti-Fascist viewpoint. Only sixty out of 2,000 inhabitants were members of the Nazi Party and through the Hitler period a few sturdy stalwarts appeared to have kept up a negative if not a positive atmosphere of opposition.

By early 1946 Peasants' Mutual Aid was being formed. A branch was set up in the village and took over the estate tractor, threshing machine, and the estate bull, all of which were available for lending out at a cost of a few shillings.

Albrecht told me that although 1945–6 season was bad and much damage was done by spring floods the total yield of the estate was higher. In particular the animals had increased more rapidly under the individual care of their new owners.

Rudolph Henkel, one of the new peasants, proudly showed me the horse which he had drawn in the share-out. A Derby winner could not have been better groomed. " Are you satisfied with your new life?" I asked. " Well, times are hard to-day in Germany. There are so many things you can't get. But I never had anything but a hard time. I worked on the estate since 1914 and I never got more than 15 marks a week (pre-war about 20s.) and a pound of corn for each hour's work. Before the war you could just about scrape along on that money, but during the war things grew much worse."

Henkel's original four pigs had increased to six and he had delivered his meat allocation to the State and also slaughtered one pig for his own use. Last year he grew wheat, rye, barley, beet, and hay, but the floods damaged the crop. When it came to deliveries to the State, he had not sufficient grain left to make bread for himself. The officials just would not listen to his story and he was very angry, but this year things would be better, for the 1947 deliveries make allowances for floods and other accidents.

In a four-roomed flat in the mansion I found Otto Sonnekalb, living with his wife and grown-up son. Before the share out he worked on the estate for twenty marks a week, and one pound of corn an hour, and had a small allotment in addition. He used to live with relatives in the village. Now for the first time he had his own home and furniture. Maybe, I said, he'd got a little additional furniture from the townspeople who wanted to exchange it for food. He merely smiled. He ploughed most of his plot with his own horse and plough and only hired the tractor for a field of heavy ground, but like all the peasants, he hired the threshing machine.

It was while talking to Sonnerkalb that I got confirmation of the release of fertilisers from Leuna to German agriculture. Although this factory has been taken over by the Russians as reparations, all fertiliser production is scheduled for Germany. Sonnerkalb told me that the bad weather had delayed deliveries and the village allocation of fertiliser, so he had borrowed the tractor and gone to Leuna to collect it. He secured it without difficulty.

On the estate new houses were being built for the peasants still living in the village and work was being done to farms and buildings. Materials were secured locally and the peasants had been fortunate. The nearby brickworks was at a standstill for lack of coal so some of the farmers took the tractor to collect coal. In return, the works gave them a priority delivery of bricks. The two gardeners proudly showed me their hothouse stocked with enough seedlings of tomatoes, celery, cabbages, and so on for the whole community.

I asked Walter Albrecht, the chairman of the land reform committee, whether they saw much of the Russians. Now and again a Russian officer looked in, he said, but he never interfered.

Did they have Russian soldiers coming along and demanding a chicken for dinner? No, that had not happened in their village since the very early days. They were too near to the headquarters of the local Red Army commander and a Russian caught at that sort of game was punished very heavily.

How far did the peasants help each other? For the most part each family tilled its own holding, but if anyone was ill the rest of the community would always organise help. If a job needed doing and the owner of the land could not do it, then the rest would always see that his crop or his animals came to no harm.

As I strolled through Nieder-Rossla, in the sunshine of a Sunday morning, the villagers were pouring out of church. I met Kate Schultz, twenty-five-year-old daughter of a farm worker, who is a "new teacher" in the village school. In every village in the Zone you find the new teachers, but Katie was a special case, for she was teaching in her own village where everybody knew her. At first she had to break down a lot of prejudice, but to-day she has won for herself a position of respect in the new community.

In Mecklenburg, Saxony, Saxony Anhalt, and Brandenburg, I saw the same picture of peasants tilling their own land. It is something new in the history of Germany and it is based on elemental forces which cannot be ignored.

Peasants' Mutual Aid plays an increasingly important part in the economic development of the Zone. How far is it a genuine peasant movement? There is, I am convinced, overwhelming evidence to prove that it grew democratically from the peasants themselves. The Russians were certainly not behind the formation of the movement, although they gave it every encouragement once it had begun. Like so many of the developments in the first months after the collapse, it really came into being to fill the vacuum created by the collapse of the Nazi regime. Many of the great landowners began fleeing to the west before the Red Army came in. Some went because they were Nazis, others because they feared the vengeance of the foreign workers they had oppressed or even of their own ill-paid German labourers. Maybe it was the ingrained German sense of discipline, but most of the estates whose owners went away just continued to operate as if nothing had happened. It was an agricultural counterpart of what happened in many factories when the owners or managers fled and the technical staffs carried on.

But with the passing of time the workers on the estates began to form their own committees and to discuss the division of the land—and in some cases to carry the proposal into effect on their own. Then all the political Parties stepped in with a propaganda drive for the appropriation of the big landowners. Thus, when the Soviet Military Administration issued the order in October, 1945, for the division of all estates over 250 acres and the taking over of the land of all war criminals, the mass movement was ready for the carrying out of the instruction. From this movement grew Peasants' Mutual Aid which now includes something like 80 per cent of the peasantry. The movement differed in the various provinces; Mecklenburg and Brandenburg, where the biggest estates and the most vicious of the Junkers were found, went forward rather more rapidly, but the same elemental forces were present all over the Zone—the hatred of the landless peasant for the landowner.

The story of thirty-one-year-old Paula Rabetke, now one of three peasants' representatives in the Thuringia Parliament, is typical of the way Peasants' Mutual Aid came into being. Paula knew the tragedy of the landless agricultural worker from the other side. She was the daughter of a rich Prussian landowner and just before the Nazis came to power she joined in an agitation to improve the conditions of the farm hands. She was practically driven from her home and went to Berlin to study agriculture. There she married an engineer which earned for her complete repudiation by her indignant family.

During the war her husband was arrested by the Gestapo for anti-Fascist activities and she got a job as a farm worker in Thuringia. By the time of the collapse she was one of two foremen on a big estate owned by a much-hated officer of the Wehrmacht. Even before the Red Army arrived she and forty farm workers had taken over the estate. They collected the 1945 harvest under the supervision of a committee with Paula as secretary. When the order came to divide the land Paula, who was hoping to rejoin her husband and therefore was not interested in taking her own plot, was busy setting up committees among the workers on neighbouring estates. That was how the peasants' movement was born in Thuringia. By March, 1946, it was possible to call a conference of peasant delegates from all the province and to set up a Peasants' Mutual Aid organisation. Paula was elected secretary.

The other provinces in the Zone were following the same course of development and by May, 1946, an inter-zonal committee to create a single organisation was set up. Paula was again a member. She told me that in Thuringia alone Peasants' Mutual Aid has 2,400 local committees and 70,000 members—including farm workers and small-holders as well as peasants.   The organisation controls some 6,000 big units of agricultural machinery, mostly tractors, which are distributed among 500 stations, each in charge of a skilled operator. " My most important job," she told me, " is to try to encourage the peasants to co-operate.   This is particularly difficult with the middle peasants—those with farms up to 250 acres who were not affected by the share out.   But even among this section we are finding a new atmosphere, for they are feeling far more secure to-day than before the division when they would always feel at the mercy of the big land-owners.   The new peasants are growing naturally into the idea of joint working," Paula added, " although there is not the slightest support for the idea of collectivisation."

Peasants' Mutual Aid has full-time officials in the head office and in the districts, and relies on voluntary officials in the villages. One of its big aims is to set up an educational department at all levels. There is a subsidiary organisation which organises the repair of farm implements. Peasants' Mutual Aid has also done a big job in re-dividing stock after the initial shareout.   Some holdings had too many of one sort of animal and not enough of another, so Peasants' Mutual Aid collected them up and redistributed on a rough valuation basis.   Some peasants had insufficient of some crops to meet the government quotation and a surplus of other.   Peasants' Mutual Aid stepped into the breach by collecting surpluses and redistributing. It also swopped seeds with the Western Zone for lorries, and organised a gift of livestock from Thuringia where devastation was much less severe to Mecklenburg which suffered badly.   Thirty tractors were being built in Thuringia in the spring of 1947 to be delivered to Peasants' Mutual Aid by July.   They represented the first tractor production in post-war Germany.

The most important task, however, has been to try to bridge the gulf between the countryside and the town.   In times of acute shortage of foodstuffs there is always a tension between the peasant and the industrial worker and even under conditions of land reform the Soviet Zone is no exception.   Parents in the towns who see their children obviously under-nourished are not likely to feel well-disposed to the villagers whose children are fat and well-fed.   I heard bitter complaints in various towns and loudly voiced demands for govern-ment action to force the peasants to disgorge more of their stocks.

The main fact, of course, is that foodstuffs production can only be increased if the landworker is provided with sufficient incentives and as a result the peasant is undoubtedly the most pampered section of

the population. There has been, however, a real development of
public spirit in the villages, not by any means universally and not
sufficient entirely to stop black market deals, but enough to make a
big improvement in the general food situation.

This has been mainly the work of Peasants' Mutual Aid. The
local Committees have carried out campaigns to persuade the peasant
to sell his supplies to factory and school canteens, to hospitals and
other public institutions. The actual sales, which are at prices far
higher than the controlled State purchase figure, but nowhere near
black market levels, are usually handled by People's Solidarity. In
some areas squads of workers from the towns have organised help
to the villages in the repair and maintenance of machinery—again
in return for food.

While food remains desperately short these movements cannot
hope to embrace more than a proportion of the peasants. The
temptations and the opportunities to indulge in black marketeering
are too numerous. But the system provides a basis for the rebuilding
of an agriculture free from the age-old tyranny of the landlord and
ending in a very real way the isolation of the countryside.

Significantly, the political Parties report a growing interest from
the countryside. The S.E.D. has gained rapidly for it can claim the
biggest share in the bringing about of land reforms and since the
conditions in the country are better than the towns it does not have
to bear so much blame for defects in administration. In the Catholic
villages, however, the Christian Democratic Party holds the allegiance
of the peasants.

Two good harvests in the Soviet Zone, an economic agreement
which eases the famine in fertilisers and other necessities, and the
delivery to the countryside of the tools and equipment now included
in the economic plan, and the world will see that almost unnoticed a
fundamental change has been carried through.

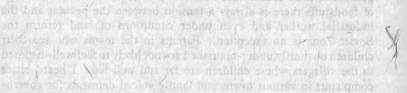

II

THEY ALL TALK FOOD

EVERYONE in Germany—except the occupation forces—talks about food. Go to any home, and however important the subject under discussion, the conversation will sooner or later turn to rations. The Soviet Zone has been hungry—no hungrier than a number of countries which suffered from Nazi aggression, but nevertheless sufficiently hungry for food to overshadow everything else in the minds of a big section of the population.

In the early months of occupation the Russians brought in considerable quantities of food to tide over the complete breakdown brought about by looting, transport chaos and other accompaniments of the collapse. Then the Soviet administration and the newly found German authorities settled down to organising a proper system of distribution. The supplies available in the Zone had to provide for the existing population, for an ever-increasing stream of new settlers and for the main demands of the occupation force.

From the beginning, ration cards were allocated on the basis of work, the various categories ranging from the heavy worker with the highest rations to the person without work (including housewives) on the lowest category. The first peace-time winter was exceptionally difficult and there were gaps in the allocations, but early in 1946 supply became more regular. During my visit I received the same reply to my inquiries wherever I went—that though rations might be late, the cards were always honoured. Whatever is on the ration card is always ultimately available in the shop.

Rations are paid out for ten-day periods, and the delays can mean hardship. Two weeks' supply of meat may come all at once, or the fat ration may be carried over to the next ten-day period so that again the housewife draws double quantities. Most families get through these double allocations in the single period and may then be left for days with little more than dry bread. Unlike Britain, there is literally nothing off the ration, except for those fortunate enough to be able to buy on the free market and those with friends in the country.

Here are the rations for the big towns: they are actually calculated in grammes per day but to enable a comparison to be made with British rations I have given the weekly allocations in pounds and ounces:—

	Heavy Worker.		Worker.		Office Employee, Housewife, Old People.		Children.	
	lb.	oz.	lb.	oz.	lb.	oz.	lb.	oz.
Bread	7	0	6	3½	5	7	4	10½
Cereals	0	12½	0	8½	0	6¼	0	6¼
Meat	0	12½	0	10	0	6¼	0	6¼
Sugar	0	6¼	0	5	0	5	0	6¼
Fat.....................	0	7½	0	3¾	0	2½	0	5
Jam or Artificial Honey..........	0	7½	0	7½	0	7½	0	7½

Milk.—Nil for adults except in special categories. Children up to 3 years, ½ litre full cream daily; 3 to 5 years, ¼ litre full cream, ¼ skimmed; 5 to 6 years, ¼ litre skimmed.

Miners receive 12lb. of bread, 1lb. 9 oz. of meat, 8 oz. of sugar, and 8 oz. of fat.

Everybody has a potato card entitling the holder to about eight pounds a week. This was paid out in hundred-pound allocations until the spring of 1947, when supplies failed in many areas because the clamps were ruined by frost. Vegetables are distributed to all groups on a special card according to available supplies. Eggs, fish, or cheese will sometimes replace meat, but quantities are increased to make up protein value. Four times the amount of cream cheese for example is issued against meat coupons.

Milk is issued for three months at a time to tuberculosis cases and is also secured on a doctor's certificate by expectant and nursing mothers.

Certified victims of Fascism receive one grade of rations higher— that is, workers receive heavy workers' and dependants receive workers' cards.

Vouchers for clothing, household articles and other consumer goods are given out by the local authority on proof of need, settlers from the former territories, bombed-out families, and victims of Fascism being given preference. These vouchers are strictly limited to available supplies, but in shop windows all over the Zone one can see articles of clothing for sale against coupons.

Gas and electricity are technically rationed but supplies have generally been so limited that households seldom get an opportunity to use their full amount. Gas is available at rare intervals and I met numbers of families who made a habit of getting up in the middle of the night in order to cook their weekly joint when gas was on tap. Electricity cuts are frequent, industry being given preference over the domestic consumer.

Some towns adopt the practice of dividing the areas into two parts. One half is allowed to use electricity in the morning and the other half in the afternoon, the whole town being switched on in the evening. Inspectors detecting anyone using current outside permitted hours have the right to switch the offender off for any period up to a fortnight without further argument. In one or two areas an experiment was made with a special fuse, which can only be fitted by the local authority and which blows out if more than a given number of electric appliances (except lights and radio sets) are in use at the same time in a block of flats. The residents are expected to sort out the period between themselves, and if the fuse blows they can wait up to fourteen days before the inspector comes along to put in a new one.

The frequent breakdowns during the times when current was supposed to be available provided the main hardship. Meetings would have to be abandoned because the light failed; scores of families simply went to bed as soon as the light went out. In a hundred ways life was disorganised because there were simply no supplies of candles or oil to provide alternatives.

Berlin gets a slightly higher ration in all sectors, although the four powers bring in different types of supply. In the villages of the Soviet Zone and in the semi-rural areas, workers not employed on the land get a rather lower ration because it is assumed they can supplement their supplies from allotments and peasant friends. Peasants receive normal rations of foodstuffs which they do not grow themselves and sometimes are given extra supplies in return for extra deliveries to the State. They take their own flour to the baker for bread, and receive butter from the dairies in return for additional deliveries of milk.

Everybody receives a quarter of a pound of ersatz coffee a month, one piece of poor quality soap and some soap powder. Various " teas " made from herbs are sold freely. Neither real coffee nor tea is available except on the black market at fabulous prices. Cigarettes and tobacco are on ration but are seldom available. An enormous number of people grow their own tobacco. There is a tax on such plants over a certain number. Peasants who bring in their crop of tobacco to one of a list of tobacconists are given cigarettes in exchange.

Coal is on separate ration cards which were honoured until the cold spell of 1947 shut down many mines. The ration is not sufficient even for one warm room during a normal winter.

The universal shortages show themselves in various ways. For example, for a shampoo at a hairdresser's the customer has to bring his own soap and his own towel. Laundries demand soap powder before accepting any work. Restaurants serve meals in return for coupons. Quite substantial meals are on the menus but they take a couple of days' meat coupons as well as those for fat and potatoes. In consequence no one can dine out except on rare occasions, and social life has transferred itself from the restaurants and tea-shops to the factory or office canteens where meals, consisting mostly of vegetables (except when supplies are coming from the peasants) are served for a much smaller number of coupons. People's restaurants were opened during the winter of 1947 because families could not cook owing to the fuel shortage. These provide meals at a low coupon rate.

A surprising number of small manufactured articles—picture frames, candle holders (but no candles), cigarette lighters (but no flints), ornaments, and so on—are to be seen in the shops. Clothing, handbags, shoes, slippers, knitted goods, can be made in shops all over the Zone from customers' own material.

The standard of living represented in these rations is low, but by no means catastrophic. Families in the Soviet Zone with some members on heavy workers' and workers' cards are probably the best off of any in Germany—always excepting those living on the black market and the peasants. The real hardship is suffered by the old people unable to work and people on the lowest ration who are living alone.

Until February, 1947, non-employed people, including housewives, were on a lower category—"cemetery ration" as it was called by the population—and those not living in families were very near to starvation. The abolition of this card, which brought several million into the present lowest category, was a tremendous concession and was made at a time when other zones were suffering cuts.

Prices of rationed goods are rigidly controlled, with the result that rations take a very small proportion of the average income. Heavy workers' rations for a month cost only 21 marks (about 30s. on 1936 values) and those of children and the lower ration groups a few marks less. Spirits are much more plentiful in the Soviet Zone than in England (or in Scotland!) but they are heavily taxed, costing 42 marks (60s.) a bottle. Beer (very weak) is served freely. These figures mean that even the poorest, including those on the lowest scale of public assistance at 90 marks a month, can afford their rations. One woman said to me, " There is less food now than after the first war, but then the unemployed could not afford to buy even the present ration."

I visited a number of hospitals and talked to many doctors in the Zone. Their reports all agreed that, though there are extensive signs of malnutrition, there is no great evidence of starvation. Hunger œdema has occurred, mostly in the older people without work who lived for many months on the old lowest ration card. When cases do occur among children and young people they are treated with a special protein food manufactured in the Zone, supplies of which are too short for all to benefit.

The children's physician at one of the big Dresden hospitals told me that young children are receiving sufficient and are able to maintain full health on their rations. Complaints due to over-feeding have disappeared. After six years of age, however, the children are showing the effects of a diet which is deficient in a number of body-building foods. Infectious diseases take a heavy toll and there is a prevalence of skin ailments. Tuberculosis is on the increase among children as in every other section of the population and is aggravated not only by shortage of food but also by appalling housing conditions and lack of cod-liver oil and vitamin preparations.

Drugs generally are desperately short. People have died through lack of insulin. Penicillin is being produced in the Zone but supplies are limited. Sulphonamides are also limited. Dr. Runja Scheuer, Pathologist at Dresden hospital, brought a small quantity of M. and B. with her from England. " I just keep it for the worst cases," she told me. " It's a terrible decision to have to make, but until we get normal supplies of drugs we have to accept the fact that patients who could otherwise be saved must die."

12

THE BLACK MARKET

On the train from Osnabrueck to Berlin, I met a Danish singer who had lived in Germany before the war and was on his way to a job in Berlin. He had called that morning on a pre-war friend in Hamburg and had breakfasted with him on eggs, bacon, white bread, real coffee, and other luxuries unknown to the German compelled to live on his rations. This particular German was a dealer in carpets and tapestry, and was trading entirely on the black market. He reckoned his weekly family expenditure on food at 10,000 marks, more than most honest persons in Germany can earn in a year after payment of tax. In Berlin I met an Englishman who showed me a beautifully turned-out cigarette case priced at 42 marks. He had paid for it in cigarettes at the current price of 7 marks each and was very proud of his bargain. It did not occur to him that his action was plain looting.

I met an English official on the way home on leave who explained to me that he had left his dog to be looked after by some German friends. "Can they feed it?" I inquired. "They're not short," he said. "They've got everything. They even keep me in cigarettes." I asked how they achieved this miracle in starving Germany. "Selling fake antiques to Americans," he replied. "They are making very good stuff and only experts can tell they are not genuine. As a matter of fact, they needn't bother, for the Yanks will buy anything. My friends are making 140,000 marks a month and they're salting the cash down in genuine antiques against the time when the American demand dries up."

"How do they get raw materials?" I asked. He chuckled. "You can get anything in Germany if you know the right way. Why, look at my hat. It was specially made by hand. My friends paid twenty cigarettes for it. Of course, I wouldn't go in the black market myself, but after all, this was a gift."

These are just cases met at random which could be repeated endlessly in Germany to-day. The pegging of wages and prices imposed by the Allies has prevented inflation in the legitimate market, but in the black market there is a completely inflationary situation. Cigarettes have become a universal currency and the newly arrived visitor is soon reprimanded by his friends if he spoils the market by tipping to the extent of more than a couple of cigarettes a time. The cigarette currency arouses far more confidence in the West than the mark, and cigarettes will pass through many hands. In fact, most fantastic of all, sometimes they will pass around to the point when they fall to pieces and are never smoked at all ! This situation means that goods are simply being looted by anyone, German or foreign, who can secure cigarettes, soap, liquor, or other commodities from the occupation troops to exchange for goods.

That is one form of black market. The other arises from exchanges of manufactured goods from the factories and sales of foodstuffs by the peasants. With black market prices ranging at 500 to 600 times the controlled price, the diversion of goods from legitimate channels, unless sternly checked, goes on increasing and with it comes a disruption of the whole economy. It becomes increasingly difficult to induce the peasant to deliver his proper allocation to the State, while absenteeism leaps in the factories and mines because it is far more profitable to concentrate on securing a packet of cigarettes or a few pounds of potatoes than to put in a week's work. As confidence in the currency declines, black market prices rise even higher and the incentive to work grows steadily less.

These problems faced the Soviet Zone equally with the rest of Germany, but the method of tackling them in the East was entirely different. The Russians began with two major measures mentioned in Chapter 3—the stopping of bank accounts and the registration at the Labour Exchanges of all holders of ration cards with the exception of old people and women with children. This meant that from the outset there was some check on the money available for black market operations and supervision over the people who would otherwise take the opportunity of deserting work for black market activity. Even those people who retained a certain amount of cash could not make it last long at the prevailing black market prices.

In one village the peasants told me with great gusto the story of one of the richer farmers who, in common with everybody else, had his banking account stopped. He discovered a method of getting some of his money paid out by a branch of his bank in the American Zone. Accordingly he got across the zonal frontier, drew his money and proceeded to have a good time. Within a few weeks he was back grumbling more than ever. He described the fantastic prices he had been obliged to pay on the black market for foodstuffs available on his own farm, and indicated that he now proposed to settle down.

It was then that he received the news that since he had been away a better tenant had been found for his land.

Others got away with it for longer, like the former manager of an insurance company in Saxony Anhalt who succeeded in making frequent journeys along the Elbe to Hamburg in the British Zone. When these trips at last became the subject of investigation, it was found that he was drawing cash from a branch of his company still operating in the British Zone and returning only after he had had a good fling on the black market.

These are examples of the small racketeers. Bigger leakages occurred through the activities of criminal gangs, many of them led by Nazis and former S.S. men. An exhibition at Leipzig Police Headquarters gives an interesting cross-section of the underworld of the Soviet Zone. It takes the form of posters published by the police all over the town with the object of bringing the public behind the authorities in the fight against the black market. Here are some of the case sheets:—

Fritz Keittel—former compositor, forged 15,000 three-pound bread coupons and a large number of meat and sugar coupons. The poster explained that he took to crime because of a " morbid desire to show off, instilled by Nazi methods of education, particularly the Hitler Youth." Fritz had three associates, all named in the poster, who traded the forged coupons in public houses for money, liquor, and cigarettes. Later, he grew bolder and, with an American uniform, secured with the help of his girl friend Annelies Wasserfall, he went into the black market in an even bigger way. " Our whole supply plan is seriously endangered by such conscienceless forgeries," the police statement declared.

Alfred Pazsch—aged twenty, had set up as a burglar and enlisted four other youths from sixteen to eighteen in his gang. " All these youths," said the police poster, " had gone through the Hitler Youth and were left without any desire to lead a decent life."

Eldebrant Schroeder—the girl who appears in the next poster, secured a haul of 3,000 pairs of stockings, nearly 1,000 yards of curtain material and half a ton of wool. She had a confederate in a factory in the Saxon town of Zwickau and disposed of the swag through another girl.

Another gang got away with a big haul of foodstuffs under the leadership of a former police officer presumably dismissed as a Nazi, who used his uniform and forged documents to enable his confederates to pose as members of the criminal police.

The file also includes the case of a butcher named Kalat who killed off dogs, selling the flesh on the black market as veal for about a hundred times the rationed price, and a gang who wore Soviet army uniforms and got away with a vast range of goods varying from jewellery to noodles.

Inevitably, in conditions of acute shortage, the black market offers rich rewards to the many criminal elements in the Zone and gives an opportunity for revenge to the large numbers of dispossessed Nazis, who are determined not to redeem their past by hard manual work. The problem of juvenile crime is also acute. Large numbers of boys and girls had no schooling at all during the last years of the war. Boys were enlisted in the Wehrmacht at fifteen and sixteen, and since the collapse have been living on their wits. Cases are constantly coming to the notice of the authorities of prostitutes at the ages of thirteen and fourteen.

To these demoralised youngsters the black market is a constant attraction and the authorities in the Soviet Zone have set up a number of youth reclamation centres where attempts are being made to bring them back to a normal life. Under a law dating from the Weimar Republic children in need of care and attention may be compulsorily sent to these homes.

" The greatest difficulty in reforming these juveniles is the lure of the ' golden West,' " a worker in one of these homes said to me. " The boys' one idea is to get over the zonal frontier and to live on cigarettes and other goods cadged from the American and British soldiers. The girls are obsessed with the idea that they may succeed in marrying a British or American soldier if only they can reach the West."

Social workers are emphatic that this youth problem must be solved, and a campaign is going on to secure more of the big houses of the confiscated estates as centres where the reform of youthful delinquents can be tackled thoroughly and scientifically. The fact that the authorities in the Soviet Zone are making a genuine attempt to deal with a problem which is acute all over Germany has not stopped certain of the Berlin newspapers from indulging in the most grotesque campaign of lies about the treatment of children in the Soviet Zone.

Shortly before the Berlin elections in 1946 the British, American, and French licensed papers came out with stories of children in the Soviet Zone being collected in the streets and taken away to concentration camps. The story began with " hundreds " but it soon increased to thousands. Mothers were supposed to be throwing themselves in front of the cars which were carrying away their children. Newspaper readers who are constantly being fed with stories of this kind must have been prepared to believe that some

Bolshevik pied piper would soon come on the scene to lure away every child in the Soviet Zone. All that really happened was that about fifty-four youths of between thirteen and sixteen were arrested in Brandenburg following the discovery of three secret organisations headed by former members of the Hitler Youth. They had several machine-guns, rifles, and other weapons, and openly confessed that they intended to carry out a campaign against the Russians.

There have also been arrests of students at the universities for pro-Fascist activity, and although these cases have been very few, they are invariably the signal for another spate of terror stories in the anti-Soviet newspapers. While I was in Dresden, stories appeared in the Western newspapers about arrests of students in the town which were denied by every responsible official to whom I spoke.

On this matter, as on others, the question may be asked how an investigator can be certain of his facts in turning down such reports. The answer again is that it is inconceivable that Germans of all parties, as well as ministers of religion, government officials, and police—who are perfectly willing to criticise the Russians on other matters—should conceal the truth, particularly on a matter affecting children. It must also be remembered that, while a big proportion of German youth is being swung into the movement for national reconstruction, the Nazi tradition is probably stronger in a section of the former Hitler youth than anywhere else in Germany. These young criminals have been detected in the other zones of Germany, and the Russians, equally with the other occupying powers, have a duty to stamp out their activities.

Hans Kahle, who commanded the German division in the International Brigade and who is now police chief of the province of Mecklenburg, told me that the problem of juvenile crime is the most difficult task he has had to tackle since he returned from London to Germany. " The moral deterioration during the Fascist period, and particularly during the war years, presents us with a constant problem," he told me. " It shows itself in widespread thefts among people who, in former times, would never have thought of indulging in petty crime, and in an acceptance of the idea of corruption in the most unexpected circles. Youngsters who have lived in this atmosphere for most of their lives and who ran wild during the war are already confirmed criminals. We have had a number of cases of murder by youths of seventeen and all sorts of other offences can be traced to these youngsters. They resent any attempt at discipline and are easy prey for the Nazi propaganda. We had one case of two boys in a country town who sent through the post crude leaflets, decorated with pictures of the Nazi leaders cut from old newspapers, and ending with 'Heil Hitler!' Maybe this was purely bravado, but it is dangerous in a country which is only just emerging from Nazi dictatorship."

The criminal underworld is one of the constant problems in post-war Germany and in the Soviet Zone it is sustained by all sorts of people who are only too anxious to sabotage the administration by undermining the economic and agricultural plans. For them, too, the black market has proved a powerful weapon. The activities of these elements consisted mainly in diverting goods from the factories to the black market. It began with apparently innocent " compensation agreements." These worked in this way:—

A factory making stockings would barter some of its output with a neighbouring factory making pots and pans or an enterprise turning out electric lamps would make an exchange for soap. Almost any undertaking would try to get coal in return for some of its products, while the miners, who in the cold winter were the masters of the whole situation, would collect foodstuffs and consumer goods from all over the Zone.

In a number of factories the shop stewards were drawn into these agreements. In many cases they acted quite innocently, thinking only of securing essential supplies or of giving some incentive to their fellow-workers. But the system soon grew into a gigantic racket and round about the end of 1946 and the beginning of 1947 the figure of production diverted in this way rose in some areas to as high as 30 per cent. There was plenty of ground for suspicion that numbers of employees saw in the procedure a method of sabotage. Some factories, for example, handed out rolls of cloth or articles of clothing to their workers, thereby drawing them into the racket. But a big part of the diverted material found its way on to the black market.

The authorities acted swiftly. They banned all " compensation agreements " within the Zone. During the cold spell the agreement under which the mines were allowed to dispose of half their production over the plan was cancelled and the trade unions were mobilised for a campaign to explain to the shop stewards that " compensation agreements " were destroying the whole economic structure of the Zone. The regional conference of the trade unions in Thuringia and Saxony took the lead by passing resolutions condemning the practice, and the zonal conference of the trade unions in Berlin followed by adopting a statement declaring that the method was " unjust and undermined economic planning."

" Compensation agreements," said the statement, " cannot safeguard the supply of industrial goods to all workers. They are unjust because only workers employed in factories producing household articles, clothing and similar goods, can profit. They endanger supplies because a fairly large quantity of goods is being withheld from general distribution." The conference suggested that, as an alternative, goods produced over the plan should be fairly distributed among the workers in all factories over-fulfilling their quota.

The campaign was not a hundred per cent successful. In an economy in which everything is short, the temptation to secure additional supplies overshadows everything else for a good section of the population, but it reduced the evil to a very large extent. Certainly, it could not have been tackled without the trade unions and the collaboration of other mass organisations. And here again one must note that, in the Soviet Zone, the creation of mass democratic movements has provided the only machinery capable of dealing with problems of this kind.

I found general agreement in the Zone that the Russian occupation troops and officials are not pumping goods into the black market to any considerable extent. One reason is that the Russians do not receive more than their minimum needs of goods susceptible to black market sales. Another is that control of the movement of all goods is extraordinarily strict. A Russian car driver might get hold of a few litres of extra petrol to swop for a bottle of schnapps, but he has no opportunity to secure any quantity. In the early months there were cases of Russian officers taking supplies illegally from the factories, but subsequently the most stringent checks were introduced.

Moreover, the control of raw material begins from the moment it leaves a factory in the Zone or is imported either from a foreign country or from the Western Zones. The central planning office has a list of factories requiring the raw material, but deliveries are only made on receipt of detailed specifications of the purpose for which it is required. Once the raw material is handed over, the factory is compelled to deliver manufactured goods in accordance with specifications. Thus, allowing for normal margins of error, it is theoretically impossible for anything to be diverted from the agreed purpose. All imports to the Zone are handled either by the Zonal Imports Board or by private firms working on direct instructions from the Board. No financial transactions with the Western Zones can take place except through the Berlin State Bank. Thus, really big black market operations which can only now be based on illegal trading involving a constant supply of raw materials have been made virtually impossible either for Germans or Russians.

Whatever checks may be introduced, the problem of corruption remains, and to counter this the Allied Control Council issued an order in April, 1947, providing drastic penalties for the illegal use of controlled foodstuffs, consumer goods, or documents concerned with these commodities. Sentences of from six months to life imprisonment may be imposed on persons concerned with the production, administration, transport, or protection of these goods if they steal or misuse them, or the documents connected with their disposal. In addition to imprisonment, offenders can be fined from 5,000 to 5,000,000 marks—a salutary way of getting back black market fortunes. Smaller penalties are imposed for neglect of duty. There is no doubt that in the Soviet Zone this law will be resolutely applied.

Diversion of foodstuffs from the countryside presented a different problem, complicated by the fact that the peasant has the right to sell his surplus above the State quota at free market prices. Methods had to be devised to ensure him this freedom, while preventing the foodstuffs getting into the hands of speculators. The practice in the various provinces of the Soviet Zone varies. Mecklenburg, for example, which had the biggest surplus of foodstuff, forbids all private sales to individuals. The peasant is allowed to sell to the co-operative societies and in the free markets held weekly or twice weekly in all the big towns. Prices are very much higher than the State price fixed at 1944 level, but nothing like black market level. In addition, he may sell to Peoples' Solidarity or to factory canteens with the permission of his local council.

These regulations are coupled with stringent police measures. Cars are stopped en route and all supplies which cannot be accounted for are confiscated, while in the towns controls are strict enough to ensure that there are no open black markets such as one finds in Berlin. At the same time, the lure of food for the purchaser and easy money for the farmer constantly defeats the authorities. For example, in the early winter of 1946–7, Mecklenburg police ignored single persons with rucksacks until they found that a black market organisation in Berlin had sent out hundreds of apparently innocent pedestrians and cyclists equipped with goods for exchange, and was raking in vast quantities of foodstuffs.

Here again, however, the main weapon against the black market is in the mass organisations. The peasant—and it must be remembered that many of them have received their land from the regime—is constantly urged to play his part in national reconstruction, and to a very large degree he is responding. Moreover, the agricultural co-operatives are offering essential services in return for the supplies purchased from the peasant. The farms sell cream to the Co-operative butter factories, potatoes for starch manufacture and so on, and in return are able to buy seeds, fertilisers and other necessities.

Black marketeers have little chance of cashing in on the free markets, for goods are sold only by the pound, and any stranger attempting to buy is usually surrounded by angry housewives.

The other provinces have not taken such drastic action as Mecklenburg and only specify certain goods in short supply which cannot be sold except to recognised institutions. Considerable trade goes on between purchasers from the towns and the farms and, in consequence, clothing, furniture, and other goods are going to the villages from the towns. Several times I heard the crack, " the peasants won't look at anything now except a new carpet for the pigsty." Peoples' Solidarity, Peasants' Mutual Aid, the Trade Unions, the Free German Youth, all play their part in a campaign to induce the peasants to divert their supplies to hospitals, factories, schools, and other similar organisations.

Again it must be said that none of these measures is 100 per cent effective. Loads of foodstuffs are constantly escaping the police control—on one occasion six coffins on the road were opened and found to be stuffed with slaughtered pigs. Although the police forces and public administration have been denazified, a great deal of corruption remains, and black marketeers can afford to pay heavy bribes. Russians going on leave, or about to be demobilised, go to extraordinary lengths to secure some goods to take home, but many of them find their loot confiscated at the frontier.

Until more goods are available, these leakages will go on. During the cold spell of 1947 hardly anyone, Fascist or anti-Fascist, would resist the opportunity if it presented itself of getting enough coal to warm a room. Hundreds of tons of coal disappeared from railway sidings. At Leipzig railway stations the police gave up attempting to stop coal-pilfering, and in the end women with bags full of coal would queue up at the railway siding to pay their fine of a few marks before leaving. Children were selling coal briquettes on the trams at two marks each (the official price of a hundredweight is just under two marks).

Nevertheless, black market in the Soviet Zone is the exception rather than the rule. Moreover, a large section of the people is consciously hostile to the black market, and the democratic organisations have created machinery for the fight against it. With a better harvest and the diversion of a greater proportion of production to the home market, the effects of this achievement will become much more apparent.

13

NO WORK, NO FOOD

THE Soviet Zone had a population of 17,300,000, excluding Berlin, at the time of the first post-war census. Since then the number has risen through the influx of refugees from the east. When the first registration of able-bodied men and women was made in October, 1945, the number reporting for work was just under 5,000,000. It was known then that millions had escaped the net and were intent on living by black market and similar methods. Then the slogan " No food without work " was rigorously applied, with the result that 9,369,736 people—4,421,874 men and 4,947,862 women—were registered by December 31st, 1946. Out of this number, 69,636 men and 48,289 women were found incapable of normal employment and 14,364 men and 75,567 women were unemployed. Thus the workless figure is less than 1 per cent of those eligible for work and less than ½ per cent of the population. At the time when this 90,000 unemployed figure was registered, there were 105,000 jobs on the books of the labour exchanges. During 1946 well over 3,000,000 were placed in jobs by the labour exchanges. It must be remembered that the population consists of a preponderance of women and elderly people.

The demand for skilled technicians, who are assured the highest grade of rations, is constantly increasing as peace-time industry develops. Mecklenburg, for example, which was formerly almost entirely agricultural, is developing ship-repairing and ship-building industries (only building of small ships is allowed by the Allied Control Council) and has vacancies for many hundreds. A large number of applications have been received from unemployed technicians from Hamburg in the British Zone. The campaign to make the fullest use of available manpower is on very similar lines to that adopted in Britain, and is based on three main principles— training and re-training of craftsmen and technicians, measures to attract women into industry, and provisions for the employment of the war-injured and partially disabled.

Training is carried out at special trade schools, students working part of the time in the factories. Courses last from six to twelve

months, and the trainee receives 80 per cent of the craftsman's rate
for the first three months and 90 per cent until the completion of the
course.   What is more important, he receives the appropriate ration
card for his new trade.   At the end of the period he passes an examination which entitles him to start work, but he is also given facilities to
qualify for the full craftsman's examination.   Those showing special
ability may go on to higher training—building workers, for example,
may qualify as architects.

The biggest reservoir for these trade vacancies is among the
clerks and other black-coated workers.   One pamphlet, issued throughout the Zone by the Central Labour Administration, gives an idea of
the methods adopted to appeal to these people.   First, the pamphlet
tells them quite bluntly that there is little hope of advancement in
their old jobs, since " Hitler's insane plans for world domination "
has multiplied the number of clerical workers out of all proportion
to German needs.   " Get used to the idea of taking up a trade," the
pamphlet goes on.   " Getting nostalgic about your old profession
won't help you."   The pamphlet points out that bricklayers, car-
penters, painters, electricians, plumbers, tailors, engineers, and
textile workers are all urgently needed, and promises " full employment for many decades and better conditions than those of office
workers for all who take up training for these trades."

I visited many labour exchanges where there were officials
assigned to the job of advising applicants for training in much the
same way as in Britain.   It is an interesting experiment in breaking
down the prejudice ingrained in Germany, as well as in Britain, in
favour of office work rather than skilled manual work.

The scheme to absorb the disabled is almost on all fours with the
one introduced by Ernest Bevin in Britain.   Every factory or other
undertaking is compelled to take on a proportion of badly disabled
workers provided the work is suitable.   Where it is not suitable,
permission may be obtained to employ two lightly disabled persons
in place of one heavily disabled.   The term " heavily disabled "
applies to men up to sixty-five and women up to sixty who have at
least 50 per cent disability.   Like all legislation of this kind the
disablement order gives legal status to the trade unions in the operation of the scheme.

The drive to bring women into industry depends partly on the
attraction of the higher ration card, but it is being reinforced by the
steady increase in the number of factory creches, by giving the
mothers time off for shopping, and by allocating to women workers
consumer goods which they otherwise could not get.   Up to November,
1946, 3,200 creches, with accommodation for 144,000 children, had

been opened; that is to say that some 15 per cent of all children between three and six were being cared for in this way. Both the Ministry of Labour and the trade unions are pressing the need for more creches on managements of factories and other undertakings. As an experiment, an "all-the-week creche" was started in Leipzig. The idea came from Russia and the German officials were at first doubtful whether it would prove popular. Mothers brought their children on Monday mornings, and took them home for the week-ends. They surrendered the children's ration cards, and the creche received some additional supplies through People's Solidarity. As it happened, the mothers accepted the idea enthusiastically and now there are six of the creches in Leipzig, and others are being set up in the rest of the Zone.

In conjunction with the trade unions, the Ministry is trying to restrict night work for women; but this has not yet proved possible, so in factories where night shifts are in operation night creches are made available to the children. Equal pay for equal work is legally enforceable, but in the long run its operation depends on the vigilance of the trade unions.

The labour exchanges have the right to direct workers to jobs, but this power is used sparingly, except in the case of active Nazis. The employment of Nazis, incidentally, has caused some difficulties. At the beginning they were sent in large numbers to the mines, but the miners protested that, while they were willing to take their share, they objected to their industry being made into a penal centre. As a result the procedure was modified so that all essential industries receive a quota. In certain essential industries workers cannot move without permission—a decision usually left to the shop stewards.

Herr Herwegen, Minister of Labour and Social Service for Saxony Anhalt, gave me a picture of how the system works out on the provincial level. The power to direct labour was not used except for rush jobs such as the dismantlement of factories (now over). Herwegen explained that when this work was ordered, he had to rush large numbers of specialists to the site. The workers got special allowances for being away from their jobs. (I heard from other sources that some of these dismantling operations were badly handled, with the result that several hundred workers were congregated together without even primitive accommodation.)

In Saxony Anhalt, and it is typical of the other provinces, there are thirty-nine Courts for the settlement of differences between employers and workers, comprised of nominees of the employers and the trade unions. The State enterprises rank as employers and have their own nominees. The employees in a State factory can bring the government to court in the same way as a private employer. An applicant has the right to bring a trade union representative to argue his case. These Courts also arbitrate between the trade unions and the management if negotiations break down. There is also an appeal Court to which any case in the lower Courts can be referred. Arbitration decisions are not legally binding, and the trade union retains the right to strike. In each of the thirty-nine areas there is a labour exchange and a department for factory inspection. If a factory inspector certifies that an accident occurred during work, the person concerned can go direct to the Social Insurance Office to collect the agreed scale of compensation. In the event of disagreement, the case has to be settled by the Court.

In the central administration for the Zone (the equivalent of our Ministry of Labour) Jennie Mattern, vice-president, gave me this summing up of her work: " We are building the foundation for a better and more equitable democracy, but we still have to fight the legacy of Fascism. We are giving to the people democratic machinery for improving their standards, but hundreds of thousands have yet to understand that they are no longer just wage slaves, but free men who must fight for their democratic rights. In our administration we are making constant efforts to ensure the greatest degree of democratic consultation. When new regulations are under discussion, we call conferences of the four anti-Fascist parties and of the provincial administrations to discuss all the problems involved. Then we seek the opinion of the trade unions, not only among the leaders but in the factories as well."

Frau Mattern certainly brings to her work the experience of many years' fighting against Fascism. Twenty-five years a trade unionist and an official of the Public Employees' Trade Union in pre-Hitler Germany, she worked in the underground movement from 1933 to 1934, but was arrested and sent to concentration camps. She was released and escaped to Prague. She got to Oslo when the Germans marched into Czechoslovakia and again escaped when the Nazi armies invaded Norway. Finally she received sanctuary in Moscow.

Social services in the Soviet Zone are more advanced than at any previous period in German history. What is more, they have been built up from scratch, for the funds of the Hitler organisations had all been dissipated in the war. The blocking of these paper assets had one very important result. It made possible the taking over of the private insurance companies and the formation of a single system of social insurance instead of the multitude of organisations which existed before the war.

The companies, like the banks, had invested all their funds in Hitler's war and were bankrupt. Their only tangible assets were a number of buildings, hospitals, and other institutions, and these were taken over by a new State Insurance Office. Instead of the mixture of State and private insurance which formerly operated in Germany, a single compulsory contribution of 10 per cent of wages from the worker and 10 per cent from the employer covers unemployment, sickness, accidents, old age and widows' pensions, hospital, dental, optical, and convalescent treatment for the insured person and his family. The fund is administered by a separate committee for each of the five provinces, on which employers and trade unions are represented. About 90 per cent of the population, including the peasants and the professional workers, are compulsorily insured. A contributor may augment his insurance by taking out an additional policy with the State insurance. Voluntary hospitals existing at the time of the collapse have not been interfered with and are still functioning.

Benefits from the Insurance Fund are extremely low, for the new office started with no assets. In 1945 the highest monthly payment was forty marks, but by the spring of 1947 the figure had been raised to ninety marks. This was still very low, and attempts were being made to raise the figure, particularly for the old-age pensioner. During the cold spell of 1947, however, an exception was made in the case of workers thrown out of work by shortages of fuel and electricity cuts. Married men received 80 per cent of wages and single men and women 60 per cent, and they retained their workers' ration cards.

Unemployment pay lasts for six months and is a statutory right, provided the applicant does not refuse work (at the moment the higher ration card is a much greater incentive to get back into a job since the unemployed automatically falls back to the lowest ration category). When insurance rights are exhausted the unemployed man has to rely on public assistance from his local authority. Scales are fixed by the administration and are again low. This burden of public assistance has brought some local councils near to bankruptcy since they have had to take the responsibility for the flood of settlers from Poland and Czechoslovakia.

Coupled with the building up of the new Social Insurance was the drive against disease which, in the early months of the collapse, threatened complete disaster. The position is still serious; the death rate still exceeds the birth rate and disease is still taking a heavy toll, but the worst dangers have been passed. Typhus and typhoid have been wiped out, syphilis has been reduced by one-third since the peak point in the summer of 1946, and gonorrhea by 45 per cent.

At the Central Administration for Health for the Zone, I met Dr. Karl Coutelle, former International Brigadier, who had come back to his homeland via France, Britain, and China. Working with him is Dr. Eva Kolmer, an Austrian now married to a German, who was imprisoned after the Dolfuss fighting and who organised the Austrian Centre in London during the war. Dr. Coutelle is in charge of the personnel department of the Ministry, while Dr. Kolmer is responsible for planning the zonal drive for improved health conditions.

This is the story they told me: When the Red Army came in the whole health administration had broken down. A considerable number of doctors and officials in public health posts were active Nazis and had earned the hatred of the population for their part in driving Hitler's war machine. They had implemented a directive from the Nazi government ordering them to compel workers to carry on even when they were ill. This directive stated bluntly that the factories must be regarded in the same way as the front, and if workers died through being forced to work when unfit they must be regarded in the same way as casualties in the fighting line. Thus, a large number of doctors had sacrificed their whole position as medical men and, in fact, many of them were quite probably killed by the angry workers, particularly the foreign slave workers, during the first days of liberation.

The administration had broken down, and simultaneously sewage, water supply, and other services were in a state of collapse. At first improvised measures were taken by the Red Army and a few groups of Germans in the localities, but as early as September, 1945, the central health administration was set up in Berlin. All available doctors were mobilised. Those in the public services who had not fled to the West were roped in, as well as doctors in private practice. An attack was made on disease in the refugee camps where epidemics were rampant. In the typhus areas, delousing squads were sent out armed with D.D.T. taken from stocks stored by the Nazis for agriculture. Each squad was given a specific area in which every house was entered and deloused. A number of doctors, nurses, and volunteers caught the disease and some score died. But the typhus curve dropped at an amazing rate, and by May, 1946, typhus was conquered. From that date no single case had been reported in the Zone.

Practically the whole population was innoculated against typhoid. All persons discovered to be typhoid carriers were registered, and special regulations were issued to control the storing and manufacture of food from which the disease might be spread. This battle was also won by May, 1946, since when only a few sporadic cases of the disease have been reported. "All the methods used in the campaign were orthodox medical practice," Dr. Coutelle explained. "The one thing which the Russians added was the idea of organising a campaign in which the ordinary people took part as well as the medical and nursing professions. It was quite new to German ideas, but it worked."

Another immediate problem in the early months of occupation was malaria. Although malaria-carrying mosquitoes exist in this part of Germany, the disease had been practically non-existent for many years. German soldiers from Africa and Russia had returned with the malaria germ, which in turn infected the mosquitoes and started a mild epidemic.

Venereal disease, however, was the biggest problem. By the summer of 1945 the figures for both gonorrhea and syphilis had risen alarmingly. Notification of the disease, which was compulsory from pre-Hitler times, was vigorously enforced. Doctors were under an obligation to assist in tracing the source of infection in every case coming under their notice. Six weeks' training in V.D. treatment were organised for the doctors, and one doctor was placed in charge of the campaign in each area. Small quantities of sulphonamides were available but there was no penicillin, and pre-penicillin methods had to be employed. Special V.D. clinics were set up, and despite the desperate shortage of hospital accommodation, an order was issued that every case of open syphilis must be forced to take hospital treatment. Police were given the right to round up people in places where prostitutes were known to resort, and they were submitted to compulsory examination. This machinery was modified after a short time and only those without identity cards were detained, the rest being told to visit the clinic for examination the next day. The register of V.D. cases was used as a basis for identifying and following up prostitutes and other obvious sources of infection. The housing shortage added to the danger of the V.D. epidemic, for, with people crowded together in one room and even in one bed, infection was spreading, apart from sexual contact. This was countered by a publicity campaign explaining the need to take precautions against infection.

The one disease still on the increase is tuberculosis and little more than ambulance measures can be taken because of the lack of adequate food. Since October, 1946, an extra allocation of food has been placed at the disposal of the health administration for T.B. victims, but it is not enough to meet demand, and in many cases the disease has assumed a virulent form against which the doctors can do nothing. The fight against T.B. has also been organised on a district basis.

L

In each of 170 districts a special T.B. officer is in charge. X-ray apparatus, which is desperately scarce, is concentrated in central clinics.

Denazification of the medical profession presented special difficulties because of the shortage of doctors. All active Nazis, however, were removed from posts in public administration and in the worst cases their certificate of registration taken away. In local administrations and ordinary practice the health authorities admit that there are still many medical men formerly connected with the Nazi Party or other Nazi organisations.

On the other side of the picture is the big drive to train new doctors. Medical faculties were reopened in five universities, and at the beginning of 1946, 3,000 medical students had begun studies. The doctors' organisation, known as the Hartmann-Bund, equivalent to the B.M.A., was dissolved. In the Weimar Republic, as well as in the Nazi regime, it shared with the Ministries of Home Affairs and of Labour in the administration of health service, and it always pursued a reactionary rôle.

Doctors were made eligible for membership of a special section of the Public Employees' Trade Union. This move met with bitter opposition in sections of the profession, as will be seen by this description given me by one who was present at a meeting of doctors, pharmacists, and dentists in Leipzig at which they considered joining the trade union: " The trade union made a mistake in the organisation of the meeting by putting up trade union banners in the skin-disease clinic where the meeting was held, and by choosing a spokesman for the union whose grammar was not of the best. Naturally, both these incidents played into the hands of the opposition. During the discussion a number of doctors got up and complained that they were becoming State officials. Others asserted that they were not interested in their salaries, but only in their ability to serve the community. There was a lot of talk about preserving their code of professional ethics, and allegations were made that they would eventually be compelled to join the union and submit to the ' dictatorship ' of the Socialist Unity Party. Then anti-Nazi doctors intervened to remind their colleagues that under Hitler they would not have been allowed to have such a democratic discussion, and that many of those most insistent on ' professional honour ' had shown little regard for it when carrying out the orders of the Nazis."

The fears expressed seemed very much like those at a meeting of the British Medical Association. Slowly, however, the doctors have been coming into the union and contrary to their expectations there has been no official pressure to make them join.

Mortality figures were high during the first months, but the death rate, the infantile mortality rate, and the maternal mortality rate have been falling, although they are still above pre-war.

A particular problem at the moment is the prevalence of abortion. In March, 1947, the administration was drawing up a new proposal for the guidance of the provincial governments, modifying the pre-war ban on abortion and permitting the operation under proper medical conditions where there are sufficient health or social reasons and nothing can be done to improve conditions. Thuringia has adopted such a proposal, and women are coming to the province from all over the Zone in the hope of securing an abortion.* Manufacture of contraceptives is being developed—although material is short.

In Schwerin, capital of Mecklenburg, I saw a poly-clinic in action which is intended as the prototype of the new State medical service in the Zone. It gives treatment to between 500 and 700 patients a day. There are ten departments for specialist treatment, each with a private waiting room and a system of fixing appointments to avoid undue delay. Twenty doctors are in attendance, each spending half the time in the clinic and the rest in private practice. Insured persons and their families are entitled to free treatment, and the municipality which owns the clinic collects from the Social Insurance. The doctor under the German system is paid for the number of treatments given, while the patient has to collect a form from the social insurance office, after which he can go to any doctor. There is nothing to prevent a patient paying privately and some do rather than bother to go for a social insurance certificate, but they are a very small minority.

Dr. Georg Pietruschka, the physician in charge, told me that at first many doctors were hostile to the change because they were afraid of being State servants and because they feared it would take away their patients. Gradually, however, most of them have become enthusiastic supporters. Incidentally, Schwerin is one of the towns in Germany where the infantile mortality rate has been reduced to the pre-war level.

The provincial governments are introducing their own improvements in the health services. Thuringia, for example, has passed a law reserving 90 per cent of holiday accommodation in the health resorts for the wage-earners.

---

* During the summer of 1946 Saxony Parliament adopted a similar measure.

14

FIVE MILLION REFUGEES

I LOST my way near Halle in Saxony Anhalt. The first three of the four Germans to whom I spoke shrugged their shoulders and explained that they were strangers to the district. That incident crystallises one of the most amazing developments in the Soviet Zone. Since 1945 between 5,000,000 and 6,000,000 refugees have come to settle in the Zone from Poland, Hungary, Czechoslovakia, and Austria. Even in the spring of 1947 the stream was still going on, and hundreds of thousands more were expected, some from Denmark, where they were dumped by the Nazis from East Prussia in the closing months of the war, and still more from the Eastern areas.

These figures mean that over-all between one-quarter and one-third of the population are newcomers. In Mecklenburg the figure is practically half and half, and in Saxony Anhalt 40 per cent are refugees. The remarkable fact is that this vast influx of people, very largely elderly men, women, and children, has been organised from the start; disease has been checked, clothing and furniture have been made available, normal rations issued and, what is more important, they have been absorbed into the population. Apart from transit camps, where the occupants stay for only a few days, there are no refugee camps in the whole of the Zone.

All the efforts of the authorities are directed towards bringing the new settlers, as they are officially called, into the normal life of the community. Just under half of the total of adults were found fit for work, and practically all of these immediately secured employment. Nearly 2,000,000 were taken into industry. Many others took on administrative and professional jobs. Some 80,000 families received land, and more were given employment on the farms. You meet the new settlers all over the Zone, as teachers, civil servants, engineers, and in a score of other capacities. From the time of arrival they have full rights as citizens and many have been elected burgomasters, members of the provincial and local administrations, shop stewards, and so on. Many thousands, particularly the skilled glass-workers from Czechoslovakia, have set up industrial co-operatives and are already bringing new techniques to German industry. Brandenburg alone has fifty-three of these co-operatives, employing 30,000 workers.

The job of moving this vast refugee army in the chaotic conditions left by the war was a real miracle of organisation. At one point they were coming in at the rate of 20,000 a day. In charge of the Ministry for New Settlers, which was set up in September, 1945, is Rudolph Engel, who was badly wounded while fighting with the German division of the International Brigade in Spain and, after a period in a French concentration camp, escaped and served during the war with the French Maquis. " At times," he told me, " our whole transport system was engaged in moving the new settlers. At first it was a two-way traffic, for millions of foreign workers conscripted by the Nazis were going back at the same time. The foreign workers were home long before the flow of people into Germany had begun to subside. Apart from a few thousands who are still in the country, some illegally, all the so-called displaced persons in our Zone are back in their own countries."

In the autumn of 1946 an exchange involving 2,500,000 men, women, and children was carried out between the Soviet and the Western Zones. This was done to reunite families, for the other zones have also taken a share of this vast influx.

In the Soviet Zone, resettlers speaking German as their mother tongue, who used to live permanently outside Germany and who have been obliged to leave their homes, at once secure the same rights as other citizens. That means they are entitled to money grants in cases of need and, if they were not active Nazis, they are immediately entitled to pensions and other social service benefits in exactly the same way as other citizens. Many thousands have already taken advantage of the State training facilities and some are in the universities.

When the new settlers arrive, they are subject to quarantine, and then after a few days in one of 130 transit camps they are sent on to the provinces, where the local government is responsible for their well-being.

The quantities of household goods brought by the refugees varied, but normally they had very little, except for the proved anti-Fascists from Czechoslovakia who came with railway wagons packed with their belongings. Others from Czechoslovakia had 100 to 200 pounds of baggage and about £35 in cash. Thus, for most of them the provincial governments had to find not only homes but practically everything else as well.

This vast movement of millions of human beings, many of them old and sick, inevitably caused great suffering. They have been found homes, but overcrowding is terrible, and it will be years before either the new settlers or those who have been forced to share their homes achieve anything like normal conditions. Suffering was inevitable, but it would have been infinitely worse but for the assistance of the women's anti-Fascist Committees, People's Solidarity, the Free German Youth, and other bodies who organised collections of food, clothing, and furniture, and did everything possible to ease the situation. In the localities special committees of the anti-Fascist parties have the task of seeing to the welfare of the new settlers. Moreover, about 90 per cent of available production of clothing, furniture, and household goods is diverted to the new settlers.

But for the policy of bringing the new settlers into the life of the community from the moment of their arrival, the problems would have been practically insuperable. Even despite this remarkable effort, there is no doubt they still form the focal point of various opposition elements. It is easy to work on the feelings of families who have been forced to give up part of their home to another family from the east. Whatever is done for them, life for the newcomers is beset with hardships. Most of the youngsters quickly find their level, but the old people pine for their homes and the life they were used to in the old surroundings.

There are some German leaders who do not hesitate to tell the population that this is one of the prices that must be paid for Hitler's war, and that it is right and proper that the burden should fall not only on the people uprooted from their homes, but also on those who have to give them refuge. Others, however, in all parties, either shirk the issue or come out openly with a condemnation of the new frontiers, for such a speech is always certain to attract wild applause. Whenever a British or American spokesman makes a statement suggesting the possibility of a revision of the frontiers, the effects on the new settlers and their neighbours is at once evident. Where they have begun to settle down to their new conditions, they become restless and unsatisfied. Anyone who has seen the human problems associated with this gigantic transfer would certainly hesitate before raising hopes which, in the political circumstances of to-day, have no prospect of being satisfied.

The other big problem is the returning prisoners of war. They, too, are being rapidly absorbed into industry and agriculture. In some cases where land was divided, the wife received a holding on behalf of a prisoner-of-war husband, but, in any case, jobs or training are waiting for all who return. It is amusing to talk to the prisoners from England, who have been fed from various sources with anti-Soviet propaganda. Some were even given pamphlets, attacking the Soviet, on arrival in Germany. There have been cases of men jumping from the trains before crossing the Zonal frontiers, and others when they arrive are firmly convinced that they will be sent on to Siberia. This propaganda, like the rest, recoils on the people responsible, for the prisoners are so surprised to find the measures taken to find them homes and jobs that they accept willingly the hardships which everyone in Germany has to endure. Prisoners from Russia usually arrive very tired after their long journey which sometimes takes as long as two months, but they make no complaint about food and general conditions. Generally speaking, there is now a bigger flow from the West Zones to the East than vice versa. Officially, anyone coming illegally across the " green frontier " should be sent back, but where a man or woman is willing to work there is usually a job available and no one bothers very much about legalities.

In all this vast movement of people the former Nazis have a good opportunity to disguise their past, and there is no doubt that many of them are loose in the Zone, often equipped with false papers.

15

OIL INTERLUDE

WHEN American armoured columns raced across Germany in the last weeks of the war, they were the first to take over three world-famous factories, Leuna and Buna, heart of the " secret empire " of I. G. Farben, the great German combine which was indicted in 1947 before an American War Crimes Court, and Zeiss, whose cartel agreements were also a potent weapon in the hands of the Nazi war-mongers. American firms were proved by the American anti-trust department to be involved in these cartel agreements. The areas in which these three undertakings were situated were within the previously agreed Zone of Soviet occupation, but many things happened before the Russian troops marched in. I first heard the story during my visit to Buna.

It was in this great factory that I. G. Farben turned out synthetic rubber from oil, under an agreement with Standard Oil of America, which deprived the United States of the "know how" of the process and kept American industry short of rubber. When the Americans first arrived the Buna workers succeeded in getting rid of the general manager who was an out-and-out Nazi. He, however, chose another Nazi to succeed him, and the appointment was confirmed by the Americans. Then, on June 22nd, 1945, a number of the foremost scientists in the firm were told by an American officer that on orders from the United States Government they were to leave next day. They were given permission to take their families with them, but only two suitcases of luggage. Twenty-four specialists were taken from Buna, and they were joined by a number of others from Leuna and from another factory at Boehlen near Leipzig. Altogether, the scientists and their families totalled 200 and were taken off in lorries. With them went blueprints, patents, and all available technical material from both Buna and Leuna.

That, as far as the workers at Buna were concerned, was the end of the matter, and they set to work to reorganise. An anti-Fascist Committee, which had already been set up before the Nazi collapse, took over. They organised the trade unions and began to sort out the Nazis. Production was at a standstill because of the transport breakdown and the general chaos, but amazingly the vast organisation kept in being. It seemed to keep going on its own momentum. The workers just went on reporting for duty. The office staff went on operating as if nothing had happened. Every week wages were paid out. And, meanwhile, the anti-Fascist Committee was organising, repairing machinery, getting some sort of production going. For a time the men made cigarette lighters and various other simple goods.

By the autumn of 1945 the wheels were slowly beginning to turn again, and then one morning Dr. Johannes Nelles, one of the " kid-napped " specialists, walked into the shop stewards' room. His visit was not a complete surprise, for a fortnight before the factory had received an S.O.S. from a village in the American Zone where the specialists had been lodged, and managed to get a lorry-load of furniture and personal supplies to them. But now Dr. Nelles had come back to ask the shop stewards to let him know which of the specialists they were willing to take back.

The story of their experiences is best told in the words of Dr. Joseph Fischer, one of Germany's foremost specialists in synthetic rubber, who now works at Buna: " Some of us protested when we were first ordered to go away," he told me, " but the American officer told us that it was a direct order of his Government. They drove us to Rosenthal, a little place new Marburg. We were billeted in various houses; some of us were in a schoolroom with no furniture and only straw to sleep on. No one took any interest in us and no one seemed to know why we were supposed to be there and on whose orders we had been brought. We used to sit together every evening, discussing what we could do. We sent some of our people out to contact various American officials, but we always got the same reply that no one knew anything about us, but we were to stay where we were. Then Dr. Nelles announced that he was going to make contact with his old firm. First of all we sent the S.O.S. to Buna, asking them to send on some of our things, and then Nelles decided to go across."

Dr. Nelles is one of Germany's most brilliant specialists in organic chemistry. He is only thirty-five, but he already has a number of big discoveries to his credit and took the job with I.G. in Buna because he was promised his own research laboratory. What was much more important to him as he stood in the shop stewards' office was that he had been a member of the anti-Fascist Committee and was thus free from all suspicion of Nazi sympathies. So the shop stewards sat down and made a list of the specialists they were willing to take back, and armed with this and a few articles of food and clothing hastily collected in the factory, Nelles went back. Two or three weeks later, he returned with two of his colleagues and then events at Buna began to move.

A meeting of all the trade union officials in the factory was called, and there were plenty of complaints that Nazis—some of them with Party cards since 1933—were still in key positions. Then suddenly someone said, " Why not have done with them ? Let's turn them all out. We've got Dr. Nelles back. Why not ask him to run the factory ? " There was no further discussion. A group of shop stewards went hot-foot to the office of the Red Army commander in the nearby village of Merseburg to ask for his confirmation. He was a little taken aback and sent them on to Halle. There they saw General Kodikov and poured out their suggestion.

" Why not ? " said the Red Army general simply, after he had heard the story. Thus the job was done. Dr. Nelles was installed in the directors' office; two of the old directors were dismissed, and the third kept on in a minor position. Dr. Nelles still runs the works under Nazarov, the Russian director who took over in September, 1946, and he still has his private laboratory.

Altogether, ten of the Buna specialists went back. One accompanied the party who was not on the list, but the trade union decided that, in view of his Nazi record, they could not ask the workers to accept him and he went back to Rosenthal. (The Russians were rather angry that they let him go.) Buna's example set the others going. Nine decided to return to Leuna and one to Boehlen.

But the strangest case of all is that of Dr. Zorn, one of the inventors of the synthetic oil process. One day, so he told visitors from Buna, he was taken from Rosenthal to Frankfurt and put on a plane to England. He came back after three months to clear up some affairs, with a contract in his pocket from Anglo-Persian Oil. But when the plane came down at Frankfurt, he was promptly picked up by the Americans and taken back to Rosenthal.

When I visited Jena, I found the shop stewards at the Zeiss works were in touch with specialists from their factory who had been taken away by the Americans and dumped in the small town of Heidenheim, in the American Zone. Two physicists were reported to have committed suicide there, and a number of others without any Nazi history were vainly trying to get permission to return home.

The Americans also took away patents and all available technical material, as well as equipment. According to a statement in the Thuringia Parliament in March, 1947, they were planning a rival Zeiss works at Oberkochem in their own zone. Thuringia sought to counter this move by officially handing the Zeiss factory back to the Zeiss foundation, which has always run the works under a trust deed.

The deed was amended to forbid manufacture of war equipment and to incorporate the rights of the shop stewards to a greater share of management. Altogether, some seventy specialists were taken from Zeiss by the Americans. Some, at that time, had started to work in a new factory using machinery taken away from the Zeiss works, but others had taken jobs on the land in order to secure enough to live.

In Jena University I found that the professors were also trying to get back a number of their colleagues who were kicking their heels in Heidenheim. The Americans took from Jena University not only fifteen technicians, but part of the technical library and a quantity of laboratory equipment. The curator of the University had just returned from a visit to them when I talked to him at Jena. " All those with no Nazi record want to come back, and I went on to Wiesbaden and supplied the authorities there with a list of names," he told me.

Dr. Bredereck, internationally known bio-chemist, was reported at the time of my visit to be keeping the wolf from the door at Heidenheim by making saccharine. He was one of those who had asked permission to return. Professor Bauersfeld was reported to have visited England to advise on the construction of a planetarium before being dumped back at Heidenheim. Professor Labes, Professor Bennewitz, and Professor Von Zybel, inventor of a new process for preserving animal foodstuffs, were living on assistance from the local council. One of the assistant professors who, in this case, was a Nazi Party member, was spirited away to Paris one dark night when the Americans weren't looking !

Zeiss itself has been dismantled by the Russians. For a time there were fears that it would be completely destroyed as a war factory, for there can be no doubt that in the Hitler period it was entirely devoted to precision instruments for war. Eventually, however, after appeals by the trade unions and the Thuringia Government, the Soviet authorities agreed to leave 10 per cent of the machinery and to give facilities for the works to be built up to peace-time requirements. Actually, rather less than 10 per cent was left, but the German technicians believe that within a year or two, with the existing machinery, some new ones, and others retrieved from bombed factories, they will be able to reach the pre-Hitler output of peace goods. In April, 1947, one small shop had begun to start work making lenses, and it was planned to start production of microscopes by the following summer. Five thousand workers were employed on this work, on the rebuilding of the factory, and in making new machinery, and another 2,000 had been promised their jobs back within a year. The shop stewards were consulted during the dismantling and assured themselves that a proper proportion of each type of machinery was left.

Some 270 workers from the Zeiss factory were taken to Russia, where they are rebuilding the evacuated machinery. There is no doubt that many of them volunteered and received well in advance clothing and other equipment for the journey. But the transfer was handled very badly by the special organisations responsible. The men were ordered to leave suddenly and a very bad atmosphere developed. The shop stewards went to Karlhorst, the Russian headquarters in Berlin, and protested in no uncertain terms that in future there must be adequate consultation. I saw letters from the transferred technicians in Russia, in which they described their living conditions as good. Some of the letters were enthusiastic, but some of the married men complained that their wives found difficulty in settling down.

In other towns in the Zone I found that the transfer of workers to Russia was handled much more intelligently, with formal contracts signed well in advance. Since the letters have started arriving there has been a rush of would-be volunteers. There were several hundred applications filed at Schwerin, in Mecklenburg, when I was there, although the Soviet authorities had announced that no further applications could be considered. When I attended a meeting at Freital, near Dresden, where a Soviet Army Officer spoke and answered questions on Russian policy in Germany, two German engineers came up to the officer after the meeting to ask whether he could recommend them for jobs in the Soviet Union.

Buna and Leuna are now Soviet-owned, but with the exception of a Russian director and about half a dozen Russian technical advisers, the works are run entirely by Germans. In these factories and the Soviet-owned mining and briquette undertaking at Espenhain, near Leipzig, I found that the agreement with the trade unions regarding wages and conditions was the general one for the industry, and the shop stewards' committee had secured the right to consultation in all matters of administration, including appointments and dismissals, and production. In each factory I talked with the trade union leaders separately and was assured that their full rights were respected and that there was no interference from the Russians.

Espenhain employs 9,500 workers. The Russian general director began life as a working miner. Production of coal briquettes goes entirely to Germany. The director handed me a pile of delivery slips showing various amounts sent to factories, schools, hospitals, and other buildings in the area. Outside I saw lorries and horse carts loading up the briquettes as they came, still steaming, from the conveyor belts.

" It is our policy," the director told me, " to encourage the workers in every possible way. We have an agreement giving full rights to the trade unions, and we sit down together with the shop stewards to discuss all questions. I have a regular discussion with the shop stewards every week. It is also our policy to promote workers to responsible jobs. One man here, who was working in a very minor capacity when I came, is now managing the briquette factory."

Walter Borsch, one of the shop stewards who was in a concentration camp from 1933-38 and who, before that, worked in the Ruhr, said that the biggest task was to replace the former Nazi specialists. " Some of them have been kept on because we have not yet trained people to replace them," he told me. " They are not allowed any administrative responsibility but they are still a danger. Most of them are awaiting for something to happen from the West. We are training workers fast, and in some shops we have weeded out all active Nazis. Some students from the factory are studying at the university. They are financed by the works and receive all extra foodstuffs supplied to the rest of the staff. With regard to the nominal Nazis, who did nothing much more than take out a party card, our policy is to draw them into the trade unions and try to win them for constructive work. So far that policy has been fairly successful."

At Espenhain, in the interim period between the departure of the Americans and the taking over of the factory by the Russians in August, 1946, the shop stewards were virtually responsible for the administration. During that time they carried out a big repair programme and got production well under way. Some thousand women are employed, and the factory has set up four creches for the children. It has its own housing plan, by which it hopes to relieve the desperate shortage of accommodation.

Working as labourers at Espenhain are a number of active Nazis, among them a former judge and a town clerk. I asked Borsch for more details. " We don't pay any attention to them," he said. " They get the ordinary pay and rations, and you can only pick them out because they are still as lazy as ever."

When I visited Leuna, where the Germans made synthetic oil under a pre-war deal between the German monopoly and Standard Oil of America, I found the entrance emblazoned with trade union slogans put up for the new election of the shop stewards' committee. They read: " Unity is the strength of the Workers " and " The Shop Stewards are the leaders in the fight for reconstruction."

I talked to the deputy director, Djomin, who held a similar post at a factory near Moscow. There were only eight Russians in a total labour force of 28,000, he told me. The fertilisers turned out at the

works were all going to the Government of Saxony in accordance with
a pledge by Marshal Sokolowski that every effort would be made to
satisfy the needs of German agriculture. Production was restarted
on a general scale in June, 1946, after war damage had been repaired,
and the Russians took over in September. To all my other questions
Djomin replied, "Ask the Germans; they deal in all matters of
administration."

I continued my talks in private with Bolle, the secretary of the
trade union in the factory (in this case the Chemical Workers'
Industrial Union), and Uterwedde, secretary of the shop stewards'
committee. They told me that the trade union agreement for the
factory was the general one for the chemical industry. " Is the
agreement fully observed ? " I asked. Both replied " Yes."

" Before anyone can be employed or dismissed, it must have our
confirmation," said Uterwedde. " All the figures relating to production and deliveries come before us, and we use this information to
prevent, as far as possible, supplies getting to the black market."

" Because of the lack of technicians, we have had to keep on some
Nazis," Bolle added, " but we have a special clause in our shop
stewards' agreement under which we appoint a committee for each
section where they are working to keep a check on them. On all
important questions the ex-Nazi has to secure the consent of this
committee. But these people are still a brake on production, and
our big job is to train workers to take their places. We have education
courses in the works, and already a number of rank-and-file workers
have qualified to take on executive jobs."

Altogether 10,000 hits were made on Leuna during twenty-two
aerial attacks. Some 83,000 bombs were dropped, about 12 per cent
hitting the works. Most of the repairs were done by the workers in
the first twelve months after the collapse.

I talked to the rank-and-file workers as well as the shop stewards
in these Soviet-owned factories. There is undoubtedly still some
feeling of hostility to the Russians, but this attitude is diminishing.
To the average worker what matters in the long run are the day-to-day
conditions of his work, and under the new regime there is certainly
more freedom and security than in the days when the great German
trusts were in control.

16

HOW THE RUSSIANS LIVE

THIS story of life in Russian-occupied Germany has been mostly about Germans. That is inevitable, for Germans, and not Russians, are largely responsible for running the Zone. But it would be completely wrong to assume that the Russians are just leaving the Germans to get on with the job and assuming no further responsibility. There is a very close watch at every stage on the activities of the German administration; in the first place to see that there is no revival of Nazism, and secondly to ensure that they do their job efficiently. Soviet authority is divided into three sections: occupation, administration, and political security. Each section has its own General working under the Commander-in-Chief, but otherwise functioning independently.

For the average German occupation means no more than the sight of Russian troops in the streets and the reminders of their presence in the various Soviet-occupied buildings, usually decorated with pictures of Lenin and Stalin, and in the Red Army memorials and cemeteries set up in many towns and villages. But, as far as daily life is concerned, all contacts are with the Germans. When the housewife queues to collect the ration cards and to present the certificates saying that the members of her family are at work, she sees German officials. If a worker is dissatisfied with his ration classification he appeals through his trade union to the German food office. If a householder uses an electric appliance during the banned period and is found out, it is a German official from the municipal undertaking who cuts off the current. A worker who wants to change his job does so through the German-manned labour exchange. All legal cases—civil and criminal—are heard by the German Courts with the one exception that cases of alleged Nazi activity are the responsibility of the Russians. Even these suspects are normally handed over to the Germans when their crimes are not against foreign nationals.

In the early days of occupation the picture was very different. The Germans accepted their new rulers with surprising docility and it was not long before everyone with a complaint, and everyone who wanted permission to carry out the most simple activity, invaded the office of the local Russian commander.

This complete lack of initiative among the ordinary Germans astonished the Russians, who, particularly during the war years, had been trained to improvise at every point. They faced appalling difficulties in this defeated, chaotic country, and here were Germans running to them meekly every minute asking whether this or that was allowed, apparently completely incapable of thinking for themselves or inspiring the mass of the people to start tackling the tremendous tasks of reconstruction. Progress in the initial stages depended very largely on the Red Army commander who happened to be in charge and on the anti-Fascists who were available in the locality. Very quickly, however, administrative machinery was created and the Germans were ordered to get on with various tasks.

The really striking achievement of the first two years of occupation is the way in which an increasing proportion of the people has been brought into active co-operation in the work of reconstruction. To the Russians the idea of stimulating a popular movement to back some urgent task was the most natural thing in the world. The Germans had been accustomed to propaganda, but not to a policy which called on them to use their own initiative rather than follow a leader. Even now the stimulus for action comes from the Russians more often than the Germans. For example, in the early spring of 1947 it was the Russians who started impressing on the people in charge of the radio stations, the newspapers and the various democratic organisations, the urgent need to launch a campaign to encourage the spring sowing. The Germans responded and there can be no doubt that the campaign made a very big increase in the harvest area.

Thus the result of two years' occupation has been to create a basis for a mobilisation of popular forces to meet emergencies when they arise. The disastrous floods in Brandenburg in March and April, 1947, were a striking example of how far this object had been achieved. In a matter of days, huts previously used in the transit camps for resettlers were rushed to the scene and emergency measures of all kinds were begun. The Free German Youth, acting entirely on its own, started various relief activities. When it was found that the flooded land could not be reclaimed in time to be sown with corn, voluntary helpers from every quarter collaborated in planting the area with potatoes.

In Mecklenburg I found that the housing department of the Government had constructed a model house made of clay and timber which could be built during the summer months with materials available locally. Apparently this particular clay had been used centuries ago to build some of the old castles and specialists had been given the job of finding out how it was done. The School of Architecture at Weimar had carried out similar experiments in providing designs for buildings which could be constructed from the materials available in the Zone. The Russians had existed like that for twenty-five years, finding new methods to overcome difficulties and, having found them, inspiring the people to see that the necessary tasks were carried out. They have been teaching the Germans to do the same.

Most of the jobs now falling on the Russians are carried out by the section responsible for administration. The occupation troops were steadily scaled down, as it became clear that the threatened underground Nazi movement was not going to materialise, and the security forces (a branch of the N.K.V.D.) have not had to deal with many serious cases of Fascist activity.

The Russian administration is a complete parallel to that set up by the Germans. That means that for each German Ministry for the Zone there is an equivalent Soviet section at Karlshorst, the Russian headquarters in Berlin. In the capitals of each provincial government there are German Ministries and an equivalent Soviet section. In the towns and rural areas every sphere of activity has its own Soviet official, except that in these cases one man may have a number of departments under his charge.

As far as numbers are concerned there is no comparison. A German Ministry will employ thousands of officials, while the equivalent Soviet section will have only a handful of specialists. In the case of the central administration for the Zone the Russians still exert an overriding authority, since they have the responsibility of seeing that the orders of the Allied Control Council are carried out. In the Lands and Provinces and in the towns and rural areas, where elected authorities are functioning, the Russians act only in an advisory capacity.

I found in almost every case, when talking to a German responsible for a particular department, that he was on the closest terms with his counterpart in the Russian administration. And almost invariably he would pay tribute to the technical competence of the Russian official concerned. The critic may reply that this is typical of the sycophancy which one finds in every zone of Germany to-day. In some instances this factor is doubtless present, but I must add that I met scores of Russians in key administrative jobs and there could be no dispute about their qualifications. University professors are in charge of education. Men and women with long experience in planning are responsible for economic affairs. Doctors are in the departments dealing with health. Through the whole administrative

machinery one finds that the Russians have picked out people with
an expert knowledge of their particular task. And these officials take
their work seriously. Many times Germans told me how they were
working until the small hours of the morning thrashing out problems
with their Russian counterparts.

The N.K.V.D. works in conjunction with the German Ministries
of Justice and it was amusing to find how the legends of secrecy and
terror which are supposed to shroud this organisation were dissipated
in actual fact. Actually, it is no more shrouded in secrecy than our
own Home Office and the officials are on just as friendly terms with
the German officials as any other department.

The average German has an almost mystical respect for technical
competence, and their discovery that the Russians were masters of
their jobs did a great deal to tide over the difficulties with which both
sides were faced. It is this impact of Russia on Germany which affords
the most fascinating study of all. The Russians, representing, as
they believe, a new and more advanced civilisation, came to rule
Germans, most of whom, despite defeat, were still soaked in the master-
race propaganda of the Nazis and were supremely confident of the
superiority of the west over the east. The clash had the most
surprising results. You meet scores of Germans who are openly
contemptuous because the Russians do not act with the assurance
they expect of conquerors. It is a legacy of Nazi ideology which
respects nothing but a display of force. One of these Germans
explained to me that Russian officers were often billeted in a couple
of rooms, sharing a flat or house with a German family. " You see,"
he added patronisingly, " the Russians aren't used to anything better.
The Americans or the British wouldn't put up with such conditions.
They would take the whole place. "

" I suppose you understand," I said, " that there's nothing to
stop the Russians turning everybody out of their houses. You are
rather lucky they haven't turned you out of yours." He looked
surprised, for this type of German always assumes that the proper
way to curry favour with the English is to start running down the
Russians. Nevertheless, he tried again. "That's true," he said,
" but they are so poor. They are quite satisfied with two rooms.
We western countries, we have much higher standards."

I have no doubt that if I had continued the conversation he would
have produced the conventional patter which one hears everywhere—
that it was a mistake for the British and Germans ever to fight each
other, that of course he didn't know anything about the concentration
camps, and that he personally always did everything he could to help
some very good friends of his who were Jews.

In the Western Zones, of course, these types are much more numerous and much more vocal. They couple their talk about the Russians with the most hair-raising stories about life in the Soviet Zone. In the East of Germany, at any rate, it is rather more difficult to explain that everybody lives under a reign of terror, when you are sitting in a town where the only display of force is a neatly dressed police girl, where shops are not only open, but with at least enough goods available to meet the demands of anyone presenting their ration cards, where cinemas and theatres are open, and where Germans, who formerly only opened their mouths to Heil Hitler, blithely run down the occupation authority !

Generally speaking it is true to say that the Russians do not act like conquerors. The division of authority between the occupying power and the German administration has been codified to a point where any Russian demands automatically go through a mutually agreed procedure. Thus, provision of accommodation for the Russians is the responsibility of the German billeting officer, and I heard of several cases where negotiations went on for weeks over a Soviet proposal to take over a number of houses. I also found an instance where the billeting officer, apparently anxious to satisfy a Russian demand, ordered families, some of them anti-Fascists, to leave at a half hour's notice. In this case the S.E.D., at the time of my visit, were trying to get the anti-Fascists put back.

The general attitude of the Russians is to minimise the burden of occupation and not to provoke the sense of humiliation which any people must feel at the consciousness of being under the supervision of a foreign power. Significantly, I never once heard the Soviet National Anthem, even at Russian functions.

The tradition of the Soviet Union regarding its own constituent republics, where the policy has always been to foster the language, literature, and culture of the non-Russian people who were formerly colonial subjects of the Tsars, inevitably found its reflection in Germany. It was expressed by one Russian commander who, when taking over a district, called the Germans into conference and explained to them " We in the Soviet Union have no tradition of colonial administration. We have never occupied a country before and we have got to feel our way. Our chief task here is to help you Germans to run your own country."

In the various meetings in the Zone, to explain to the Germans the policy of the Soviet authorities, this note was the predominant one. The Russians speaking at the meetings appear to have taken the greatest care not to antagonise the audience. Even in one case when a woman got up to ask why Russia didn't send Germany food from the Ukraine, the Soviet speaker explained very patiently what the German armies had done in that part of Russia.

There is a close watch on the Press and broadcasting. At the radio stations a Russian official is always available for consultation. The newspapers are subject to certain regulations—for example, they are not supposed to criticise the occupation power or Allied policy—but there is no pre-censorship, and the editor has to bear responsibility if faults are found after his paper has appeared. I found in practice that the newspapers were inclined to ask advice from the responsible Russian official before publishing anything likely to give offence. In one case, a picture newspaper proudly showed to the Russian officer a page devoted to the Soviet Theatre. "Very interesting," he said. "Now take it away and think over the fact that you are a German and not a Russian newspaper and bring me back a page about the German Theatre."

The Zone has its own station sending out Russian language broadcasts for the occupation forces; the other stations are directed entirely to the German listener. Religious services are broadcast on the German radio every Sunday; Leipzig radio gives forty-five minutes on three Sundays in the month to the Lutherans and one to the Catholics. Political Parties have the right to equal time on the air and there are direct broadcasts of political meetings—a procedure which sometimes has unexpected results as in the case of a Liberal Democratic meeting where hecklers collared the air instead of the advertised speakers. When instructions are given over the air to the public, they invariably come from the Germans and not the Russian authorities. In fact, I found that in nine months only one Russian had spoken on the Leipzig radio and that was to give a fifteen minutes' talk to celebrate Red Army Day.

The real iron curtain between the two races is the barrier of language. Very few Germans speak Russian, and at the beginning of the occupation only a small minority of the Russians knew German. Many incidents resulted, some of them amusing. One local Red Army commander in the first week of liberation gave orders for posters to be printed emphasising that there was to be no interference with religion and that all churches would be open. The interpreter did not quite understand and the bewildered population were confronted with enormous notices, telling them that by order of the Soviet authorities every citizen must attend divine service on the following Sunday! Another story, which I could not check, is worth repeating as it was told me with hearty chuckles by a German anti-Fascist, for it is an example of the misunderstandings that can occur through the language barrier.

A German, well known as an author, died, and the local Russian official responsible for encouraging cultural activities called on prominent local people to discuss the funeral ceremony. He at first suggested that pictures of the dead man might be carried in the procession. The Germans explained tactfully that while this was a good Russian custom it would not appeal to the Germans. The Russian agreed and then suggested that, at any rate, they could have a statue in time for the ceremony. The Germans tried to explain that it was impossible to provide a statue in so short a time, but the Russian waved them aside and said that surely they could provide this small tribute.

The Germans went hot-foot to the only sculptor in the town. He refused point blank to consider a statue, but, after being assured that the Russians would be most angry if he did not do something, agreed to try to produce a bust. In the end, however, he had to confess that the job was impossible. So the Germans went back to the Russian official on the funeral morning to explain that a statue was impossible.

" Statue," said the Russian. " That is a very good suggestion, but, of course, it would take many months and we should have to appoint a commission to decide on the best design. But why do you bring up this question now ? "

" You insisted on having a statue in time for the funeral," said a German. " I suggested nothing so ridiculous," said the Russian. " I merely proposed that we should send a special wreath." The story did not say what happened to the interpreter.

I had an experience of how the language barrier can work, when driving with some German Co-operative officials through a town some miles from Leipzig, at the time of the Fair. A round-faced Red Army boy who looked no more than nineteen ordered us to stop. He asked for the papers of our Russian driver who, incidentally, could not speak a word of German. Then he looked at my British passport. Without a word he clambered into the car happily waving his tommy-gun, and gave peremptory orders to the driver. I squeezed up so that he could sit down with the gun perched precariously between his knees. Then I discovered that, although his German consisted of only a few words, he had learned French at school. It turned out that he was twenty-one-and-a-half years old. He joined up with the guerillas in Kiev at the age of fifteen and a half and then went into the Red Army. He had spent four years fighting and had been in Germany since 1945.

When we arrived at the local commander's headquarters I produced my papers : there was a quick check-up on the telephone and we were bowed out. Later, when a Russian friend was able to get the story from our Russian driver, I found the reason. Our round-faced boy was suspicious at finding a Russian driving Germans and an Englishman, and was convinced he had come across a black market conspiracy. An incident like that between Germans and Russians, neither of whom could speak a word of each other's language, could clearly be magnified into one of the many anti-Russian stories that are constantly being circulated through the Zone. In fact, I have no doubt that some of the people who witnessed the incident were quite ready to tell the world that we had been taken off to Siberia.

Back in Berlin, I was talking to an Englishman: " I suppose they followed you about all the time ? " he said. " On the contrary, I went exactly where I liked," I replied, " and no one followed me."

" They didn't, of course, let you talk to Germans on your own," he asserted. " In fact," I said, " I spent nearly all my time talking to Germans on their own. Germans even came to see me to tell me about all the faults of the Russian administration."

" You must have been arrested," he said. " Yes," I said, " I was arrested." He breathed a sigh of relief and waited expectantly for details. Then I told him about my round-faced Red Army boy. " Was that all," he said, with an air of disappointment.

The language difficulty is being overcome much more by the Russians than the Germans. Time and again I met Russians speaking fluent German who hardly knew a word in 1945. Others explained to me that, although they did not trust themselves to use German, they had learned enough to be able to check up on the interpreters. Once a Russian has learned German he quickly gets in much closer touch with the people. I attended a conference of the Free German Youth in Mecklenburg, at which the Russian responsible for maintaining contact with political and cultural activities came to give a greeting. He spoke in German, which he had learned since the occupation.

" I've just left the President of Mecklenburg," he told them. " I wanted to have a word with him about a wild pig." The audience listened expectantly. " Yes," the Russian officer went on, " this wild pig is dead and it was killed by a member of the Free German Youth. Now wild pigs are damaging the peasants' crops, so this young man dug a pit and in fell the wild pig. Do you think that young man did a good thing or a bad thing ? " The audience shouted, " It was good."

" So I thought," said the Russian, " but there is a law in Mecklenburg which says that wild pigs can only be killed by shooting. So a policeman came along. He looked up his book of law and he said: ' You killed a wild pig without shooting him, and therefore you must be put on trial and you will probably have to go to prison.' That policeman was administering the law, but it was a law made in the days when Mecklenburg was ruled by the great land-owners, and it was designed to protect the wild pigs for the pleasure of the land-lords when they went hunting.

" I went to your President and told him that your peasants haven't time to go hunting and that in Mecklenburg to-day the landlords aren't there any more to kill the wild pigs. I said that, far from putting that boy in prison, they ought to reward him, and that if the policemen find bad laws in their books, they must be replaced by good laws." The audience shouted their approval and the Russian officer added: " I hope you go on killing wild pigs." When I saw the President later he assured me gravely that the young man would not be charged and the law would be amended. It was an amusing illustration of the unorthodox way in which problems are often settled between the two sides.

The Russian approach to cultural questions is another factor in the development of relations. When the Red Army took over Weimar, one of the first acts of the Soviet General was to arrange for a ceremony at Goethe's grave, at which he himself made a speech on the place of Goethe in German literature. The Germans organising cultural activities can often count on support from the Russians against their own officials.

Paul Dornberger, secretary of the Cultural League in Thuringia, told me how, after unsuccessfully arguing with the German authorities about the need for a cultural headquarters, he enlisted the help of the Russian commander. He was given a list of houses, taken over by the Russians early in the occupation, which they were handing back, and told to take his choice. No sooner had he arranged to take over the house than one of the German Ministries protested that it had a prior claim to the building. The Soviet commander called a conference and at the end said, " The Ministry was guilty of a very long delay in asking for this building and since it is not yet handed back by us we have a right to a say in its use. We cannot neglect the claims of the cultural organisations, so I rule that the Cultural League should have it."

During the winter months the Soviet authorities frequently intervened to secure supplies of coal for theatres and other buildings where entertainments were presented. They also insisted on supplies of petrol being made available to members of repertory companies and other artists.

When it comes to the allocation of paper for books, except for the quota for school books which was an order of the Soviet administration before democratic governments were formed, decisions are left to the Germans, but the Russians constantly press the claims of classics and the fact is that German, French, English, American, and Russian classics are appearing in the Zone in a greater volume than ever before in German history. It is another of the lesser-known differences between East and West that the Russians do not consider it good democracy to waste paper on cheap sex novels when the people are without supplies of decent literature.

There are book-shops everywhere, and they are usually crowded with Russians as well as Germans. I met one Russian officer speaking perfect English who produced from his pocket a tattered volume of Burns's poetry. " I was given the job of blowing up a library in 1941 as the Germans were advancing on a town," he told me. " As my men were setting the fuses I picked up this volume of Burns and started to read it. The beauty of the poetry was in such contrast to the barbarism of war that I was almost unable to give the order to blow up the library. Right through the war I carried this book with me. Somehow it remained as a symbol of civilisation through all those years." That officer is far more typical of the new Russia than the comparatively few Soviet troops who got out of hand, and yet all over Germany you hear talk about western culture and eastern barbarism !

Soviet occupation troops receive the same rations as during the war. That means they are regarded as being on active service and live at a rather higher standard than the Russian civilian and a good deal better than the German population. These rations, however, are by no means abundant, and since Russia cannot afford to send much from her own country local shortages are felt by the occupation forces as well as the population.

Both military and civilian personnel are paid half in marks and half in roubles. They can spend the marks in their own shop where clothing, household equipment, and food is available on the rations, and some consumer goods are on sale at high prices. There are also a few shops in the Zone similar to those in the Soviet Union where rationed goods are obtainable without coupons at very high prices.

Officers live mainly in flats and houses and are allowed to bring their wives and families. Other ranks are in barracks. The men may not bring their families. It was explained to me that this rule was not intended as a differentiation between the two, but was due to the fact that the occupation troops are mainly conscripts who will go back home after their period of service, whereas most of the officers were in Germany for a period of years. The Soviet soldiers have lectures on various questions, including some on the rôle of their army in

Germany in which the attitude of their country to any form of race hatred is stressed.

Fraternisation between the Russians and the Germans was permitted from the beginning and many friendships have grown up. I could not, however, trace any cases in which marriages had been permitted. For the Russian children schools are provided in various towns with a curriculum similar to that of their home country. The Leipzig school alone has 400 pupils.

That is a general picture of how east is meeting west in this Zone of Germany. The barriers are still there but they are being broken down. And a foundation has been laid on which mutual respect and co-operation can be built up in the future. The Russians are acting on three basic principles. They believe that it will be very many years before the occupation forces can withdraw. They do not, however, intend to waste precious manpower doing jobs which the Germans can do themselves. They are convinced that no policy can succeed if it accepts the oppression of one race by another. They know that in the final analysis only the Germans themselves can win their way back to freedom and the respect of the world.

17

UNITY OR CONFLICT?

WHAT is to be the future of Germany? What impact on the rest of Germany and the world will result from the changes—economic, political, and social—which have been made in the Soviet Zone.

The facts set out in the foregoing chapters cannot give an answer to these questions. The future of Germany will be decided in the long run by the measure of agreement or disagreement, of co-operation or conflict, between the great Allies, and by their ability to stimulate the best and not the worst in the German people. But the changes which are being made now, partly by agreement between the occupying powers and partly unilaterally in the different zones, are already influencing the structure of Germany and, with it, Europe.

As I said in the foreword to this book it is not my task to draw comparisons or contrast between zones. But in assessing the possibilities of the future it is impossible to avoid consideration of how the general developments in the zones affect each other.

The observer in Germany, like the German people themselves, falls easily into the habit of viewing the position in the light only of immediate problems. In the Soviet Zone he sees the effect of the dismantlement of factories and the obvious impossibility of building up full production without new sources of raw materials. He is over-shadowed by the prevailing food shortages. Since these factors colour everything, he forgets that they are the least permanent aspects of the situation. Dismantlement would remain a perpetual grievance if it brought with it prolonged unemployment, but in the Soviet Zone this is certainly not the case and many of the dismantled plants are already back in production on the basis of the percentage of machinery left by the Russians. Therefore the loss leaves no more trace than the other blows inflicted by the war.

The shortage of raw materials provides a much more permanent problem. In fact, I have heard it said both in London and Berlin that since the Soviet Zone is unable to develop without hard coal and steel from the west, it can safely be left alone until it is forced to join the other zones on the American and British terms. No policy could be more fallacious and in the long run more dangerous.

In the Eastern Zone all the democratic organisations, with quite open support from the Russians, are campaigning for the breakdown of the zonal barriers and the economic and political unity of Germany. The Russians believe that, given production in the west of Germany to the standard reached in the east, coupled with stringent measures to prevent goods' being swallowed by the black market, German production within the new frontiers would be sufficient to pay for necessary food imports, to ensure an improved standard of living for the German people, and still provide reasonable reparations from current production.

They believe that any solution tending to perpetuate the present economic division will be bad for Germany and bad for the world. But, in my view, the facts show clearly that if disagreements between the Allies were to force this division, if the Eastern Zone were to be permanently deprived of the resources of western Germany, it would not collapse. It would be driven to re-orientate its economy to the east. Here, too, the problems must be viewed from the long-term viewpoint. Some British observers in Moscow may conclude that Soviet economy is collapsing because they find there a scarcity of certain goods and a still desperate housing shortage, but locomotives and tractors and machine tools in the long run represent a much greater form of wealth and it is these and other capital goods which are pouring from the factories of the U.S.S.R.

The new democracies of south-eastern Europe are going forward at varying paces, but all of them are building up an agricultural and industrial potential far higher than before the war. Bad harvests can hide these developments but they cannot change the long-term effects. Within this area there are raw materials in sufficient supply to keep the industry of the Eastern Zone of Germany going. It is not essential for Germany to recover Silesia, to have Silesian coal. The Russians took away a good deal of German mining machinery to help rebuild the devastated Donbas, and so intensified the difficulties in their own Zone. But when the Donbas is producing again at full blast—and it will reach that point—transport difficulties would not prove insuperable to Russia's supplying fuel if there were no other way to keep the factories of eastern Germany going. Russian cotton, leather, and wool have kept a number of eastern German towns alive during the first two years of occupation. These commodities and many other raw materials will become available in increasing quantities as the Soviet five-year plan develops.

I have heard the statement made in Berlin that the dismantlement of German factories has turned the Soviet Zone into a desert, and that it can therefore be ignored as an industrial competitor. It was even added that the Russians were getting ready to withdraw, since they had sucked their Zone dry. These statements are being disproved every day and will be more obviously proved wrong as the Zone emerges from its initial difficulties. The fact is that Germany, despite war devastation, is still a highly industrialised country, with a labour force and a technical level which in a matter of years could quickly enable her to resume a substantial position. Of her pre-war industrial capacity about 32 per cent (excluding coal) is in the British Zone, 20 per cent in the American, 25 per cent in the Soviet, 12 per cent in the French, and the remainder in Berlin. The British Zone has 76 per cent of the total coal. This enormous industrial capacity has never yet been fully used for peace production.

The Russians, having made sure that war industries are eliminated, are helping the Germans to transform the Zone into a going concern. How far they have already gone will be seen when the demands of the millions of refugees who, so far, have taken most of the supplies available in the Zone, have been satisfied. The goods produced in this area are going to be put on the world markets and if they are cut off from the west they will go to the countries in the planned areas of Europe which are ready to absorb them. These countries do not fear the revival of peaceful German industry. They fear the growth of a new aggressive Germany, but they are not concerned to prevent the rise of a competitor, for they can absorb manufactured goods without putting their own factories out of action and creating unemployment.

For the German worker and his family security from unemployment far outweighs the disadvantage of having to work some of his time to repay a fraction of the suffering inflicted by Hitler's war. In fact, a period of depression and consequent unemployment would reduce German production and consequently her ability to pay for imports of food and raw materials far more than the annual payments demanded by Russia and the other Allies on reparations account.

Temporarily, these simple economic truths are hidden by the food shortage and the fact that America has a virtual monopoly of available foodstuffs. This situation will not last. In the not-distant future, Russia, Poland, Rumania, and other food-producing lands in the area of planned economy will be able to supply foodstuffs and other goods in return for manufactured goods from countries without sufficient agriculture to maintain themselves.

These facts must be borne in mind in considering the economic questions to be settled by the great powers, but the Russians so far have taken meticulous care to avoid any step likely to draw their Zone within their own economic area. If they wanted to see eastern Germany " bolshevised " they would support the tendencies in the west which appear to be aiming at a permanent division of Germany. They have not done so. First, they know that to deny Germany's aspirations for national unity is to fly in the face of history. Secondly, they realise that if division between the Allies were to force the economic division of Germany, it would, at the same time, create a permanent division between the east and west of Europe, accompanied by an ever-increasing tension between the Allies instead of the co-operation which alone can ensure the full recovery of Europe and the building of permanent peace.

But if this economic unity is to be achieved it is waste of time to present Russia with the ultimatum to join the fused American-British Zone in its present form or to stay outside. A great deal of hard thinking will be necessary before ways and means are found for getting over the unequal economic development which has already taken place between the zones. These difficulties will increase the longer a settlement is delayed. How is financial reform—essential to the economic recovery of Germany—to be achieved when banking accounts have been stopped in the east, while in the west the profiteers of Hitler's war have multiplied their fortunes by operations in the black market?

How are the Lands and Provinces in eastern Germany, which are planning their economic development and which have incorporated the duty to plan in their new constitutions, to fit into a united economy with other provinces still based on the old ideas of private enterprise? What place will the State-owned factories of Mecklenburg, Brandenburg, Saxony, Saxony Anhalt, and Thuringia take in a united economy? Any attempt by the rest of Germany to return them to private enterprise would provoke the most violent resistance, and in any case is no more possible than would be the restoration of Britain's mines to the coal-owners. Perhaps more important still, how can the two parts of Germany work together when, in one shop, stewards are taking part in management, while in the other they are still vainly fighting for this right? Will employers' organisations be re-established in the east or will they be abolished in the west?

All these questions must be answered in the industrial field, and there are equally fundamental issues in regard to agriculture. The land reform in the east can never be undone and any policy based on the belief that it is temporary is the sheerest fantasy. But if the present farm holdings in the east are to be part of a unified German agriculture they must be fitted into a national German economy with the western agricultural areas in which land reform—if and when it comes—is visualised in quite a different form.

The differences go deeper. The Eastern Zone of Germany, like the south-eastern European States, has operated on the assumption that the war was caused by Fascism and that therefore the main task of the democratic forces must be to eliminate Fascism from the whole national life. In the west, generally speaking, this has not been the case. Whatever machinery has been operated for the denazification of the country, there has been no basic policy of creating, in place of the old administration, a new anti-Fascist administration.

When Germany tried to establish democracy after 1918, the Weimar Republic, behind the form of democracy, left the real sources of power in the hands of the financiers, the trusts, and the land-owners. Like other governments with progressive programmes, it found that the actual machinery of administration remained under the control of people hostile to its professed aims and ready to sabotage its policies. The Eastern Zone of Germany has not repeated this mistake. The fact that the great majority of those responsible for reactionary policy in the past eagerly backed the Nazi Party gave the opportunity for a clean sweep.

There was a loss of efficiency in the east while this drastic switch-over was made, but now the initial difficulties have been successfully overcome. The surgical operation has given the opportunity to the patient to recover from the cancer of twelve years of Fascism. New people are in the key positions. Education, freed from the worst Nazi elements, will steadily produce a stream of men and women able to play their part in rebuilding a democratic community. For some years the effectiveness of the changes will be conditioned by the scarcity of real conscious democrats, but the conditions for rebuilding have been created in the east and the opportunities for sabotage by reaction have been minimised. In the west these essential reforms have hardly begun.

These are the divergencies as they affect the Allies, but what is their impact on the German people ? Here, again, it is idle to look at the problem only in the light of immediate post-war conditions. Apart from a few sporadic outbursts of pro-Nazi activity there has been a general acceptance of occupation in all zones, but the urgent desire, on the part of the best elements of the German people, to co-operate with the occupation authorities in rebuilding their country has waned very considerably in the west.

The democratic forces in the Soviet Zone have suffered disappointments and setbacks as well, but I think there is no doubt that, whereas the western Allies have been losing ground, Russia is slowly but steadily overcoming the bitter hostility with which her armies were first greeted. This fact cannot be concealed indefinitely by the anti-Soviet propaganda in the west.

The Soviet Union, whatever her critics may say to the contrary, is not attempting to colonise her Zone of Germany. On the contrary, she is trying to give to the German people an opportunity to regain their self-respect and to rebuild the German nation on a new democratic basis. As I have said before, she bases her policy on the certainty that Germany can never be destroyed as a nation. She is seeking to assist the democratic forces to lead these national aspirations away from the old ideas of aggression into a sincere patriotism. An occupying power with that policy can make many mistakes and still recover the respect of the people, but an occupying power which attempts to deny so fundamental a principle cannot fail to lose ground.

In these early years of occupation the extent of the backing for these principles in Germany may well be concealed by hunger and privation, and the nauseating sycophancy which so many Germans show to their particular occupying power, but they will grow. If an occupied Germany is not led towards a sincere patriotism based on peaceful, democratic reconstruction it will inevitably move towards a sullen hatred and new hopes of revenge.

Already it is showing itself in the west in the slogan "Total victory, total responsibility": in other words, " the Allies defeated us, let them now take on the job of clearing up the mess." The slogan in the Eastern Zone is "for a united, democratic Germany," and, despite the propaganda against all the organisation in the Soviet Zone, that is an appeal which will go on mobilising support in every part of Germany.

The Russians believe that attempts to set up federal states with a weak and ineffective central administration will not only play into the hands of the reactionaries but will also eventually provoke the united opposition of the German people. Therefore the Soviet Union backs the demand for a united Germany. Refusal of such a demand by the western Allies would eventually give to Russia a position of moral leadership in the west as well as in the east.

A stark alternative faces all the occupying powers; either help the German nation to its feet, enlisting the progressive forces for the rebuilding of a free, peaceful country, or hold down a rebellious people by force in circumstances which would restore to authority the nationalist reactionary forces which created the Nazi regime. For every lesson of history shows that any people will eventually struggle for its liberty. Germany cannot be kept in the status of a colony any more than any other people, however much some countries may fear her revival as an industrial competitor.

To rebuild the German trusts and cartels as a subsidiary of western capitalism is to court the same disaster which enveloped the Weimar Republic.

Can the Allies still hope to work together for the rebuilding of a democratic Germany which will no longer be a menace to her neighbours, but instead will put her skill and resources into the common pool? The answer to that question is that the Allies must accomplish this task. Disagreements between them, deep-rooted as they are, must be solved. A Germany divided between Allied occupying forces, or a Germany feeding on the disagreements between her conquerors and sullenly awaiting the day of revenge, would bring the shadow of world war number three over the world.

It is my hope that this study of life in the Soviet Zone will make a small contribution to an understanding of the problem. Russia has pointed some of the paths which must be trodden by the Allies if they are to succeed. She has shown that the German people can be enlisted in the common tasks of peaceful reconstruction. The work she has done, her successes and her setbacks at least merit the attention of the rest of the world.

RUSSIAN ZONE OF GERMANY

RUSSIAN ZONE OF GERMANY